W9-AFY-725

MODIPLOMACY

MODIPLOMACY
Through a Shakespearean Prism

T.P. Sreenivasan

Foreword by

Pranay Gupte

2020

Konark Publishers Pvt Ltd
New Delhi • Seattle

Konark Publishers Pvt Ltd
206, First Floor,
Peacock Lane, Shahpur Jat,
New Delhi - 110 049
Phone: +91-11-41055065
Mob: +91 93552 93900, +91 93552 94900
e-mail: india@konarkpublishers.com
website: www.konarkpublishers.com

Konark Publishers International
8615, 13th Ave SW,
Seattle, WA 98106
Phone: (415) 409-9988
e-mail: us@konarkpublishers.com

Copyright © T.P. Sreenivasan, 2020

All rights reserved. No part of this book may be reproduced or utilised in any form or by any means, electronic or mechanical, including photocopying, recording, or by any information storage and retrieval system, without the prior written permission of the publisher. The views and opinions expressed in this book are the author's own and the facts are as reported by him, which have been verified to the extent possible, and the publisher is not in any way liable for the same.

Cataloging in Publication Data—DK
   Courtesy: D.K. Agencies (P) Ltd. <docinfo@dkagencies.com>

Sreenivasan, T. P., author.
   Modiplomacy : through a Shakespearean prism / T.P. Sreenivasan ;
foreword by Pranay Gupte.
      pages cm
   Includes index.
   ISBN 9788193555446

   1. India—Foreign relations—21st century. 2. Modi˜, Narendra, 1950-
3. Shakespeare, William, 1564-1616—Criticism and interpretation.   I. Title.

LCC DS449.S64 2020 | DDC 327.54   23

Edited by Preeta Priyamvada
Cover Jacket by Dushyant Parasher
Cover image courtesy: Ministry of External Affairs, India
Typeset by The Laser Printers, New Delhi
Printed and bound in India by Thomson Press India Ltd.

To

Sreenath, Roopa, Sreekanth, Sharavati

Durga, Krishna and Shivaay

Contents

Comments by a Preview Audience

"

T.P. Sreenivasan has added a literary bent to his established reputation as one of India's most distinguished diplomats. He is fascinated by Modi, who he believes has grounded India's international relations more firmly on their domestic base. *Modiplomacy* is a reflection on Indian foreign policy, and especially on Modi's foreign policy, built on the template of a classic 5 act Shakespearean play. It is densely packed with engaging observations. I was especially struck by his comment that Modi's idea of foreign policy is 'transactional' clearly a compliment in this case but a word that has been applied to US policies more as a criticism.

—**Teresita C. Schaffer,**
Former US Ambassador

***

T.P. Sreenivasan has given us a fascinating and engagingly written account of Modi's foreign policy in the form of a Shakespearean play. He does not explicitly call it a tragedy or comedy, but his overall appraisal of Modi's diplomacy is positive. Irrespective of whether or not the development of the present situation, particularly in our neighbourhood, and the course of events bear out this reading, the book covers all the significant and relevant themes, and is a thought-provoking and stimulating read for anyone interested in Indian diplomacy and policy.

—**Shivshankar Menon,**
Former National Security Adviser

***

Using analogies spanning from Hindu Mythology to Shakespearean Drama, this scholarly book is an interesting, informative and insightful read. T.P. Sreenivasan's erudition is matched by his engaging narrative skills. Prime Minister Narendra Modi has his squad of staunch fans and foes, but *Modiplomacy* sidesteps the minefields of abject adulation and crass condemnation to provide an objective appraisal of Modi's foreign policy – commonly a sphere of bipartisan support in India. Seasoned analysis is leavened with anecdotes of Modi's courage and unconventionality, successes and failures, positive actions triggering negative reactions, ironies, surprises, stalemates and setbacks. As Sreenivasan eloquently illustrates, governance is usually a process of caution curbing certitude, results rewarding resolve.

—**Anita Pratap,**
Journalist and Author

***

It is only a brilliant student of English literature and an accomplished diplomat who could think of a most innovative way of narrating the saga of Modi diplomacy as a Shakespearean drama in 5 acts. This gives the book, *Modiplomacy, Through a Shakespearean Prism* a unique narrative as well as analytical structure making it a most readable account. A must read book for those looking for deep insights into what drives India's foreign policy and the unique flavour Modi has imparted to it.

—**Shyam Saran,**
Former Foreign Secretary

***

A brilliant, objective and professional assessment of the diplomacy during first five years of Prime Minister Modi, cast in the mould of a Shakespearian play. It is also an easy read, despite weaving in and out of time zones and mixing of earlier articles with current analyses.

—**T.P. Seetharam,**
Former Ambassador

***

Foreword

A Writer For All Seasons

WHILE it was an honour to be invited to contribute a foreword to this latest book of former Ambassador T.P. Sreenivasan, it was also daunting to attempt its composition. After all, a foreword is what readers typically see first before they move on to the book's body. I was conscious of the need to strike the right tone, of the need to pay tribute to the author without seeming to be obsequious, of the need to convey the book's essence without misrepresenting it. A foreword writer is not a co-author: He's merely a town crier ringing the bell alerting readers to expect—certainly in this case—a unique reading experience.

Although I have been a journalist and author for five decades, I hadn't received any specific training in writing forewords to books. An old publisher once told me that a good foreword should draw attention to the book and its author, and not to the writer of the foreword. While I have known Ambassador Sreenivasan for almost as long as he's been a diplomat, I was surprised—albeit pleasantly—

when he asked me to contribute a foreword. Truth be told, I was a tad unsettled because I was immediately aware that whatever I wrote, it would be scrutinized carefully in the context of his book. I did not want to let the ambassador down, but I had trepidations.

It was particularly daunting to write a foreword after I read a draft of the manuscript: Sreenivasan's treatment of Prime Minister Narendra Modi's foreign policy is so thorough, so seamless, and so creative (imagine, a serious tome of political science presented in Shakespearean architecture) that the foreword writer cannot help but gasp in sheer admiration. (Didn't I warn myself against seeming to be obsequious?)

A foreword was also daunting because of Sreenivasan's vast professional accomplishments over four decades representing India in various capacities in Tokyo, Thimphu, Moscow, New York, Yangon, Suva, Nairobi, Washington and Vienna. Writing about his book inevitably meant taking into account this record. International observers have characterized his service as distinguished, and there's general agreement that Sreenivasan is one of the very best diplomats that India produced. He has been variously called 'scholarly,' 'thoughtful,' and 'incisive.' What other encomiums could the foreword writer add? Indeed, was there any point in heaping more praise on the author—however well-intentioned—without endangering one's own credibility?

One device that presented itself in order to at least partially insulate the foreword against diplomatic hagiography was recounting Sreenivasan's career beyond diplomacy: in addition to his books— some of which were bestsellers—Sreenivasan has authored acclaimed articles in newspapers and magazines. The ambassador is a sought-after speaker at major conferences in India and abroad. He was on the National Security Advisory Board; he served as a Senior Fellow at the Brookings Institution in Washington; he was Vice Chairman of the Kerala State Higher Education Council; he teaches at various universities. He has received several awards and prizes. Sreenivasan is currently Director General of a foreign policy think tank, the Kerala International Centre, in Thiruvananthapuram, Kerala; he founded the institution.

Still, I was committed to writing a foreword. A book is a book, and—make no mistake about it—this is a glorious one. As someone who's known Ambassador Sreenivasan for long years, I am not the least bit surprised, and I would expect nothing less from him. It is not my place to hoist expectations for this book, but Sreenivasan has delivered. He has turned out a riveting examination of the twists and turns of Modi's first term dealing with India's neighbors and with the global commons.

Of course, ultimately readers will have to decide for themselves how effective Sreenivasan has been in tracing Modi's narrative. But I venture to predict that their judgment will be solidly in support of the ambassador.

What is there not to support? Sreenivasan mixes his personal exposure to Modi with a gimlet look at the drawbacks and deficiencies of Indian foreign policy before Modi was elected prime minister in 2014.

There are some revealing anecdotes, such as the time that Sreenivasan was Charge de Affaires in India's Washington embassy in 1999, and Modi, then General Secretary of BJP, was visiting the American capital. Sreenivasan decided to host a dinner at home for Modi, and the latter cannily requested that perhaps key officials of the World Bank and International Monetary Fund be also invited. Pakistan and India were at odds at the time because of the Kargil conflict. Modi instinctively knew that a combination of pressure from the White House and the US Congress, and possibilities of diminished assistance from the World Bank and IMF, would persuade Pakistan to abandon its errant ways. In the event, Modi's intuitiveness was borne out.

Such anecdotes, related engagingly, enliven Sreenivasan's book.

But, of course, the value of the book lies not only in its anecdotes but also its cogent analysis. Some may opine that perhaps he focuses too heavily on India's relationship with the United States.

Sreenivasan explains: The greatest success of Modi was the 'new symphony' he choreographed with the United States from 2014 to 2016, taking India closest to the United States as a 'close defence partner' of the US as part of the 'Make in India' programme, including co-designing and co-manufacturing of defence equipment. He signed defence agreements with the United States, which his predecessors had hesitated to do.

'The ... [visit of US President Barack Obama] to India in 2015 resulted in a historic agreement on cooperation between the two countries in the Asia-Pacific. The "Quadrilateral" for cooperation among the US, India, Japan and Australia began to take shape. Investments grew and it appeared that India-US relations would reach unprecedented levels. Both China and Russia watched these developments with concern and began showing signs of diversifying their relations in South Asia.'

The advent of President Donald J. Trump may offer new opportunities for India, in Sreenivasan's view, although Trump can be notoriously unpredictable.

Listen to Sreenivasan: 'Trump has already indicated his willingness to work closely with Modi. These advantages, together with Modi's penchant for international affairs, a congenial economic climate and a broad consensus inside the country in his favour, should give his foreign policy a new thrust and vigour.'

And what about Modi's second five-year term?

Here's Sreenivasan's take:

'India has long dreamt of becoming a fourth pole in an emerging global order. [The other three poles being the United States, China, and Russia.] The time has come for us to pursue this dream, now that the world is in a flux and the three existing poles are not able to cover the entire globe.

India, having experimented with embracing the United States till 2017, feels it necessary to find an alternative and neither China nor Russia holds any attraction for us.

India too has no constituency of its own, either in our neighbourhood or elsewhere, as the glue of non-alignment has withered away. The emergence of Narendra Modi as the leader of the biggest democracy presents an opportunity for India to build a string of friendships with common aspirations for beneficial cooperation.

'Even in the absence of overwhelming economic and military power, India may be able to build an affinity with a variety of countries across continents and ideological affinities. Countries like Japan, Germany, Australia, Brazil, South Africa, Indonesia, Malaysia, the UAE, Saudi Arabia and Israel come to mind.'

Sreenivasan writes: 'Modi is faced with a number of tough foreign policy challenges in his second term. The US has indicated that it would be willing to work with Modi on the basis of the foundation laid by the previous Presidents of the United States and that it would continue its strong partnership with India. At the same time, on issues like trade, immigration and defence cooperation, Donald Trump's views would prevail.'

'The dangers of a tight embrace with the United States were all too evident in Modi's first term. China has made no concessions on any of the problems that have plagued bilateral relations since the Sixties. Russia's steadfastness also cannot be taken for granted. Steering clear of these inherent hazards even while cooperating with them and finding a niche for India in the emerging multipolar world should be the objective of Modiplomacy 2.0.'

Sreenivasan's book will surely be read in the offices of power in New Delhi and other major capitals. The everyday reader who follows current affairs will also find 'Modiplomacy' appealing. The book should be required reading in colleges and universities.

Ambassador Sreenivasan's great gift to readers of all persuasions lies in his sharing of personal experience and hard-earned knowledge of global and regional issues.

I am not only honored that he asked me to write this foreword, I am thrilled.

I have an important question for Ambassador Sreenivasan: 'What is it that you have for breakfast that gives you such incredible energy to be so prolific?'

—**Pranay Gupte**

*

(Pranay Gupte was a foreign correspondent with *The New York Times*, a columnist for *Newsweek International*, and a contributing editor at *Forbes*. He is the author or editor of 15 books.)

Introduction

THIS book has been in the making for the last five years. Ever since Narendra Modi emerged as the leading contender for the post of Prime Minister, I have been following his fascinating forays into foreign policy. Though I knew he was not a novice in international affairs, as I had seen him in action in Washington in 1999 during the Kargil conflict, the new initiatives he took in foreign policy and the assertive manner in which he projected India to the world surprised everyone. No other Prime Minister of India except Pandit Nehru had given so much attention to international affairs in the early months of his first term. He had a clear vision of what he wanted to accomplish and led the country from the front to attain his objectives, overcoming the hesitations of history, which had restrained India in the past.

PM Modi's journey around the world had the flavour of the 'Aswamedha Yagas' of yore, in which a ceremonial horse was dispatched to conquer kingdoms by goodwill or force. His rise as a global player and a man of action was spectacular. It struck me then that he had the makings of a Shakespearean hero, who, with many qualities of head and heart, makes his mark on the stage and faces complications and challenges imposed by circumstances as well as by some tragic flaws in his own character. I began to see the pattern of a Shakespearean play, consisting of early successes, some complications, a climax, the emergence of a major event or a character which changes the course of events, leaving the hero to disentangle the situation and emerge victorious as in this case, or fall victim to the forces at work.

At the end of five years, I found it possible to neatly organise the foreign policy successes and frustrations of Narendra Modi into five Acts of a play. His impressive victory in the 2019 elections has shown that he is in the mould of a Shakespearean hero, who overcomes his problems by the sheer dint of his wisdom and courage and emerges victorious in the end.

This book also contains my real time commentaries, which appeared in *The Hindu*, *The Indian Express*, Rediff.com, PenNews and others on the events that unfolded during the last five years. They give the readers an opportunity to read my assessments at the time, together with my considered opinions recorded for the book.

Shri K.P.R. Nair of Konark, a veteran publisher, visualised four independent works to cover Prime Minister Modi's contribution in different fields and chose me to deal with foreign policy. The credit should go to him and his team for ensuring the quality and authenticity of these volumes.

I am indebted to Pranay Gupte, my friend of many years and my favourite journalist and author, for writing a generous Foreword, which has enhanced the value of this book. A galaxy of experts chosen to be part of the preview audience of the book has also been gracious with their words. Former US Ambassador Teresita C. Schaffer, legendary journalist and author Anita Pratap, former National

Security Adviser Shivshankar Menon, former Foreign Secretary Shyam Saran and former Ambassador T.P. Seetharam are among them. Others who read the manuscript and gave various suggestions are my wife Lekha Sreenivasan, my son Sree Sreenivasan, Divya Iyer, Lakshmi Krishnakumar and Shalini Goyal Bhalla. I am grateful to all of them.

T.P. Sreenivasan

A Note on the Structure of Plays

'The play's the thing wherein I'll catch the conscience of the king.'
(*Hamlet* Act 2, Scene 2, 578-79)

ACCORDING to Aristotle, the beginning of a play consists of the presentation of a character, someone the audience can identify with. That is a beginning—an opening, a first act. The character makes a decision and performs an action, which moves the play on. That action has consequences, and so it goes on until that initial action results in a climax, followed by a reversal and then a resolution. All that will make the audience hold its breath and then release it at the end in a kind of catharsis.

Shakespeare's plays have five acts and several scenes, and each scene indicates the location of the action in that scene. Gustav Freytag (1816–1895), a German novelist and playwright, did a study on the 5-act structure of drama and found it to be rational. He laid out a model for drama, dividing it into five parts or acts—the first act is 'exposition', which introduces the characters and the setting; the second act is 'the rising action' section, which has a series of events leading to the climax; and the third act is the 'climax', which is the turning point of the story where the fortune of the protagonist reverses. The fourth act is the part of 'falling action or resolution' where the final outcome of the conflict begins to unravel but is not clear; and the fifth and the final act is called 'dénouement', which ties up the loose ends and presents the consequences of the resolution.

Prologue
Enter Narendra Modi

INDIA-US relations plunged into a 'nuclear winter' following the nuclear tests of 1998, but blossomed into a 'Kargil spring' in 1999, when the US, for the first time in history, stood by India at the time of the Kargil conflict and demanded that Pakistan should withdraw from Kargil and go behind the Line of Control, which it had crossed. This was the cruellest time for the Indian Embassy in Washington as we had to defend the nuclear tests and subsequently convince the US Government of Pakistan's perfidy in planning aggression in Kargil in the middle of a peace offensive by India.

In the midst of these preoccupations, I received a call from Narendra Modi, who was in Washington and wished to meet me in my office. Ambassador Naresh Chandra was out of town and I was in charge of the Mission. The name was familiar, but I did not know what his mission was. But I agreed to meet him and he came to my office. He looked like a common politician dressed in a kurta pyjama, but after a short conversation on the latest developments in India-

US relations, particularly the efforts we were making on the Hill to build opinion against the Pakistani aggression in Kargil, I was so impressed with him that I asked him whether he would come home for dinner for a longer chat. When he readily agreed, I asked him whether there was anyone in particular he would like to meet at the dinner. I was surprised that he wanted me to invite some senior officials of the World Bank and the International Monetary Fund (IMF). I did not ask him the reason, but was intrigued that the response was positive from both the organisations. By evening the guest list grew, as many Indians wanted to join the party when they heard that Modi was in town.

At the dinner, Modi spent a long time with the World Bank and IMF officials and chatted with the Indians. He was pleasant and polite to everyone, but he seemed preoccupied. He told me that he was meeting several Congressmen and Senators and I suggested some names of friendly Congressmen to meet. Modi did not reveal to me what he was trying to do, but I presumed that he was trying to win friends and influence people on the Capitol Hill. This was the only time I met Modi face-to-face, but he left a deep impression as a man with a mission.

Many years later, after Modi burst on the global scene as a foreign affairs savvy Prime Minister and arrived in Washington on his first visit to the US, documents surfaced in Washington which pointed to a hitherto unknown role played by Modi in securing the withdrawal of Pakistani forces from Kargil at the heavy prodding of the then US President Bill Clinton. It became clear that Modi was not a stranger to foreign affairs even in 1999 when he visited the US as a *pracharak* of the RSS.

According to K.P. Nayar of *The Telegraph*, it was Modi who managed to strengthen a draft Congress resolution with the help of

BJP activists. At meetings on Capitol Hill, Modi asked for reopening of the text of a draft private resolution (HR 227) arguing that it was toothless and would not do anything to persuade Musharraf to call off his dangerous Kargil adventure. Modi said the only thing that would hurt Islamabad was a financial crunch and he called on the US to work towards cutting off funds for Pakistan from the World Bank and the IMF. He directed an onslaught by overseas friends of the BJP on the Congressmen to adopt a strong resolution.

By July, two days after Modi had his meetings with Congressmen, at a 'mark-up' session of the committee, Bruce Ackerman moved an amendment to HR 227 which substituted portions of the original resolution. In part, Ackerman's amendment read: 'President should consider all alternatives, including instructing the US representatives to various international financial institutions such as the International Monetary Fund, the World Bank and the Asian Development Bank to oppose any loan applications from Pakistan, except for food or humanitarian assistance, until it withdraws its forces from the Indian side of the Line of Control.' As the Ackerman amendment made its way through stages on Capitol Hill, Sushma Swaraj arrived in Washington and was personally on the Hill during the period the amendment was passed. It is believed that it was the Ackerman amendment that strengthened Bill Clinton's hand in demanding that Pakistan should withdraw from Kargil. As requested by Clinton, Pakistan Prime Minister went to Washington on 4 July, America's Independence Day, and agreed to withdraw and end the Kargil war. Clinton had also invited PM Vajpayee to Washington, but Vajpayee declined. However, the US State Department kept the Embassy informed of the developments and Clinton made several calls to Vajpayee to apprise him of his progress with Nawaz Sharif.

I can believe *The Telegraph* story that Modi played a role in shaping the Congressional Resolution as I had noticed his interest in meeting the World Bank officials and the US Congressmen when I had first met him. I also met Sushma Swaraj who visited Washington after Modi and gave me hints of the efforts of the BJP. When Modi became Prime Minister and plunged straight into foreign affairs, I was not surprised as I had seen him in action in Washington in 1999.

I had seen Modi in action also at several Pravasi Bharatiya Divas gatherings as the Chief Minister of Gujarat. He had realised the potential of overseas Indians in promoting Indian interests abroad and had cultivated them during his visits abroad and at their gatherings in India. Many Chief Ministers addressed these gatherings, but none gave the overseas Indians as much attention as Modi did and it was at these gatherings that the first whispers were heard about him being a potential prime minister. Although people did not expect that he would become prime minister, based on his accomplishments in Gujarat, many wished that he would be prime minister one day. The overseas constituency that he cultivated during the Pravasi conferences became the backbone of the crowds abroad which gave him a rock star image during his initial visits abroad.

Most observers expected Narendra Modi as Prime Minister to engage in some theatricals, but felt that there will be more continuity than change. The projection I made a month before the formation of the government was as follows:

> 'A dream foreign policy that enhances India's power and prestige will be part of the upcoming government in India. Aspirants to the post of national security advisor might be burning the midnight oil to fashion foreign policy and security strategies. They may have many ideas to revamp policy, reshape institutions and open new chapters in relations with other countries. But once the initial euphoria is over and the new government settles

down to business, there is likely to be continuity rather than change.

No government makes foreign policy in solitary splendour. The broad strategy outlined by any government will not be different from the traditional foreign policy that has enjoyed general consensus. The insight, judgement and instinct of professional diplomats will prevail, as has been seen in times of change in the past.

The Morarji Desai government's policy of "genuine" non-alignment and the Atal Bihari Vajpayee government's nuclear tests are cited as instances of fundamental change brought about by new governments in their initial stages. But neither of these was fundamental or unanticipated. "Genuine" non-alignment simply meant distancing India from the Soviet Union. But the government soon discovered the extent of our involvement with the USSR and quietly went about its business as usual. I travelled with Morarji Desai to Moscow in 1979 on his only visit to the Soviet Union. On his way to Moscow, he had every intention to distance India from the Soviet Union, but having realised the depth and breadth of India-Soviet relations during his stay in Moscow, he came back fully convinced that the relations should be strengthened rather than weakened.

The 1998 nuclear tests were not spontaneous. Since Nehru's days, successive governments had maintained the nuclear option and invested in explosive technology. The timing of the 1998 tests was determined more by the Comprehensive Nuclear-Test-Ban Treaty (CTBT) than by ideology. India chose to face sanctions for tests rather than for not signing the CTBT. The fact that subsequent governments endorsed the tests is enough proof of continuity in nuclear policy. Talk of a new government possibly reviewing the "no first use" doctrine provoked widespread reaction. But that proposal seems to have been dropped now.

Practical matters rather than ideology have determined our relations with neighbours, including Pakistan. Changes in policy have only been triggered by negative incidents. No government has advocated war as an option against Pakistan. The Kargil War came after a peace offensive by Vajpayee and, for all its tough talk, the Indian side refrained from crossing the Line of Control. A new government may criticize Manmohan Singh's "extra mile" policy, but it will not abandon the principle of reciprocity, as war is not an option between two nuclear-armed neighbours.

Changes in the Sri Lanka policy will depend on where the DMK and AIADMK stand after the election. But even if the Prime Minister is in a coalition with one of these parties, there will only be a war of words with Sri Lanka. The case is similar with our other neighbours—the more concessions we give, the more will be asked for. The more we deny them anything, the more blackmail there will be. Any government in Delhi will face these pressures.

The Vajpayee cabinet had at least one member who characterised China as "enemy number one". Vajpayee himself took Bill Clinton into confidence about the threat from China. But he also sought a strategic dialogue with China. Similarly, Manmohan Singh had dealt with China with restraint despite provocations, based on the logic that China is too big to threaten India. A new government may give defence preparedness more importance, but it will not be more assertive with China than its predecessor.

The relationship with the US will be a priority area for any incoming government. But the grievances that the US has against India, like the nuclear liability act, the fighter aircraft issue and the liberalisation of the economy to protect US interests, are not easy to deal with. Still, friendly gestures in the Asia Pacific region, such as joint exercises with the US, Japan and Australia, will be sufficient compensation for the US. A new government will have the advantage of being able to distance itself from the Devyani Khobragade fiasco and begin relations afresh.

Indications of institutional change, hinted at by some political parties, betray a lack of insight. Diplomats have been handling economic and trade issues for years. But merging the external affairs and trade portfolios will have adverse implications. Long-term policy planning and strategic thinking, which, according to some, India lacks, might be attempted. But soon, routine issues will start to dominate foreign relations again. No one disputes the importance of military leaders having a greater role in policy issues, but civilian control of defence is equally important. Regional satraps may become prominent if a multiparty coalition gets formed, but they will not be allowed to dabble in foreign policy beyond a point.

Change will be part of the agenda of any government that comes to power in India later this month. A dream foreign policy that enhances India's power and prestige will be part of it. However, as Barack Obama found out in the US, the power to change is not limitless, especially in foreign policy. Moreover, the wish lists that the new government will have to accommodate will be enormous. After the initial declarations of innovative policies, the new government will reconcile itself to ground realities. It is likely to focus on the primary purpose of foreign policy—to ensure peaceful domestic development.'

On 14 May 2014, I recorded my views on how Modi might change India's foreign policy:

'A tough line towards Pakistan, greater attention to building of Brand India, and a bigger role for the states in foreign policymaking are the proposed modifications of foreign policy put forward so far by Narendra Modi. His promise to allow states a bigger say in strategising and building foreign policy is unexceptionable.

The making of foreign policy cannot be shifted out of Delhi; and the regional satraps, who do not have a national perspective, should not be allowed to dominate foreign policy. But regional inputs should be integral to foreign policymaking at every step of the way. If regional leaders, think tanks and media are fully briefed, they will become partners in foreign policymaking and implementation rather than becoming hurdles.'

ACT I
THE EXPOSITION

Modi Storm Grips India

NARENDRA Modi is nothing if not theatrical. He is his own playwright, choreographer, scriptwriter, director and actor. Plays, however well-choreographed, do go off the track for reasons beyond the control of the people in charge because of unexpected developments or advent of characters, even *deus ex machina (god from the machine)*. Modiplomacy of five years falls into five acts on the pattern of a Shakespearean play. Now that the fifth act has been played out after the uncertainties of the third and fourth acts, it is clear that he has emerged victorious. Like in a Shakespearean comedy, there are celebrations all around.

Shakespeare has two categories of heroes in the way he introduces them. In the first category, the hero does not jump on to the scene at the very beginning with a flourish, but is introduced slowly by some minor characters, who bring out the best and the worst in him. It is Rosencrantz and Guildenstern, rather than Hamlet or Ophelia who come on the stage first. The audience is thus prepared to absorb the hero's appearance when he arrives and begins to delve into his story and share his agony and ecstasy. But there are also some plays where the hero opens the action.

Like the heroes in the second category, Modi stormed on to the national and international scene, making the exposition dramatic, eventful, riveting, awe-inspiring and game-changing. It was like the unleashing of a ceremonial horse for an 'Ashwamedha Yaga', which was expected to conquer every land it traversed on the strength of the might of the conqueror who followed. An unstoppable whirlwind appeared to have gripped the nation. The most dazzling of his early actions was in the sphere of foreign policy when it was announced that all the leaders of South Asia had accepted Modi's invitation to attend his swearing-in ceremony. This was a master stroke as it highlighted the 'neighbours first' policy Modi had announced during the campaign and showed his penchant for leading the battle from the front rather than banking on the bureaucratic and diplomatic machinery to grind their way to policymaking and action.

The array of South Asian leaders lined up in the forecourt of the Rashtrapati Bhavan made the ceremony appear as though it was the coronation of an Emperor, where the small kingdoms came to pay obeisance. Except for the Prime Minister of Bangladesh, who happened to be in Japan at the time, all South Asian leaders, including Pakistan's Nawaz Sharif, Afghanistan's Hamid Karzai and Sri Lanka's Mahinda Rajapakse, were in attendance. Much to the annoyance of the Chinese Government, the 'Prime Minister of Tibetan Government-in-Exile' Lobsang Sangay attended the ceremony. Navin Ramgoolam, the Mauritian Prime Minister was a natural choice from outside South Asia. The mere spectacle of the South Asian show was a departure from the past. Like a Shakespearean hero, he strode the stage with confidence and a sense of invincibility.

Modi held separate meetings with his counterparts in South Asia, which revealed to him the extreme complexity of the geopolitical situation. None of them was fully satisfied with bilateral relations and the list of grievances was getting longer. The extent of their embrace of China also became evident during these meetings. The fact is that they came more to seek solutions to their problems than to declare loyalty. Since it was the first meeting, the discussions were cordial, though Modi had a sense of the problems in his neighbourhood.

Modi's first speech from the ramparts of the Red Fort on the Independence Day in 2014 was considerably influenced by his interaction with the South Asian leaders. He said:

> I clearly believe that India's foreign policy can be multidimensional. But there is an important issue to which I want to draw your attention, the way we fought for freedom, we fought together, we were not separate at that time. We were together. Which was the government with us? What were the weapons available to us? There was a Gandhi, a Sardar and lakhs of freedom fighters and such a huge empire. Didn't we win in the struggle of freedom against that empire? Did we not defeat the foreign powers? Did we not force them to leave India? We were the ones, they were our ancestors only who showed this might. If the people of India could remove such a big empire without the power of the government, without weapons and even without resources, then friends, if it is the need of the hour to eradicate poverty, can we not overcome poverty? Can we not defeat poverty? My 125 crore dear countrymen, let us resolve to eradicate poverty, to win against it. Let us move with the dream of poverty eradication from India. Our neighbouring countries are also faced with the same problem. Why not get together with all the SAARC nations to plan out the fight against poverty? Let's fight together and defeat poverty. Let us see at least for once as to how wonderful the feeling of being alive is, instead of killing and getting killed. This is the land where incidents from Siddharth's life happened. One bird was shot with an arrow by one brother and the other took out that arrow to save it. They went to their mother and asked: whose bird, whose swan? Whether the killer's or the saviour's? The mother replied, the saviour's. The saviour has more power than the killer and that makes him Buddha in future.

And that's why I seek cooperation from neighbouring countries for fighting against poverty in concert and cooperate with one another, so that together with SAARC countries we can create our importance and emerge as a power in the world. It is imperative that we work together with a dream to win a fight against poverty, shoulder to shoulder. I went to Bhutan, Nepal, all the dignitaries from SAARC countries took part in oath-taking ceremony; this marked a good beginning. This will definitely yield good results; it is my belief. The thinking of India, in the country and the world, is that we want to do well to the countrymen and be useful for the welfare of the world. India wants a hand to be extended. We are trying to move forward with these dreams to achieve them.

No Indian Prime Minister had envisaged that India would emerge as a power in the world together with its neighbours. Thus came about the 'neighbours first policy', which, however, lay shattered by the end of the First Act of the Play as the dramatis personae had their hearts in China, not in India.

Modi's logic in emphasising the importance of the first concentric circle of its neighbours was impeccable, but the evolution of India and its neighbours, after all of them became independent had not become conducive to close economic and political cooperation. Regional cooperation was new to the smaller neighbours of India, who saw India as a big brother from whom they had to extract concessions. Landlocked countries expected that their access to the sea and customs arrangements were their privileges, which should not be challenged. India was aware that any regional institution will end up as ganging up of the smaller countries against India. The Pakistan conundrum was a constant inhibitor of regionalism and the other countries did not want to side with either Pakistan or India. For these reasons, Prime Minister Indira Gandhi was not enthusiastic about a regional organisation when it was proposed by Bangladesh. When she finally accepted it, she insisted on several conditions such as no bilateral matters would be discussed, the agenda should consist of economic and trade issues and that all decisions would be by consensus. SAARC is not a multilateral body, but a web of bilateral relationships. Modi, as a disruptive innovator, had thought that these historical impediments would be overcome by his sense of purpose and transparent interest in creating a new South Asia.

Even his soft power diplomacy did not make much of an impact. Our hardy neighbours were not moved by gifts of sarees for their spouses or appearances at weddings or hugs. When India organised a new round of talks in a major departure from the policy of 'talks and terrorism do not mix', the Pakistani delegation arrived in Delhi and demanded a meeting with the representatives of the Kashmiri rebel movement, the 'Hurriyat'. Modi was taken aback by this. He was not aware that such a practice existed and genuinely thought it was illogical that another party should be involved in a bilateral dialogue between India and Pakistan. Thus, a heroic initiative by Modi to resume the stalled dialogue suffered a setback in Act I itself.

Modi also visited the other neighbours and began to realise that Pakistan was not the only impediment to realising his dream of cooperation among the South Asian nations. The stage was set for a long and strenuous effort in the following years.

In pursuit of his other priorities such as security, investment and overseas Indians, Modi launched his goodwill offensive with the US early in Act I, soon after he had visited close neighbours and Japan. Like a Shakespearean hero embarks on a mission to conquer hearts or land, he revealed his intention to make the US the centre of his global strategy, considering that it was a unipolar world, even though there were theories about the diminishing importance of the US. The US-India ties were at a low ebb when Modi took over as Prime Minister. Barack Obama was not very enthusiastic about the nuclear deal as a Senator, having moved some killer amendments against it in the Senate, but as President, he had gone along with it as a national commitment. He visited India in 2010, just before his second election campaign in the expectation that he would bag two contracts of USD 10 billion each for nuclear reactors and fighter aircraft and thus reduce the unemployment rate in the US. He was rebuffed on both—nuclear reactors, on account of the controversial Indian Nuclear Liability Law; and fighter aircraft, on account of the Indian decision to purchase the French Rafale rather than F-16 or F-18. The Devayani Khobragade incident, in which an Indian diplomat was arrested and humiliated, was a symptom of the poor state of US-India relations. The charge was that the diplomat had mistreated her Indian domestic assistant, but in a bizarre development, the State Department had taken the maid's parents to the US and given them green cards! Modi had not only supported the Government's retaliatory steps, but also condemned the US for its provocative action.

Modi decided to visit the US despite all these setbacks and the fact that he did not hold any grudge against the US for denying him a visa for nearly five years was testimony to his sense of purpose and determination. I wrote at that time that Modi's 'Amercayaan' will be as spectacular as India's 'Mangalyaan', which was just accomplished:

> 'The doomsayers are saying that Modi will not accomplish anything during the visit. Modi will not bring a bagful of goodies from Washington. He is not going there to seek anything. Unlike Japan and China, the US has a long relationship with India. He is going there to fly the Indian flag in a gesture of friendship. He is going there as a strong nation in strategic partnership with the US. This is a journey like none other, meant to signal that the two democracies are in a defining relationship of the 21st century.
>
> Though it was not planned this way, Prime Minister Modi is leaving for the US soon after the spectacular victory of 'Mangalyaan', after India 'dared to reach into the unknown and

achieved the near impossible'. The best memento that he can give President Barack Obama is the latest picture of Mars, which may be new even to NASA scientists. They will look at India with envy, not in condescension to Third World country technology. Americayaan will be an unqualified success. His journey has begun soon after he reshaped the way India does business with the world by announcing his vision of 'Make in India', which will have a magnetic effect.

The latest measures announced by India will automatically tackle the issues that the US has raised such as market access and trade restrictions that militate against the American trade perspective. The warmth of the welcome for Modi will be doubled after the measures announced as part of the 'Make in India' vision. The assurance of red carpet rather than red tape has already gladdened their hearts. 'Make in India' is a vision that they will welcome, provided the promises are kept. The US has as much to gain from India as India does.

India-American relations are not transactional anymore. The US does not do business like China or even Japan. China does business at the bidding of the political leadership and even Japan has a business community, which acts in accordance with State planning. The US business has nothing to do with the government. Even at the height of the Cold War, business flourished between India and the US. What we need to do in order to do business with the US is to create the conditions in India itself to make it irresistible for the multinationals. We need to improve the investment climate, stop being unpredictable about taxes, eliminate scams, increase transparency and increase productivity and efficiency and even Obama cannot stop the US firms from coming to India.

These are the promises that Modi is carrying and they will be music to the ears of the US corporate world. The welcome being organised by the Indian-American community in the US will be unprecedented. The influence of the community has grown by leaps and bounds to the point of the US appointing one among them as the ambassador to India. Modi will not seek favours from the community, but will invite them to participate in building a modern India. Apart from the community's intellectual contribution, Indian FDI in the US is a strength for India.

As for the issues to be resolved, the visa issue of Modi was buried when John Kerry distanced the Obama administration from the decision, which was taken in 2002. The Khobragade fiasco is behind us. A New York court has just paid compensation of $250,000 to another innocent Indian, Krittika Biswas, who was jailed without reason. Such an action is not unthinkable in Khobragade's case in the US judicial system.

The nuclear trade is a priority for US businesses and the failure of the two countries to tackle the issues relating to the nuclear liability act has agitated the business community, which lobbied hard for the nuclear deal. But the US, in its heart of hearts, does not wish to export nuclear material to India. As long as defence cooperation expands and it triggers job creation in the US, the US will not shed tears for not having nuclear trade. India has several other sources for nuclear material and reactors. After Fukushima, the nuclear market belongs to the buyers.

The Pentagon has moved centre stage in the relationship after Defence Secretary Chuck Hagel's offer of co-production and co-development of weapons with India. No improvement of relations with our neighbours will obviate the need for strengthening India's defence capability. India will buy weapons only for its requirements and if our imports benefit the US industry, we do not need to be concerned. Moreover, our good relations with the Pentagon will reduce its involvement in arms supply to Pakistan to a certain extent.

On the political front, the US has many concerns like Ukraine, ISIS, the South China Sea and Afghanistan. Our core national interests are not in conflict with any of these. We do recognise Russia's legitimate interests in Ukraine, but the annexation of Crimea under the guise of a referendum is contrary to our own principles.

The dangers arising out of ISIS in West Asia will reach our shores sooner than later, if its progress is not checked. We too have commercial and maritime interests in the South China Sea.

The advent of a national government in Afghanistan has increased India's space in Afghanistan. The US will not push India for India's involvement in these issues, but will certainly expect our understanding, which will not be hard to promise.

Modi has more similarities with Obama than with Shinzo Abe or Xi Jinping. Both Modi and Obama have broken the glass ceiling of birth and upbringing and are products of the established democratic process. Both are orators with vision, who can sway public opinion. Together, they should be able to develop a common vision for themselves and the globe. In that sense, if nothing else, Modi's "Amercayaan" will be a success.'

The visit was more successful than anticipated. What impressed President Barack Obama was that Modi had a grip on a significant section of his voters as demonstrated at the rock star reception that he received at the Madison Square Garden even before he visited Washington. Having enthralled the Americans and the Indian American community, Modi's US visit marked a new direction in strengthening of Indo-US ties. In a four-day visit, Modi not only met US President Barack Obama, but also sought to invite investment from prominent CEOs and urged the Indian-American community to take up a greater role in the development of India.

The highlights of Modi's US visit were a Modi-Obama joint statement which sought to reset ties between India and the United States, a Joint editorial, the first instance of the two leaders putting forward a common point of view, the Madison Square Garden performance of Modi, his UN General Assembly speech, promise of lifetime visas for people of Indian origin, a breakfast with CEOs and an op-ed by Modi in the *Wall Street Journal*.

Addressing the Indian Americans at the Madison Square Garden, Modi said:

'Just like Mahatma Gandhi made freedom struggle a national movement, we have to make development and progress a people's movement. 1.25 billion people should work for the betterment of India. I am sure that now an atmosphere has been created where every Indian wants to work for the nation.'

Like you, Mahatma Gandhi was an NRI. I implore you to do something in your capacity for the country ... India has the demographic dividend to succeed. There is no reason for gloom. I am sure that India is going progress at a rapid speed, led by the strength and capabilities of its youth ... A day will come when the world will not have young workforce. We will be able to supply the requisite manpower to all,' Modi said.

Modi said that people kept asking him for a grand vision. 'I am an ordinary, small person. But I want to do big things for small people. People have exaggerated ideas about what a PM should do. I want to break that misconception,' Modi said.

In the *Wall Street Journal* op-ed, describing America as India's 'natural global partner', Modi said the complementary strengths of the two democracies can be used for inclusive and broad-based development to transform lives across the globe.

I wrote on 22 November 2014:

'The announcement that Barack Obama had accepted Narendra Modi's invitation to be the chief guest at the Republic Day parade in 2015 is like Nixon's visit to China in 1972, an unexpected and uncharacteristic initiative by a politician.

The visit will be immensely symbolic, but there is enough time for both sides to work out substantive agreements to transform the relationship. Modi has produced another rabbit out of his magician's hat, unleashing immense possibilities for India, the US and the world.

No one will know whether India had ever invited a US President to the Republic Day, ever since India began the practice of inviting foreign leaders to the parade in the fifties. Most likely, this is the first time that such an invitation was extended and, of course, this is the first time it was accepted.

Dr Manmohan Singh may have thought of inviting George W Bush, but the political climate may not have been propitious for such an important initiative. President Bush had to go to Purana Quila, next to the zoo, to address the Indian people, as an address to Parliament was considered sensitive even after the nuclear deal was concluded.

Finding a politically correct Head of State or government year after year for the Republic Day must be a minor headache for every Prime Minister. The chosen guest inevitably raises questions of appropriateness and propriety. Availability of the right dignitary is an issue when most heads are peripatetic. When the jigsaw is finally resolved, the result may not convey the right message. We cannot go wrong with Bhutan, Mauritius and Russia, but even Sri Lanka can be tricky, depending on the temperature in Chennai and New Delhi.

France has been a favourite and has the unique distinction, with Bhutan, of having been invited four times. China and Pakistan are out of the question, particularly since 1962 and 1971.

There have been occasions when a dignitary backed out at the last minute and we had to resort to getting our all-weather friends like Bhutan and Mauritius to fill in. Japan's Shinzo Abe's arrival last year was the most important political signal out of Vijay Chowk in recent years.

Modi's thought process in inviting Obama can be traced to the days when Modi was persona non grata in the United States. Having erased that chapter after the rock star reception he received in the Madison Square Garden, the next medal he could strive for was a visit to India by Barack Obama. It did not matter that Obama was considered a lame duck President by many.

Being a man in a hurry, he could not have waited till a new President was elected in the US. He calculated that Obama could not refuse the honour of being the chief guest at the Republic Day parade when India's hard and soft power would be on display. As for the domestic reaction, Modi is confident that the Congress will not oppose the visit and the Left parties are too weak to make much of a noise.

A visit to India at this time makes sense to Obama. He has just lost the mid-term elections and he is in a mood to assert his Presidential authority, as he has shown in dealing with immigration. Earlier, he had hesitated to take the immigration bull by the horns by saying that he was not an emperor, only a President.

American Presidents tend to behave like emperors in the last two years of their Presidency, whether they lost the mid-term elections or not. In a short ceremonial visit there is little risk of failure as it can be explained away. On the other hand, if substantive decisions are taken, it will be another feather in his cap.

Obama is free of the compulsions of the hyphenation of India and Pakistan, which prompted Bill Clinton to visit Pakistan almost stealthily for five hours after spending five days in India. No American President can even think of visiting Pakistan at this time. But Obama took the precaution of telephoning Nawaz Sharif to inform him of his visit to India and made a proforma promise that he would undertake a visit to Pakistan 'as soon as the situation normalises in the country.' They also discussed Afghanistan during the conversation.

Pakistan made an inevitable reference to India, including the suspension of the dialogue and firing on the border and urged Obama to raise the Kashmir issue with India. The visit is likely to be substantive rather than ceremonial, given the developments between Modi's visit to Washington in September and now. Although some of our foreign policy experts said Modi got nothing out of the visit to New York and Washington, the signals were clear that the relations were on the upswing as Modi's priorities, foreign investment and strengthening of security coincided with America's strategic approach.

Many processes were set in motion during the visit and there are already signs of rapprochement like in the case of the WTO controversy. Having been rebuffed by China and Pakistan in his peace efforts, Modi chose to build bridges not just with the US, but also with Japan, Vietnam and Australia. He has not jumped on to the US bandwagon, but he appears to have developed linkages to counter China in the whole of the Asia Pacific, including the island States in the South Pacific.

Obama's decision to visit India must be a result of his judgment that Modi is a man of action and he is capable of taking decisive action to resolve the problems that have bedevilled India-US relations.

The Nuclear Liability Law was a hard nut to crack even for Obama and Modi. Moreover, it was Modi's party that deliberately introduced the bill in this regard to prevent nuclear trade with the US, which the nuclear deal was supposed to usher in. Obama too was not very keen to sell nuclear reactors to India for fear of accusation by the non-proliferationists that India was being encouraged to violate the NPT. Still, both of them did not want to leave the issue untouched. They gave the impression that the issue was resolved by an agreement to set up an insurance to cover the claim for damages, if any and that both sides would continue the negotiations. The sudden removal of the then Foreign Secretary Sujatha Singh after she said that the deal was done added some mystery to the affair.'

My assessment of Modi's visit on 2 October 2014 was the following:

'Prime Minister Modi is not a modern day Swami Vivekananda to conquer the West on his first visit nor is he Pandit Jawaharlal Nehru to dazzle the world with his charismatic diplomacy.

He is the new prime minister of India, a leader of the Bharatiya Janata Party which opposed the India-US nuclear deal first and supported the Nuclear Liability Act to deny US nuclear trade with India. He became prime minister at a time when India-US relations were at a low ebb and he himself was denied a US visa.

To expect that he has a magic wand to resolve all differences and announce breakthroughs in all issues during his first visit to the US is to be unrealistic.

As anticipated in these columns, Modi made a mark in the US, where the image in the media and the public mind matter; he established rapport with President Obama, reached agreements on the way to resolve difficult issues and identified new areas of cooperation, in keeping with his agenda for India's development and security.

The Vision Statement and the Joint Statement contain the way forward in specific areas. Instead of going for the low-hanging fruit to show immediate achievements, the two sides decided to work diligently to transform the relationship from the transactional to the strategic.

Nuclear and arms trade on mutually acceptable terms, the combat together against terrorism and fighting climate change are long-term goals, which will immensely benefit the two countries and give the right signals to the rest of the world. The joint op-ed in the *Washington Post*, a novel diplomatic tool, showed that the two leaders share a global view.

Nothing in Modi's domestic or foreign policy was a matter of concern to Obama. Modi's domestic agenda, consisting of a liberalised and foreign investment friendly economy and a strengthened defence sector is conducive to the growth of India-US cooperation.

His neighbourhood policy and interactions with Japan, China, Russia, Israel and Australia have given no reason for concern to the US.

His position on international terrorism that it is a crime against humanity and that the ISIS's activities is a challenge to mankind, against which all people should unite, coincides with Obama's own worldview.

His assertion that terrorism in India is not home-grown and that Indian Muslims will defeat Al Qaeda was much appreciated. On

Afghanistan, he hinted at a continuing role for the US in the troubled nation.

Modi's maiden speech at the United Nations was striking for its restraint and realism, though his using a prepared text detracted from his usual oratorical flourish.

He was firm on Pakistan when he made it clear that India will engage in a dialogue with Pakistan only in an atmosphere free of violence and terrorism.

He dealt with the issue of terrorism in the larger context of the world and called upon the United Nations to adopt a comprehensive convention against terrorism, which India had proposed years ago.

He stated that India's whole philosophy is one of treating the whole world as a family. He was restrained even when he spoke of the need for expansion of the UN Security Council, as he did so without reiterating India's own claim. He urged unity in the United Nations suggesting that instead of breaking into various groups it should act as a "G-All".

The unprecedented rock star reception accorded to Modi at the Madison Square Garden reflected the genuine admiration and expectation on the part of Indian Americans that he will transform India.

Indian Americans extend support to India selectively. They were critical of Indian policies at times, but fully supportive on other occasions, like at the time of the nuclear deal.

The Indian-American population, which is not only prosperous, but also in crucial professions, has considerable influence. That explains why several Senators and Congressmen, including the Chairman of the Senate Foreign Relations Committee and the equivalent body in the House and a Governor, were at hand to greet Modi.

The India caucus in Congress and the friends of India in the Senate are the offshoots of the growing clout of Indian Americans in US politics. President Barack Obama cannot but take into account the tremendous enthusiasm of the significant one per cent of his people for the new leader of the largest democracy. The very purpose of the Madison Square Garden extravaganza was exactly that.

The Madison Square Garden event was more important for its symbolism and implications for the future than for what was said or done there. But Modi could be trusted to say the right things at the right time.

He harped basically on three themes—(i) how the overseas Indians, particularly Indian Americans, have raised India's standing and prestige abroad; (ii) the greatness of India, old and new; and (iii) his personal promise to meet expectations by sheer dint of hard work.

Modi's image of the Indians of today playing with the computer mouse rather than the proverbial snake was a compliment not only to India but also to overseas Indians who spearheaded the IT revolution in the world. He thanked Indian Americans for keeping awake with bated breath during the Indian elections, even though they could not participate in the vote. Many had even gone to India to provide support to him, he said.

Modi was at his best in waxing eloquent on Indian heritage and its potential. Gandhi created the freedom movement and he is determined to create a clean India movement. India is a young nation with an ancient history. With his penchant to create alphabetical soups for all occasions, he spoke of three Ds this time—Democracy, Demographic Dividend and Demand—which would drive India.

As expected, Modi spoke eloquently about Mangalyaan, the highly successful Mars mission, which took India to the galaxy of four Mars explorers. In Gujarat, an autorickshaw ride costs Rs 10 per kilometre, but the journey to the Mars cost only Rs 7 per kilometre, an argument against the charge of extravagance voiced by some. Though the Mars mission was launched before Modi's emergence, he took full credit for it.

Modi announced some consular concessions to overseas Indians, but not the dual citizenship, the long-cherished dream of Indian

Americans. Many had expected him to announce it, going beyond the Person of Indian Origin card and the Overseas Citizen of India card put in place by previous governments.

He must have explored it and realised that dual citizenship was not feasible for various reasons, including constitutional constraints. A lifelong visa for PIO cardholders is, however, an improvement. His own visa issue appeared to be behind his comment that India was offering visas on arrival to those who are reluctant to give visas to Indians.

Pepsico's Indra Nooyi encapsulated the American response, when she said, "Great Prime Minister, answers questions brilliantly. He is very focused on improving India and we are ready to work with him."'

A hint of the serious problems facing Modi's neighbourhood policy came in the Act I itself. From choosing 26 November to commence a SAARC summit, to not knowing the likely outcome of India's initiative in a small group of countries, to not anticipating the pressure building up in favour of China's membership, everything went wrong for India at the Kathmandu summit of SAARC in November 2014.

The reverberations of gunfire across the border and the encounter with Pakistani terrorists were audible in the conference hall, preventing the prime ministers of India and Pakistan from shaking hands or even smiling at each other. The net result was a further deterioration in India-Pakistan relations and an unnecessary confrontation with China on the issue of its status in SAARC. This was a summit India could have done without.

Another year of waiting would not have made any difference to SAARC or to India's relations with its member nations. The kind of optimism expressed by politicians and former diplomats alike even a few days before the commencement of the summit was astonishing.

They betrayed a lack of appreciation of the history of SAARC and the obvious built-in impediments to its success.

The Gujral Doctrine, which was acknowledged as a failure, was virtually resurrected by the argument that India had to define its role, from seeking reciprocity in bilateral relations to being prepared to go the extra mile in meeting the aspirations of all the other SAARC nations. To ask for a conflict-mediating or conflict-resolving institution on multilateral and bilateral issues is nothing short of suicidal.

Equally unrealistic was the suggestion that the time was opportune for a new regional architecture and that the time had come to reconnect with India's neighbours. The Indian resource position was not so robust that India could invest in SAARC as Germany did in the European Union. India had never been unsympathetic to the aspirations of its neighbours. Therefore, the advice that India must build trust with its neighbours, showing solidarity and forging with them a habit of cooperation, seemed unwarranted. There were many instances of India bending backwards to satisfy its smaller neighbours. Kachativu and Teen Bigha were obvious concessions we made for friendship.

The sense of optimism that India could work with SAARC countries to alleviate poverty and build a coalition to advance Indian interests, which characterised the initiatives of the Modi government from day one, had already been proved wrong. Nawaz Sharif's visit was followed by a sharp deterioration of relations, leading to heavy firing across the border and encounters with terrorists. The display of animosity between India and Pakistan in New York cast a shadow on both countries. Under the circumstances, a SAARC summit was doomed to fail. To expect that Pakistan would accept Indian initiatives on energy and road and railways at this time was incorrigible optimism.

The claim that the summit enabled India to isolate Pakistan was exaggerated. The normal reaction of all countries, particularly our neighbours, to an India-Pakistan confrontation was to become peacemakers, not to take sides. The greatest favour that they showed us was to say that all matters should be resolved bilaterally.

The Nepalese Prime Minister, enthused as the host to ensure the success of the summit, pushed the two sides to compromise, not to find fault with either.

The spectacle of Indian and Pakistani leaders avoiding each other amused the others, even after the 32-second handshake and the acceptance by Pakistan of the energy agreement. In fact, India was on the edge of isolation when the other seven showed willingness to accept China as a member.

The suggestion that India should promote SAARC minus Pakistan was impossible. SAARC was established on the basis that every decision had to be by consensus, not by vote. Although this provision was made at India's behest in the first instance, the others were sure to quote the same provision to prevent a break-up.

The point to note about SAARC is that it is the sum total of India's bilateral relations with the other countries, though it has a multilateral flavour. The clout that we had with them has been reduced, with the emergence of China as an alternate source of strength and money.

The ambition of the founder of SAARC, Zia-ur-Rahman, was not to forge a genuinely multilateral organisation, but to create a front to extract concessions from India and that was the reason why Indira Gandhi resisted it as long as she could. Today, SAARC is moving in the direction that its founder had set for it.

Kathmandu showed for the first time that India cannot keep China out of SAARC for long even if we argue that China is not a

South Asian country. The moment China enters SAARC, the Indian role will change dramatically. This is another reason why we should gradually reduce the central role of SAARC in South Asia.

The association is not of any particular importance to us in cultivating our neighbours and Pakistan's negativism should be seen by the countries concerned as the reason for India losing interest in SAARC. In a sense, we do not have a major stake in projecting SAARC as a viable regional forum.

Prime Minister Modi did well to signal in Kathmandu that we will work with our neighbours, regardless of SAARC. Unless Pakistan sees the economic compulsions of a regional organisation to tone down their political animosity towards India, our focus should not be on SAARC, but on the individual South Asian States.

There, the competition will be with China and not with Pakistan and it will be an uphill task. But, with Pakistan out of the game, we may have a better chance to build partnerships with the others.

As to the question whether the Prime Minister's vision of SAARC was turning out to be an illusion, it should be admitted that it was indeed so. It was time for him to play down the importance of SAARC and reach out farther for strategic partnerships.

His success with the United States, Japan, Australia and even the South Pacific States was encouraging. He should recognise the inherent weaknesses and dangers of SAARC and devise an alternative strategy to deal with his neighbours.

A mixed bag of triumphs and trials in foreign policy marked the first hundred days of the Modi government. The list includes an unprecedented invitation to SAARC leaders and the Prime Minister of Mauritius to attend the swearing-in of the new government; a visit to India's steadfast friend, Bhutan; support to BRICS and its new bank; assertion of friendship to Russia; stress on economic and commercial ties in a meeting with the Chinese President, a signal that India would be even-handed between Israel and Palestine, even while reiterating support for the Palestinian cause; meetings with three ministers from the United States; rejection of the WTO Agreement as it endangers food security plans in India; a historic visit to Nepal; an invitation to the world to manufacture in India; and a decision to resume the dialogue with Pakistan and its cancellation and shying away from signing a trade agreement with ASEAN.

As he completed a hundred days, Modi had paid a game-changing visit to Japan and on the cards were meetings with the leaders of Australia, China and the US. A newcomer to diplomacy, Modi had taken care to stress continuity, but without making it a fetish. He let the MEA mandarins prepare their briefs and used them to great effect in his conversations, echoing more or less the same language that Dr Manmohan Singh used.

The strategy was to appear steadfast in the consensus positions, which had evolved over the years. Instead of formulating and announcing new policies in advance, he decided to let his thinking to evolve as he met world leaders and measured the efficacy of his policy.

Modi spoke to Pakistan about terrorism, to Sri Lanka about the need for a political solution of the Tamil issue, to Bangladesh about illegal migration, and generally stressed the primacy of India in South Asia. Continuity for him was an anchor, as he came to grips with each situation and developed his own nuance for it. Like in the case of the nuclear doctrine, which the Bharatiya Janata Party had vowed to review, he resorted to the argument of continuity and national consensus to gain time.

Modi, however, was keen to put his stamp on diplomacy.

Innovation in diplomacy was already visible in Modi's moves. The invitation to SAARC leaders for the swearing-in was innovative and their actual arrival was a triumph.

Distancing himself from the neighbourhood policy of his predecessors, he made the innovation that India would fight poverty with SAARC and rise with SAARC in the global arena. This was a calculated risk, given the history of the bedevilled relations that India had with several neighbours.

He tried his personal diplomacy with Nawaz Sharif, bringing in the two mothers and exchanging gifts for them. Similar innovative contacts may have been initiated with the other leaders. He is known to choose personal gifts for his counterparts.

Innovation was very much on display during his visit to Nepal. The most dramatic was his offer to Nepal to consider any change that Nepal may want to see in the Treaty of 1950. This was a way of confronting the issue squarely and finding a solution his predecessors had shied away from in the past. He succeeded to remove the deep suspicion that the Nepalese had about India's designs on their water resource. The decisiveness, which Modi had shown in taking domestic political decisions, could be seen in his diplomacy also. After agreeing to resume talks with Pakistan, marking a departure from India's position that talks were contingent upon action against terrorists, Modi did not hesitate to call off the talks when Pakistan went back to its old ways of hobnobbing with Kashmiri dissidents.

Continuity came to his rescue when he put forward the Simla Agreement and the Lahore Declaration as the basis of the dialogue in the future. The decision to block a debate in the Rajya Sabha on Palestine even at the risk of paralysing the Upper House was a part of his decisiveness.

Equally, he did not hesitate to vote in favour of Palestine at the UN Human Rights Council, when he realised a change in Palestine policy would not be nationally acceptable in the face of the ongoing Gaza war. He stunned the Americans and the rest of the world by standing firm on the WTO issue at a time when the strategic partnership with the US was being discussed.

Secretiveness and the element of surprise in announcing decisions marked the Modi style of diplomacy. From being a voluble politician, Modi became a reticent statesman. He did not believe that he needed to explain each of his actions in diplomacy and open it to scrutiny by the press and the public.

The process of decision-making remained private even after the decisions were announced. He made a departure from the established practice of wining and dining journalists on board his flights precisely because he did not want to be influenced by the prejudices and predilections of the press.

At the same time, he did not maintain the sphinx-like silence of his immediate predecessor. His activism in the social media had made him less dependent on the conventional media to spread his message. Messages in social media were carried without the interference of editorial scissors and pressures of time and space.

His visuals with sartorial signals like different garbs and headgears also conveyed a vibrant image. In other words, his silence and speeches were measured and orchestrated for maximum effect.

The Modi mystique remained even after his hundred days in office because of the control he exercised on information and his continuous visibility. China and the United States were unsure as to what they could really accomplish in their encounters with Modi. They would articulate their positions on the basis of the general framework of his policy approaches, which were outlined.

US Defence Secretary Chuck Hagel did precisely that when he outlined the co-production proposal as a bait to get defence contracts. China would naturally stress investments in infrastructure and trade. Still in the stage of wooing India in the formative stages of the new government, these countries offered several diplomatic bargains.

The first hundred days of diplomacy raised the hope that Modi's diplomatic talents would be an asset to him. But the diplomatic dance was performed on thin ice and his adroitness was still to be proved.

Act I was a period of visibility, speech-making, vision-building, daydreaming, sloganeering, fashion-setting, innovating, posturing and promising change. Modi looked impressive as the leader of a resurgent India, an inspiring speaker, a man of promise and a man of integrity. He emerged as a true brand ambassador of India, often appearing bigger than the brand.

Even without any concrete results to show, both Obama and Modi won approbation in the first year itself. Obama won a Nobel Prize for Peace and Modi came close to becoming *Time* magazine's Man of the Year. He made it to the cover of the *Time* magazine before completing his first year, portrayed as a man of action and vision, a messiah to uplift India from poverty. The likes of Moody's raised the rating of India even before the economic liberalisation was put in place.

Indian foreign policy remained unchanged, without anyone noticing it, very much like US foreign policy at the end of the first year of the Obama administration. The world expected Modi, however, to do wonders before he completed his first term as prime minister. Modi had his moments of disillusionment throughout the year, partly because of his illusions of grandeur, clearly a tragic flaw, about India and himself. The invitation extended to the leaders of SAARC countries had a touch of arrogance, associated with an emperor inviting lesser monarchs to his coronation. But still they came, perhaps because of curiosity to measure the man, whom they had heard so much about.

Modi's hope that his gesture would be reciprocated by the neighbours with a new warmth and respect was belied because he had nothing to offer except to repeat the old refrain of friendship and cooperation with plenty of caveats. They repeated their woes of frustration felt at the hands of India, which was like a stone wall, when they made their demands of their big and powerful neighbour. One initiative that Modi made to resume the dialogue with Pakistan turned sour when the latter decided to test the waters by meeting the Hurriyat leaders. India and Pakistan were back to square one when they hurled accusations against each other at the UN General Assembly.

The encounter with the Chinese president in India was even more of disillusionment for Modi. The charm and warmth he unleashed on Xi was reciprocated with an incursion on the Line of Actual Control, something that the Chinese did whenever anything significant happened between the two countries. Having advocated a tough policy towards China during the election, Modi was constrained to tell the Chinese leader to his face that war and peace were not possible simultaneously. The situation was barely salvaged by the economic promises China held out during the summit.

Having burnt his fingers with SAARC and China, Modi was determined to make a success of his US visit. He could have delayed that journey by sulking over the visa issue, the Devyani Khobragade incident, which he had resented and the BJP sponsored nuclear liability law.

But he put those impediments behind to pursue with the US his twin objectives of securing investment and strengthening security.

The deftness with which he raised the relations to a higher level showed that the issues that bedevilled relations were not insurmountable.

He unleashed the money power and influence of the Indian-American community to provide the backdrop of his visit even before he reached the White House and overwhelmed Barack Obama. Madison Square Garden witnessed the Modi magic, which was not lost on the Washington elite. What impressed Obama was not the immediate solution of the problems, but the determination of India to overcome past animosities and move forward. The success of the US visit came in the form of a return visit by Obama on Republic Day to become the first US President to visit India twice. The new understanding on the liability law appeared to be the big-ticket accomplishment initially, but the bigger deal was on the Asia Pacific.

And even bigger was the avenue opened for greater defence cooperation. The strategic partnership with the US assumed new dimensions and a new dynamism. Modi overplayed his personal rapport card and Obama's parting shot on religious intolerance came as an unkind cut. The jacket fiasco was nothing but a comic interlude. The unprecedented mutuality of interests discovered between India and the US was Modi's biggest foreign policy success.

The multitude of the other trophies on Modi's wall is testimony to his virtual Odyssey across continents, from Japan to Australia to Fiji and from Germany to France to Canada. They were more than ceremonial or symbolic because he had a specific agenda for each, much of which was welcomed by his hosts. Modi took in his stride Japan's adamant stand on the nuclear agreement and the Italian machinations, which sabotaged a possible EU summit. Modi's assertion that India had a right rather than mere eligibility to be a permanent member of the UN Security Council did not carry conviction.

It is to the credit of the Foreign Service that there were no protocol snafus or crossing of wires, though the visits must have strained the resources of our missions abroad. The scaling down of the retinue of the prime minister may have helped, but the pomp and show has only increased. Air India One showed signs of fatigue, but it did not cause any disruption to the epic journeys.

The visit to China came as a fitting finale to the first year of the Prime Minister's feverish foreign policy forays, which took him also to uranium-rich Mongolia and a model of industrial development, South Korea. By stressing the primacy of economic cooperation with China, Modi covered up his disappointment over the lack of any breakthrough in the burning strategic issues like the border.

But his forthright demand for progress in festering issues must have made a deep impression on the Chinese leadership. Modi played the ball straight into the Chinese court though Xi Jinping and Li Keqiang were keeping it in the air so far.

The truth is that India is more a target than a partner in China's worldview. Evidently, Modi carried with him not only Nehru's dream of Asian solidarity, but also Patel's scepticism of China.

India's place in the global puzzle that China is assiduously putting together was yet to be determined. Though there was nothing new in India-China encounters, Modi certainly set the Yangtze on fire.

If Rajiv Gandhi rediscovered the Indian Diaspora and the subsequent governments vied with each other to cultivate it, Modi made it a priority concern in India's diplomacy.

The initial response of the community was overwhelming, but they continue to have their bodies in their cozy homes abroad, their hearts in India and their wealth in Swiss banks.

Ironically, in the midst of Modi's Herculean efforts to bring investments to India, reports came that Indian investments abroad reached unprecedented heights. The success of Diaspora Diplomacy does not depend on the concessions India keeps giving to the community, but in the community adopting a 'Look India' policy, when it comes to investment.

Modi's promise of change during the election campaign was on the domestic front, but his first year in office focused on foreign policy beyond all expectations. At the heart of his approach was the conviction that the world had become interdependent and that his domestic success would depend on the resources he could muster from abroad. And hence the slogan, 'Make in India' rather than 'Made in India' or 'Made for India'.

Apart from fulfilling the promise of change, the future held the challenge to deal with India's traditional friendships. India had promises to keep in Russia, the UK, the Gulf and Africa. While he had to slow down his pace of foreign visits to eliminate the red tape and to lay the red carpet he had promised his invitees, he still had to traverse many paths that beckoned him. He could not rest on his laurels and the Odyssey must continue. Modi earned the name 'peripatetic Prime Minister with his early journeys, but apart from neighbours, the United States, Japan, and other major countries, he went only for multilateral meetings. The places were carefully selected to project his international agenda. It was the waves he made that created the impression that he was travelling all the time. There were demands for him to stay home and deal with domestic issues.

As the curtains fell on Act I of the Modiplomacy drama, the hero was on stage larger than life with a dazzle that is unusual in classic plays. The objective of the play was laid out and the important dramatis personae made their appearance and the hero began to feel on top of the world. He had a glimpse of the difficulties ahead, but the adulation at home and abroad gave him a sense of security. He became ready for the action ahead of him and the audience was quite excited about the prospect of seeing him in action. 'Well begun is half done', shouted his admirers and 'it is only half done', retorted his detractors.

ACT II
THE COMPLICATIONS

Contours of Modiplomacy Emerge

THE Act II of Modi's diplomacy opened with the most dramatic result of Modi's visit to Washington, a game-changing visit to India by President Barack Obama, the first ever US President to be the Chief Guest at the Republic Day Parade in New Delhi. I anticipated the outcome of the visit in the following manner on 21 January 2015:

'Success is inevitable in the end as President Obama's presence at the Republic Day Parade on Rajpath will signify a landmark in India-US relations. Never has an American President shown up for the Republic Day Parade and nobody had even thought of inviting one of them, not even John F Kennedy or Bill Clinton. Significantly, nobody has questioned the Narendra Modi initiative and Barack Obama's ready acceptance of it. No black flag demonstrations are expected. No 'Yankee go home' placards, even with the addition, "Take me with you!" will appear in Delhi.

This is remarkable, considering that the one American President, who signed the nuclear deal, George W Bush, could not even address the Parliament. It looks as though there is a consensus today on the importance of seeing Barack Obama in Delhi, the first US President to visit India a second time in office. The deterioration of our relations with Pakistan and China is the catalyst for this consensus.

The brouhaha over Modi's Madison Square Garden and Central Park performance deflected attention from the very substantive agenda Obama and Modi set for themselves in their joint statement. Never before has there been such a comprehensive wish list, with clear indications of the way to go. A mere action report on that agenda will be sufficient to make the visit a success. Even if a few of them are brought to fruition, what is essentially a ceremonial visit will turn out to be a sensational success.

In the old days, US Presidents came to India with gifts or promises of gifts. The last among them was George W Bush, who came to enjoy the glow of his nuclear gift. The situation changed in 2010, when Obama came not with a bundle of gifts, but with rolls of wish lists. His own re-election appeared to hang on the jobs to be created out of expected fighter aircraft and nuclear reactor deals with India. In fact, the disappointment over the non-consummation of these deals may have made Obama indifferent to India till he discovered the "Man of Action" in Modi.

Obama's wish list this time has three main items—a 10-year renewal of the defence agreement, dilution of the nuclear liability law and an agreement on climate change, which will bury the Kyoto Protocol. The litmus test of his success lies in achieving these three, and there is expectation that at least a certain amount of progress is possible in each of them.

India's wishes are broader and less daunting—trade, immigration and anti-terrorism, apart from political support on Afghanistan, Pakistan and China. Here, the interests are mutual and have the possibility of gradual resolution. The balance sheet of the visit therefore must please both Obama and Modi.

Given Modi's twin objectives of foreign policy, namely, FDI and iron-clad security, the US is a natural ally. He cannot get either of these in adequate measure from any other source. No wonder, then, that India and the US are burning the midnight oil to find satisfaction on the US wish list. Getting a robust defence agreement on our terms with the possibility of co-designing and co-production fits in well with the 'Make inIndia' initiative. Defence imports in recent years have already reached $10 billion and it can multiply under the Defence Trade and Technology Initiative (DTTI). There is even talk of cancellation of the fighter aircraft deal with Rafale to bring back F-18 into consideration.

As for the nuclear liability law, Obama has no heart in nuclear trade with India, even though he is under pressure to pursue this issue. Left to him, Obama would be happier if he did not have to strengthen India's nuclear capability. Moreover, dilution of the liability law may not remove the last obstacle in nuclear trade with India. American lawyers have been saying, however, that there is no legal issue without a legal solution to it. A mix of relaxation of the law, together with a package of insurance policies, is the way they are seeking to put together. But even if there is a delay in a solution beyond the visit, it will not detract from its success.

Obama will attach greater importance to an agreement on climate change than to nuclear liability. For him, it is a matter of great domestic importance. His historic achievement in Copenhagen of moving the world away from the Rio and Kyoto agreements was with the implicit support of India, though India has tried to renege on it in Bali and Peru. To bring India around in Paris is a dire necessity for him. Like he did before Copenhagen, he has already struck a deal with China. With no hope of imposing mandatory cuts only on the developed countries, India is likely to cave in and accept voluntary cuts for all, particularly if there is adequate compensation by way of trade and technology transfer. A substantial investment in environment-friendly industries and adaptation measures will be irresistible.

Progress on more nebulous Indian wishes will not make or break the visit. Most of them can be covered by innovative formulations. On terrorism, the US and the UK have already won Indian approbation by demanding action against Zaki-ur-Rehman Lakhvi (26/11 mastermind).

A stern warning has been issued to Pakistan not to engage in terrorism during President Obama's visit. The trade figures are already hovering around $100 billion. Obama has taken bold initiatives on immigration, paving the way for similar initiatives to meet Indian expectations even in the face of opposition in the United States Congress. On Afghanistan and Pakistan, finding acceptable formulations is not beyond the negotiating capabilities of Indian and American diplomats.

Modi has not shown great attachment to the US position on India's permanent membership of the United Nations Security Council or on the Indian entry into the Nuclear Suppliers Group (NSG), Missile Technology Control Regime (MTCR), the Wassenaar Arrangement and the Australian Group. These will drag on as India's Non-Proliferation Treaty (NPT) status is a factor in them and the US cannot act decisively alone, even if it wishes to do so.

The chief guests do not come to the Republic Day parades with heavy agendas. The occasion is ceremonial in nature and reflective of the warmth in bilateral relations. The guests come to celebrate special relationships, not to engage in tough negotiations. By his very presence in Delhi on Republic Day, Obama is revisiting the most defining relationship of the 20th century after a period of stagnation. With the advent of Narendra Modi and his experiments with China and Pakistan, President Obama at the parade will mark a game changer for India and the US.'

In actual fact, the visit of President Obama was a game changer in many ways. It was the high point of the Act II of the Modi drama. President Barack Obama would not have changed the date of his State of the Union Address, flown over the oceans, taken the risk of letting the world know more than a month in advance that he would be under the open sky in Rajpath for more than two hours, exposed himself to Russian aircraft flying too close to him for comfort, learnt many Hindi phrases, savoured Gujarati dishes and spent two nights in Delhi to secure a 'breakthrough' on the nuclear liability issue or to renew a defence agreement. Nuclear trade with India was not his priority. He could well have accomplished them without leaving the White House.

Modi too would not have walked for an hour on the Hyderabad House lawn, talking about the minute details of the insurance pool to let the American companies off the hook on liability law. Nor was it necessary for him to spend weeks together to make a 'lame duck' President's visit historical. They both had agendas that went beyond these mundane matters. The threat from the chilly Himalayas had to be tackled in the warm waters of the Indian Ocean. Obama came in search for a legacy for himself as the man who took the dragon by its non-existent horns. He had sensed that India was ready to be the kingpin of the Asian Pivot he had proposed earlier.

He had also sensed that Modi's disappointment with China and Pakistan would drive him to an American embrace. The legacy Obama wants to leave behind is a new map of the Asia Pacific, in which India, Japan and Australia would find common cause with the United States rather than with China. He came close to making a beginning by handing a draft declaration on Asia Pacific to Modi, which the latter could not resist. Modi made it known in his joint presser that the visit was in the context of the increased relevance of the Asia-Pacific and the Indian Ocean.

India did not sign on to a US-India-Japan-Australia axis, but as the Chinese caught on in no time, Modi revealed his inclination to bank on the US for India's security and prosperity. The message came loud and clear in the statement on the Asia Pacific, which stated: 'Regional prosperity depends on security. We affirm the importance of safeguarding maritime security and ensuring freedom of navigation and overflight throughout the region, especially in the South China Sea. We call on all parties to avoid the threat or use of force and pursue resolution of territorial and maritime disputes through all peaceful means, in accordance with universally recognised principles of international law, including the United Nations Convention on the Law of the Sea.'

As against this forthright statement of intent and the progress over liability law and defence agreements, Obama's disappointment over disagreement on climate change paled into insignificance. Obama, therefore, played up the personal chemistry, though he addressed Modi as "NaMo" only a couple of times, while Modi insisted on addressing Obama as Barack repeatedly. Both knew that, at least for the next two years, they would have to work together, given the start that they have made in identifying the complementarities. They have to walk and talk longer to fashion an arrangement, which would ensure that China rose as peacefully as possible and did not threaten peace in Asia and the world.

Yet, the volumes of words generated in Delhi, perhaps the largest in any India-US summit, did not add up to a containment of China alliance. Space was left for other nations, including China, to be part of the new configuration that was envisaged. The vision of Shinzo Abe was also incorporated into the framework. The fact that the major countries in the region had more engagement with China than they had with each other weighed heavily in the formulations.

For this reason, the Chinese reaction was not only a blend of surprise and indignation, but also expectation that the US-India partnership would not turn hostile to it. Those who believed that the visit would not be substantive were stunned by the breadth and depth of the understanding reached between Obama and Modi.

It was a reflection of the new intimacy that Obama, in a parting shot, spoke of the need for religious freedom and tolerance in India. It was meant not for Modi as much as it was for the fringe elements, which threatened to destroy the heritage of the Mahatma. If Obama had glossed over the obvious danger of religious obscurantism, he would have no credibility back home.

The blanks and the brackets in the various pronouncements, written and spoken, were no less significant than the issues, which were spelt out with clarity. Pakistan remained an imbroglio in the US calculations. China did not forget to drag Pakistan straight on to the centre stage by highlighting its perennial friendship with Pakistan. The message was that the Pakistan factor should not be forgotten, as China would operate through Pakistan to disturb the new cosiness in India-US relations. Climate change and intellectual property rights (IPR) issues could not be wished away even with the new bonhomie. Obama made it clear that India should play its role, if the strategies of the future should be beneficial in combating climate change.

The unfinished agenda remained daunting. India's permanent membership of the United Nations Security Council was not even close to fruition after the parade. In fact, Obama may well have opened his eyes to the Russian tanks that rolled in front of him and the Russian aircraft that flew over him.

The US showed some flexibility on India's membership of Asia-Pacific Economic Cooperation (APEC), but even that was not a done deal. India had stopped asking for it because of the adamant opposition of the US for many years. The non-proliferation regimes were still out of reach for India, as highlighted by the Chinese.

The 'Joint Strategic Vision for the Asia-Pacific and Indian Ocean Region' did not offer a solution for the security threats that India faced. But, together with the robust economic ties developing in the region, it might enhance our capacity to play our legitimate role.

The contours of 'Modiplomacy' became clear in 2015, after his initial encounters with the world leaders. His was a transactional approach as against Pandit Nehru's approach of projecting India's requirements as those of the world itself. Decolonisation, disarmament, equitable distribution of wealth and human rights were as much in our interest as in the interest of the world. But India was leading the newly independent countries rather than making deals with individual countries. Modi, on the other hand, spelt out national interests clearly and sought to secure them by direct negotiations. I wrote on 28 October 2015:

'To characterise the foreign policy of the most peripatetic Indian Prime Minister as "nationalist" may appear contradictory. The popular demand is that he should be in India more often, to deal with the crying needs of the country. He is selective in his eloquence on domestic issues, but he is opening out his heart to foreign audiences. He is seen more in the company of foreign leaders, not only political leaders, but also leaders in technology, finance and economics. But the core of his agenda is domestic, not international. His arena is international, but his concerns are domestic.

The transformation of India's foreign policy from an "internationalist" one to a "nationalist" one may well have begun after Jawaharlal Nehru and V.K. Krishna Menon. Domestic preoccupations were brought to centre stage, though the old tradition of engagement in world affairs remained alive. The torrent of international issues—such as the conflicts in Indo-China and Korea, the Suez Canal crisis and even the conflict in Austria—in all of which India played a role without any specific agenda for itself, became a trickle.

Perhaps our early-day interventions happened because of the activism of the Non-Aligned Movement (NAM), which pronounced itself on every major international issue in its declarations. By shaping those pronouncements, mainly by balancing and moderating them, India found fulfilment in playing its international role. It did not find it necessary to take initiatives to resolve disputes or avert conflicts, except in its own neighbourhood. Our insistence on bilateralism in resolving issues may also have been an inhibiting factor.

In the post-Cold War era, India's internationalism began to be confined to regional and other groupings, most of them economic. Concerns about the protection of the global commons, such as the environment, assumed importance. We began looking at protecting our own interests, taking positions like "no mandatory reduction of greenhouse gases for the developing countries". We realised that our interests coincided with those of the great powers and the large developing countries like Brazil and even China. Copenhagen was a real turning point in our environment policy when we virtually disowned the Kyoto Protocol except in name. Our nuclear tests in 1998 and the subsequent nuclear deal with the United States left India with no like-minded countries in disarmament. It was the arm-twisting by the US that made the NSG provide us an exemption.

We had earlier used the non-aligned position that only non-permanent membership should be increased until comprehensive reform is accomplished, just to thwart the US-sponsored quick-fix solution of Germany and Japan being made Permanent Members. However, we then moved on to the G-4 initiative—under which India, Brazil, Japan and Germany would seek permanent membership—which has very few takers among the small developing countries. The G-77 virtually disappeared from many forums because India's leadership in it withered away.

India continued to take a global view in G-20 and the World Trade Organisation (WTO), primarily because of the reputation of Dr Manmohan Singh as an economic guru, even for Barack Obama. Dr Manmohan Singh's withdrawal from the international arena and his close relationship with the US in India's interests changed the Nehruvian view that India's dreams coincided with the world's dreams. During our last term at the UN Security Council, India seemed to be in a dilemma as to whether we should work with the non-aligned caucus or plough a lonely furrow; we ended up in flip-flops. Both the Permanent

Members and the non-aligned caucus found our term a mixed blessing.

A study of Prime Minister Modi's visits and speeches revealed that his strategy was that of a businessman, one who made deals only for benefits. His neighbourhood policy was an example.

Modi's surprise initiatives in foreign policy from day one seemed to project him as an internationalist. As C. Raja Mohan summarised in his book *Modi's World: Expanding India's Sphere of Influence* (2015), "he warmed up to America, recast the approach to China and Pakistan, sustained the old friendship with Russia, deepened the strategic partnership with Japan and Australia, boosted India's neighbourhood policy, wooed international business leaders and reconnected with the Indian diaspora."

We could add to this his championship of the reform of the Security Council; his stress on the environment; and his taking initiatives on getting closer to France, Germany, Canada, the island states and now Africa. But the change was not only in style and eloquence, but in turning Indian foreign policy inward. He had abandoned internationalism, genuine in the case of some of his predecessors and a cloak in the case of some others. In any relationship, the litmus test now is: what India can gain for itself, not what India can contribute to humanity.

Focusing on national interests in formulating foreign policy is fundamental for all countries. But turning statesmanship into salesmanship is a new phenomenon in Indian foreign policy. Our tradition has been to provide leadership to the world, not to demand it as our right, as Modi did in the case of the permanent membership of the Security Council. Speaking of our eminent qualifications is one thing, but claiming it as a right may drive our supporters away. Our case was that we were willing to serve on the Council to restore the balance there and to make it more relevant, not to claim membership as a right to protect our interests. Even the Permanent Members never claim that they have a right to be there.

A close study of the choice of countries Modi visited and the speeches he made would reveal that his strategy was that of a pragmatic businessman who will make deals for his benefit, but the moment the profit dwindles, he will go in search of new clients. His neighbourhood policy is a case in point. He started off with the ambition to remove poverty in South Asia through a renewed South Asian Association for Regional Cooperation (SAARC), but soon discovered the perfidy of Pakistan. He persisted for a while as India had much to gain from a transformation in India-Pakistan relations. However, SAARC was no longer a priority in his development agenda. Nepal is another case where his hopes were belied. Remember the cordiality and the oneness he projected with Nepal in the name of the eternal values the two countries shared! However, today he has virtually imposed an embargo on Nepal for not listening to our advice. Indira Gandhi did the same once, but she had explained repeatedly to the international community the rationale for her actions and had restored normalcy after a while. The world will watch our policies and make conclusions on our reliability and statesmanship.

The common elements in Modi's speeches abroad can be clearly identified. First and foremost, it is the grandeur of India and his own role as its man of destiny. Second, he claims that things have changed dramatically since he took over and that India is now ready to receive investments and recognition as a global player. He feels the world has a stake in India's development and security and that it is imperative for other countries to work with India.

He does not offer any specific concessions but expects the others to respond to his initiatives for their own benefit. According to him, "Make in India" and "Digital India" are opportunities for the world to promote India and derive benefits for themselves. In other words, the logic is one that is applied to an honest business in which every partner makes profit.

Statesmanship demands every national leader to have a global vision—he should place his country in the larger context of the well-being of mankind. In Modi's case, India is at the centre of the world. In his speeches at the UN, he claims that what the UN does today was anticipated by India long ago. If India considers the Earth as the mother and calls the whole world a family, it has nothing to learn from sustainable goals, so meticulously put together by other nations.

Modi raised the reform of the Security Council even in the sustainable development session, without saying what India would do as a Permanent Member for the world. His sticking his neck out on this issue, when there was little hope of progress in the near future, seemed ill-informed at best. Modi also seemed to take the diaspora's loyalty for granted and expected the Indian community abroad to extend support to him at all times. History has taught us that the diaspora can be critical of India on occasions. The very people who supported the nuclear tests and the nuclear deal were critical when the deal appeared to fall through. Recent events in India have already sparked adverse reactions from them. In Dubai, they were disappointed that their issues were not addressed directly by the Prime Minister.

Whether or not a foreign policy which is premised on seeking advantages for India—without projecting a grand vision for the world—will benefit India, only time will tell. However, for an India that had once taken greater pride in giving to the world than taking from it, Modi's foreign policy is strikingly new.'

In 2015, Narendra Modi's government had sprung another surprise with its outreach to Pakistan. The larger trajectory of Indian foreign policy remained robust with an effective team at the helm led by the Prime Minister himself. India was projecting a much more robust profile on the global stage than it managed to do over the previous decade. It was the new leadership that had made all the difference. A joint statement between the Prime Ministers at Ufa, Russia, on the margins of the Shanghai Cooperation Organisation (SCO) was an effort to revive SAARC and to ensure that India would participate in the Islamabad summit of SAARC.

After the Kathmandu Summit, where India was virtually isolated over the issue of China's admission to SAARC, Pakistan was not at all sure that Modi would travel to Islamabad. Moreover, India had already started thinking of a SAARC without Pakistan, given the possibility of Pakistan not allowing any progress to be made in the SAARC agenda. The plethora of measures announced in Ufa made it incumbent on Modi to attend the Summit.

The Islamabad Summit was likely to be an embarrassment for India if it continued to maintain its position that China had no place in SAARC as a country outside the region. India's admission to the SCO is the trump card China would play to find itself in SAARC. If India conceded the point to China, SAARC would be another forum where we would have to confront a China-Pakistan axis, which would be warmly welcomed by the others. Modi appeared to have ignored the dangers of the next SAARC Summit in his enthusiasm to show progress on the Pakistan front.

Neither the previous government, nor the present one had been able to take a consistent stand on Pakistan. The Nobel Prize Syndrome, the urge to take credit for resolving an old and festering issue and thus gain recognition and fame, seemed to haunt Indian leaders, while the Pakistan establishment, whether civilian or military, remained committed to its core interests. For the Indian leaders, applause from the West becomes important and encouraging. The more concessions we make, the more the applause. But since concessions cannot be given beyond a point, the governments take hesitating steps towards concessions and then step back. For a prime minister, who promised a tough line towards Pakistan, Narendra Modi gloating over the five points read out by the two foreign secretaries was an anti-climax.

The points read out, which included a meeting of the National Security Advisers (NSAs) to discuss matters relating to terrorism, a meeting of the directors general of BSF and Pakistani Rangers, a meeting of the directors general of military operations, release of fishermen and promotion of religious tourism, were not particularly significant. Of course, a pious declaration of intent to speed up the Mumbai attacks trials was welcome, though the onus seemed to be on us to give more evidence. Pakistan believed that Modi would visit Islamabad in return for these cosmetic moves.

At that time, I made the following observations in one of my columns:

'Of course, much will happen between now and the SAARC summit and the agreement to attend it may be the biggest weapon we may have to get Pakistan on track. Someone once said in all seriousness that unless we fix meetings, how can we cancel them to show our displeasure? The Prime Minister's presence at the SAARC summit should have been negotiated on the basis of SAARC-related issues. First and foremost, a consensus should be reached on China's admission. It should not appear as though India has succumbed to pressure from others to get China in.

We should insist on continuation of China's observer status as those outside South Asia have no place in SAARC as members. It might even be desirable to impose a moratorium on new members, like APEC did, now that the region has been fully covered. Secondly, there should be a commitment from Pakistan to strictly observe the SAARC rule that bilateral issues should not be brought in even obliquely. Thirdly, there must be progress on trade issues. Fourthly, the agreed declarations of SAARC on various issues should be respected and implemented. Such an agreed agenda would help Modi to participate effectively in the summit without any risk of any embarrassment.

It may well be possible that both sides may have thought that arranging Modi's visit under a multilateral guise may be less risky than doing it bilaterally. But the multilateral format would entail expression of views by others and bring pressure on us to act in a particular manner. Bilaterally, we could remain consistent with our positions, if we wanted to.

On the broader issue of resumption of dialogue, Modi had compulsions of previous positions articulated by him and his party. Previous prime ministers had modified their earlier positions, either because of external pressure or a change of heart. Objectively, there was nothing that Pakistan had done which deserved a resumption of dialogue. The assurances made in Ufa contained no commitment except a whole range of talks, which could take place without the paraphernalia associated with a joint statement of prime ministers.

The only plausible reason for Modi's change of heart could be the forthcoming election in some states, which dictated that the party cadres had something to show as Modi's triumph, which will not be tested before the elections. On the other hand, knowledgeable voters would see Ufa as a surrender to Pakistan and hence a diminution of the Hindutva agenda. Will an erosion of the Muslim vote bank of the Congress and other opposition parties make that up?

If the motivation for Modi is geopolitical calculations, the message that gets through is that the situation is not favourable from our point of view. Russia may not have suggested another Tashkent to India and Pakistan, but there are indications that Russia too has joined the Western bandwagon, which wants India and Pakistan to strike a bargain.

Pakistan is on a winning streak in Afghanistan, which causes us some concern. China is all set to make its presence felt in Afghanistan. If the idea is to speak from a position of strength, this does not look like the time to strike a deal. But Modi's readiness to visit Islamabad may well have helped him with the atmospherics, not only in Russia, but also in the Central Asian Republics.

Much will depend on the outcome of the several meetings and minor initiatives agreed upon by Modi and Sharif. The run-up to the SAARC summit promises to be active and eventful. India had already started thinking of a SAARC without Pakistan, given the possibility of Pakistan not allowing any progress to be made in the SAARC agenda.

No one should be surprised at the turn of events. It should have been clear to India that no government in Pakistan would send its National Security Adviser to India to receive the bulky dossiers on its misdeeds. It was equally clear for years that the Pakistan Army would not have any dialogue with India without Kashmir on the agenda. Pakistan had always linked terrorism, which it calls "support for the liberation movement" to its Kashmir policy.

Since India has an inflexible position on Kashmir, an integral part of India, and Pakistan cannot expect to win a war on that account, Pakistan has virtually accepted that it is engaged in terrorism to force India to change its position on Kashmir.

Nawaz Sharif did not overstep the Pakistani position when he agreed to the decisions taken at Ufa. Both Sharif and Modi agreed that India and Pakistan have a collective responsibility to ensure peace and promote development. To do so, they are prepared to discuss all outstanding issues. Both leaders condemned terrorism in all its forms and agreed to cooperate with each other to eliminate this menace from South Asia. They also agreed on a meeting in New Delhi between the two NSAs to discuss all issues connected to terrorism.

Pakistan clearly had no intention to discuss terrorism, but only "to discuss all issues connected to terrorism". Sharif's motive behind the commitment was to secure Modi's attendance at the SAARC summit in Islamabad, which he succeeded to do. Both India and Pakistan believed that each had trapped the other. The drama that followed, which ended at midnight of 22 August, demonstrated that the more India-Pakistan relations had appeared to change, the more they remained constant.

Pakistan took time to devise a credible strategy to wriggle out of the Ufa commitment and remained firm, while India harped on the claim that Pakistan had indeed agreed to have a one-item agenda for the NSA talks. The Hurriyat meeting, Pakistan knew, would be a sure way of sabotaging the talks as the Modi Government had earlier cancelled the talks at the foreign secretary level for that reason. Pakistan expected that India would promptly call off the talks, but the surprise was that instead of cancelling the talks, India arrested the dissident leaders to avoid the meeting and still wanted to hold the talks. Pakistan, caught in a bind, went back to the argument that the dialogue would include Kashmir and, therefore, a meeting with Hurriyat was essential.

India would not cancel the talks and External Affairs Minister, reinvigorated by her survival in the trial of fire lit by Sonia and Rahul, got her chance to blast Pakistan at a press conference, virtually sealing the fate of the talks of the NSAs, but still leaving it to Pakistan to back out. She said, "I have only a two-pointer message for them: please respect the Simla Agreement and do not involve any third party; second, as agreed in Ufa, the talks should only be on terror. Pakistan has only till tonight to give an assurance that the talks will only be on terror. If Pakistan does not agree, the talks will not happen."

The cancellation of the talks was a foregone conclusion, but the two sides engaged in shadow boxing till the very end to prove that the other side was responsible for the cancellation of the talks. This aroused suspicion that both were keen on satisfying some third parties that prompted the Ufa arrangement in the first place. The prompt expression of disappointment by the State Department spokesman let the cat out of the transparent bag. In their eyes, the arguments were irrelevant, but it was important that neither Pakistan nor India should be guilty of cancelling the talks. Both India and Pakistan tried to put the blame on the other, but the jury must have found them equally guilty.

The match was played, after all, for a draw. Since neither side lost the match, the search is on to figure out whether India or Pakistan gained anything from the latest bout of talks on talks. The defence on the part of the BJP was that the whole exercise was with good intentions and all was fair in love and war. But no country can afford to reveal the chinks in its own armour even with good intentions. Particularly serious is the evidence that we do not understand our adversary well enough.

Two other questions arise from the whole episode. How is it that the information in the dossier leaked out days before the talks were to be held? It was quite possible that Pakistan developed cold feet even more after they got wind of the evidence of the presence of Dawood Ibrahim in Karachi. Another question is whether External Affairs Minister Sushma Swaraj unwittingly gave a new interpretation of the Simla Agreement when she described the Hurriyat as a "third party". Since the original intention was to keep other countries and the UN out of the bilateral negotiations, considering an organisation of Indian citizens as a third party has already raised eyebrows.

The entire Ufa fiasco was predictable and predicted. The situation on the diplomatic front as well as the ground is worse today than before Ufa. The Ufa venue had created international interest in the initiative and its failure may have implications for both Pakistan and India. What remains for Modi to do is to produce a prettier rabbit out of his hat next time to deal with the Pakistan imbroglio.'

The Indian government's biggest success in the realm of foreign policy and national security in 2015 was its ability to keep its interlocutors on tenterhooks. The unpredictability of a nation whose responses had become all too easy to predict over the last few decades was generating a new sense of expectation among its interlocutors. From Pakistan to the United States, from Africa to ASEAN, there was an expectation that the new dispensation in New Delhi meant business and there could not be business as usual with the Modi government. This sense of drive and purpose was what India had been lacking in the recent past.

The bedrock of a nation's strength in contemporary global politics is its economic strength. By putting the Indian story back into reckoning after the final years of the Manmohan Singh Government, marked by scams and policy paralysis, the Modi government had shored up India's previously dwindling credibility. The fact that it had been able to do this despite an obstructionist opposition was even more remarkable. For all the disruption of the Parliament by the Congress Party, the image of a business-minded Modi government remained intact for the outside world. And that was a testament to an adept foreign policy management by the government and the energy and vigour with which the Prime Minister and his team, led by Sushma Swaraj, conducted the country's external affairs.

Modi government carefully nurtured major power relations with deft management of an ever-shifting global and regional balance of power in Asia and beyond. The political vacuum in the United States, with the Obama administration as lame duck and no clarity about his successor, was being exploited by Russia, the Europeans, the Chinese and even some middle powers. Hillary Clinton was the most likely nominee of the Democratic Party and the Republicans were still searching for one. The Modi government managed to carve out a robust relationship with the United States, even as it stabilised ties with Beijing and Moscow. India's engagement with Europe too had now become more forward-looking and devoid of the unnecessary rhetoric of perpetual inferiority. A clear message went out that India would act on its own terms and conditions and would skilfully play the role of a balancer in Asia.

The Modi government's regional outreach also made a difference as India was perceived as a credible balancer at a time when China's maritime assertiveness in the South China Sea had grown, creating space for Indian diplomacy. New Delhi's relations with like-minded states in the region such as Japan, Australia, Vietnam, Singapore, Philippines and Malaysia had grown in Act II. India sought to enhance its footprint in Africa, Latin America and the Middle East to underscore the distinct advantages that India possessed in comparison to China's more mercantile approach. The focus was on delivery of the commitments that India had made to other regions, an area where India lagged behind China and other major powers.

Asia had posed the greatest challenge to Modi in his second year, with turmoil in India-Nepal relations and India-Pakistan ties. Modi grasped the compulsions of history in charting out a new course in South Asia and managed to project a benign image when he said he was ready to change the old treaties to accommodate the aspirations of the smaller countries. The relations with Bangladesh improved dramatically as he showed magnanimity in resolving its long-pending disputes with Dhaka. Relations with Sri Lanka were also on an upward trajectory under the new Sirisena government. In Afghanistan, India's considerable investments began to make an impact, even though it was clear that the likely advent of a Taliban-led government would wipe out both the money and the goodwill.

Nepal remained a problem, largely because the political elites in the country had not managed to reconcile internal differences. India remained an easy target to channel domestic grievances; and perceptions of overbearing Indian interference had gained ground in the country. There are signs that some sort of reconciliation is beginning to shape up and India can play a role in making that happen. But New Delhi should be wary of playing an overt role in Nepal and let the domestic constituencies resolve their constitutional agenda. Furthermore, the Modi government was ending the year on a high note with its dramatic outreach to Pakistan. After carefully working throughout the year to isolate the Pakistani military globally as the epicentre of terror, New Delhi reached out to the civilian government in Pakistan to encourage the moderate elements to come to terms with the ability of India to be able to help Pakistan. But the complications of Act II had already begun to emerge towards the end of 2015.

ACT III
THE CLIMAX

New Symphony in India-US Relations

MODI enjoyed the climax that came to Shakespearean heroes in Act III when the complications of Act II appeared like opportunities rather than challenges. Realising that most of his priorities, development, security and the diaspora hinged on good relations with the United States, PM Modi put the past of his relationship with the US behind and built an equation with Barack Obama, going to the extent of tackling the intractable issue of the Nuclear Liability Act and claiming to have solved it. Though the envisaged nuclear trade with the US never materialised, the understanding reached between India and the US on the Asia-Pacific and close cooperation in defence matters, together with liberalisation of foreign investments, India-US relations reached a new high, characterised by PM Modi as 'a new symphony' in June 2016.

In early 2016, swift and determined action on both sides led to an unprecedented agreement on India becoming a major defence partner of the United States. President Obama's Indian pivot to the Asia Pacific became a reality and Modi saw his vision of 'Make in India' materialising, particularly in the defence sector. One of the reasons for promoting 'Make in India' project was to remove India's dubious reputation as the biggest importer of weapons in the world. He was expecting that by co-designing and co-production of arms in India, imports could be reduced and they could even be exported to third countries.

In a historic address to the US Congress in June 2016, Prime Minister Narendra Modi said: 'Our relationship is primed for a momentous future. The constraints of the past are behind us and the foundations of the future are in place. In the lines of Walt Whitman, the orchestra has sufficiently tuned their instruments, the baton has given the signal and to that, if I might add, there is a new symphony in play.' He said that India and the US had stepped out of the hesitation of the past and that India-US relations would embrace the totality of human endeavour. He recalled how the Civil Nuclear Agreement of 2008 had changed the very colour of the leaves of the relationship.

The question remained, however, whether India-US relations would cease to be the 'roller coaster ride' it had always been and would reach a plateau and take a predictable, beneficial and peaceful trajectory. It was by no means certain that the geopolitical configuration of the world would keep the two countries together as natural allies. The US-India-China-Russia equations would change constantly like a kaleidoscope in which pieces of glass shift positions with every turn of the device. A US spokesman described the new relationship in the following words: 'The era of alliances? We are not in that era. Why have that shackle? The "friends with benefits" model is probably satisfactory. I don't think anyone in the US government or in the Indian government feels a compulsion to form a treaty alliance.' He then pointed to the fact that the US had declared India 'a major defence partner' and made significant policy changes to flesh out the concept. The benefits would be close to that of a treaty partner.

The US has a fondness for patenting descriptions of its relations with various countries and these change from time to time except when a treaty relationship like NATO membership is in place. Non-NATO allies like Pakistan come next and strategic partners and others get benefits commensurate with situations brought about by a balance of considerations. By characterising India and US as 'friends with benefits', the indication was that the relationship would still be subject to fluctuations of loyalty even if India had been designated as 'a major defence partner'. The US response to the Uri attack and the Indian surgical strikes in September 2016 indicated that India and Pakistan were equated at best and the US was tilted to Pakistan at worst.

The new relationship was challenged in no time when efforts to enshrine the defence partnership in a Congress resolution failed and Modi's oration was characterised as his doctrine. The deterioration of India's relationship with Pakistan on account of major terrorist attacks in Pathankot and Uri and India's publicised surgical strikes across the Line of Control in Jammu and Kashmir showed that the US made no allowance for the new relationship. As before, the US did its tight ropewalking by condemning terrorism and asking for restraint on all sides. India's efforts to isolate Pakistan were viewed with scepticism in Washington.

As the US prepared for a change of guard in Washington early in 2017, the relationship remained steady. It was believed that whoever wins the election, there should be no change in the trajectory of the relationship except for unexpected complications in US interests in China, Pakistan or Russia. The bipartisan nature of the relationship was stressed, as it was believed that any President would be a reliable partner of India in the fight against terrorism. Hillary Clinton, it was believed, would follow the same policies as Barack Obama.

The new administration would take time to formulate its policy, but engaging it is important to maintain continuity. Several studies came up in India and the US on the issues that the new administration should consider on priority basis with regard to India. A report of the Centre for Strategic and International Studies (CSIS) suggested that Washington should undertake six 'must-do' tasks: (i) the new President should meet Prime Minister Narendra Modi in the first 100 days to stress the importance of the relationship; (ii) get India to sign the remaining foundational agreements after Logistics Exchange Memorandum of Agreement (LEMOA) on defence supplies; (iii) establish a quadrilateral dialogue with the US, India, Japan and Australia (earlier known as the concert of democracies); (iv) enhance India's naval capabilities in the Indian Ocean; (v) encourage India to raise foreign direct investment (FDI) in the defence sector to 100 per cent; and expand technology cooperation under the Homeland Security Dialogue.

On the Indian side, there would be demands for more liberal immigration policies, reform of WTO, increase in trade and supply of nuclear reactors. It was already decided that Westinghouse would set up six nuclear reactors in India even though the liability issues had not been sorted out. India had joined the concerned Vienna Convention and proposed an insurance scheme to cover compensation, but the US companies did not relent on their decision not to have nuclear trade till a solution was found to resolve the liability issue.

Even as Modi anticipated a new symphony in India-US relations, it was clear that there would be hurdles along the way. The greatest challenge would be New Delhi's continued wariness about US support to Pakistan and American concerns about India's close relationship with Russia. But in a twist of fate, Pakistan and Russia were getting closer, presenting new challenges to both India and the US. Russia was hurt by India's closeness to the US, while Pakistan was thrilled to embrace Russia and drive a wedge between old friends.

There was speculation that with the US planning to reduce its presence in Afghanistan, Pakistan's importance will also reduce, increasing the possibility that Washington will cut ties over an incident of state-sponsored terrorism. But in the meantime, ongoing US-Pakistan military cooperation created a brake on India-US cooperation and trust development. The best case scenario for regional peace lies in the potential for an agreement between India and China to cooperate in working for peace in Afghanistan should the United States withdraw. But that scenario would require the impossible to happen—China going against the wishes of its all-weather friend Pakistan. In fact, the opposite was happening—a China-Russia-Pakistan axis in Asia posed new challenges to both the US and India. It required serious attention by Washington but there was no discussion on the implications of the three coming together.

Taking the metaphor of friends with benefits further, it might be time for the US to think more radically about India as a friend with real benefits. The report cited India's 'sustained interest' in buying US unmanned aircraft such as the Predator. Even though India joined the MTCR, apparently it was not enough because the US 'holds a highly restrictive view of its own responsibilities under the MTCR' and the result is denial of this technology even to countries within the MTCR. The US had sold the Predator only to a handful of treaty allies who were engaged in 'ongoing operations with the United States', the report said. This does raise questions about the thesis that the era of treaty alliances is over. India as a friend with benefits is not about to get the Predator anytime soon. The US Congress too always uses India's unwillingness to participate in American-led military operations as a litmus test of sorts. This was a potential problem in relations down the line.

In terms of increasing FDI in the defence sector, India had concerns about becoming captive to US defence companies who could pull the plug should relations sour for any reason. The Americans also wanted assurances that the weapons built by US firms in India would be used only in ways consistent with US strategic goals.

The CSIS report also cited ongoing problems in the areas of counterterrorism and cyber security cooperation where trust was low. Although signed in 2010 and re-emphasised in 2015, the bilateral counterterrorism initiative had suffered mainly because the shadow of Pakistan fell darkly. Americans were reluctant to act against terrorist groups that mainly attacked India, something that lowered Indian confidence levels.

The new level of friendship envisaged between the US and India entailed consideration of several issues. These included the expectation that the new administration should take up these issues without delay and India should be prepared to make substantive proposals for bilateral cooperation. The tendency in India to hold relationships hostage to the positions on terrorism and to demand isolation of Pakistan did not augur well for full development of India-US relations. The US preoccupation with China and Russia threatened to downgrade relations with India. But the emergence of a strategic arrangement in Asia Pacific with the participation of India, Japan, Australia and the US showed promise of giving priority to India and the emergence of a new pattern of cooperation.

The general distrust that many in India had towards the US had not disappeared even though Obama had shown no great enthusiasm for regime changes and cronyism. The gradual withdrawal of the US from the Middle East may present India with new opportunities and challenges. If the US begins to see India as a partner in their world view, there is hope for India-US relations to grow dramatically. The

US should also recognise Indian aspirations to join the UN Security Council as a permanent member and the APEC as a member as gestures of goodwill. But the inability of the US to push for India's admission to the NSG in the face of Chinese opposition reveals its inability to influence the emerging world order. India's success lies in forging a partnership with the US on the basis of equality and mutual benefit.

Prime Minister Narendra Modi spelt out the possibilities of India-US cooperation in one of his speeches. He said: 'In this world full of multiple transitions and economic opportunities; growing uncertainties and political complexities; existing threats and new challenges; our engagement can make a difference by promoting cooperation not dominance, connectivity not isolation, respect for global commons, inclusive not exclusive mechanisms and above all adherence to international rules and norms.

Modi said India was already assuming her responsibilities in securing the Indian Ocean region. A strong India-US partnership can anchor peace, prosperity and stability from Asia to Africa and from Indian Ocean to the Pacific. It can also help ensure security of the sea lanes of commerce and freedom of navigation on seas. But, the effectiveness of our cooperation would increase if international institutions framed with the mindset of the 20th century were to reflect the realities of today, he said.

With these developments, both encouraging and frustrating at the same time, Act III opened, characterised by acute complications in the story with no clear indication of future events. The situation got from good to bad and from bad to worse and the spectators breathlessly watched things go wrong in a bewildering manner.

Prime Minister Narendra Modi's foreign policy in the middle of his term was very much like Act III of a Shakespearean play. The entry was dramatic, full of surprises and even exciting. He strode like a colossus on the world stage with his freshness, energy, decisiveness and oratorical skills. India became visible, active and even assertive. His optimism was contagious and the whole country began anticipating the good times he promised. India would not be a mere spectator on the seashore of world affairs but a participant, claiming its legitimate place on the table. He took the bull by the horns, whether it was Pakistan, China or the United States. Lack of diplomatic experience appeared to be an asset rather than a liability; the first act was perfect.

But in the second act, when Modi began encountering complex issues, rivals and adversaries, things appeared complicated. Hesitations of history loomed large and quick fixes were not available. There were too many boxes crying out for standard solutions as he searched for out-of-the-box outcomes. All the charms he tried on Pakistan and China went unrequited. But there was joy in the progress made in certain countries, where he followed the path laid by his predecessors.

With Pakistan, neither the charm offensive nor the surgical strikes made any difference. The situation was worse than it was in 2014, when the ceasefire was in force and the terror attacks were not frequent. The policy of the previous government that no comprehensive dialogue was possible without ending terrorism, often violated by India itself off and on, was completely disregarded by Modi when he invited Pakistan's Prime Minister Nawaz Sharif to India, proposed Foreign Secretary-level talks, held National Security Adviser-level talks and sent the External Affairs Minister to Islamabad to propose a comprehensive dialogue. The surge in terror attacks prompted the surgical strikes, which Pakistan refused to even acknowledge. Intermittent shooting on the border, expulsion of diplomats, and India's open support to Baluchistan and boycott of the SAARC summit brought the two countries to the brink of war. The lesson learnt was that 70 years of animosity and conflict could not be wished away without major concessions on either side.

The whole castle in the air that Modi built in his first address from the ramparts of the Red Fort about the progress to be achieved by the combined efforts of SAARC countries lay shattered as the future of SAARC itself was uncertain. India invited Bay of Bengal Initiative for Multi-Sectoral Technical and Economic Cooperation (BIMSTEC) members to interact with BRICS and not SAARC precisely to encourage a regional group without Pakistan in it. Another latent issue in SAARC was the possible admission of China. A majority of the members argued that since India and Pakistan were made full members of the SCO, a similar courtesy should be extended to China. Had the Islamabad summit been held, India would have been alone in opposing China's admission.

The bilateral scene with China looked less troublesome, but nothing had changed for the better in India-China relations in the last 30 months. The China-Pakistan collusion continued and the long-term measures being taken by Beijing such as the Belt Road Initiative (BRI) were designed to dominate the whole of Asia. Modi, on his part, had made no secret of his inclination towards the US, Japan and Australia and his concerns about the South China Sea. But happily, there were very few incidents on the border and the economic activities continued, though the balance of trade was in China's favour.

The situation on the Western front should be a matter of satisfaction for Modi. The designation of India as a major defence partner took India-US relations to a higher level, which entitled India to the same facilities for technology transfer as the allies of the US. The mixed picture on foreign policy that we saw at this time was an inevitable consequence of extraordinary global developments and initiatives taken by Modi. Modi appeared entangled in a web of intricate issues in the third act and it was clear that the remaining acts would determine his impact on the global scene.

A fiasco in the second half of June 2016 was reminiscent of the tragic flaw of Shakespearean heroes. Each one of them had many good qualities, which elevated them to the heights of greatness in their respective fields, but they also had a tragic flaw, which caused their undoing—if it was jealousy for Othello, ambition for Macbeth, vanity for King Lear and indecision in Hamlet. In the case of Modi, the streak of overconfidence may have been the tragic flaw. Modi launched an ill-advised campaign for India's membership of the NSG. In June 2016, I wrote:

'India's 30-year-old effort to secure a permanent seat on the UN Security Council has been characterised as the pursuit of a diplomatic holy grail. The chance of success in that pursuit has been receding like a mirage, though there have been tantalising signs of progress. A similar but less intense effort is on to seek admission to the APEC, a body which should have included India in the first place. Here again, there is no sign of India being invited, even as the 10-year moratorium on new membership has expired. India has now embarked on another quest, this time to seek membership of the NSG. The Prime Minister himself has travelled to Switzerland to seek support and he will also go to Mexico for the same purpose. It is surprising that India is investing much diplomatic effort on this issue when there is little chance of India being invited to the group.

India seeking membership of the NSG is like Russia seeking membership of the North Atlantic Treaty Organisation (NATO). The NSG was invented to prevent Indian advance towards possession of nuclear weapons after the technology demonstration test of 1974. If India joins it, the very nature of the NSG will change and dilute its fundamental position that all members should be signatories to the NPT. Though the US has stated repeatedly that it would like to see India in the NSG, it cannot be expected to be a party to the fundamental alteration of the NPT regime.

Interestingly, it was a US think tank which brought up the topic in a Track II discussion with some of us in 2007. The suggestion was not that India should be given membership of the NSG, but that India should join all multilateral export control regimes like the NSG, MTCR (which it is set to join later this year), the Wassenaar Arrangement for control of conventional weapons and the Australia Group for control of chemicals that could contribute to chemical and biological weapons. It appeared then that the whole proposal was to drag us into Wassenaar Arrangement and the Australia Group by presenting them as a package. We had refrained from joining both, for our own reasons, though they were open for us from the beginning. Our response to the US proposal was guarded as we did not want a bargain on all the groups together. We did, however, emphasise that India's membership of the NSG would be helpful as it had received an exemption from the NSG guidelines. As a member of the group, we could contribute to the discussion if it sought to amend the guidelines in any manner. In other words, it was not an Indian initiative to press for admission to the NSG.

US President Barack Obama formalised the proposal in 2010, as though it was a concession to India, in his bid to win various contracts, including nuclear supplies. Perhaps, he was aware that a decision on the NSG was not in his hands, but promised to take up the matter with the others just to win some goodwill in the process. As was expected, the fundamental requirement that every member should be a signatory to the NPT was brought up not only by China but several others. There was similar opposition in the case of the exemption from NSG guidelines at the time of the nuclear deal also, but our bilateral efforts and heavy lifting by the US, including a final phone call from the US President to his Chinese counterpart, resulted in the exemption. The strength of the argument was that this would be a one-time exemption with no strings attached.

Interestingly, the NSG is an informal grouping, which is referred to in the International Atomic Energy Agency documents only as "certain states", and there is no precise procedure for seeking admission. But since the group takes all its decisions by consensus, it follows that new members should also be by consensus. For those outside the group, there is an outreach programme which is being pursued vigorously. The outreach programme is meant merely for conveying information and not for consultation. New Delhi hosted an outreach meeting a few years ago, but it was found that the exercise was not of much use in influencing the guidelines.

The pursuit of membership of the NSG by India at the highest level has aroused suspicion that India is aiming to be in the group to deny entry to Pakistan. Such an interpretation is the result of lack of any clarity as to the benefits that will accrue to India by joining the NSG. In fact, membership of the group will not immediately open up nuclear trade as India has already pledged not to transfer nuclear know-how to other countries. If we attempt to dilute the guidelines to liberalise supply, it will be resisted by the others. Membership of the NSG will only mean greater pressure on us to sign the NPT and the Comprehensive Nuclear-Test-Ban Treaty (CTBT) and commit in advance to a Fissile Material Cut-off Treaty, which would impose restrictions on existing stockpiles of fissile material.

China has given scant attention to the NSG guidelines and has violated them in the case of Pakistan by claiming to act under an agreement reached before China joined the NSG. Unlike India, Pakistan has not even sought an exemption from the NSG. To say, therefore, that India and Pakistan should be equated on nuclear matters is unreasonable, to say the least. But the NSG did not even challenge the supply of two new reactors to Pakistan by China. The NSG's ineffectiveness in countering proliferation makes it even less attractive as a group India should join.

The green signal for India to join the MTCR came when Modi was in Washington purely by coincidence, as the last date for filing objections happened to be that day. Italy had held up its approval on account of the Italian marines issue, but did not file a formal objection because of the decision to let the marines go home. Membership of the MTCR, which restricts the weight and range of missiles, is being projected as clearing the way for NSG. This is not likely because of China except that we can now threaten to veto China if it applies for membership of the MTCR.

When India is not anywhere near the permanent membership of the Security Council and even APEC membership remains elusive, the high-level pursuit of NSG membership may give the impression that India is unrealistic in its expectations from the international community. Support by Switzerland and Mexico will not make any difference as there will not be a vote on the issue. The US may reiterate its support, but the objection will come from China and even some others. It will be better for India to concentrate on one or two fundamental objectives rather than fritter away our diplomatic resources on matters of marginal interest.'

I wrote again on 29 June 2016.

'Brexit, a seismic moment in Europe, came as a blessing in disguise for India as it came on the same day as the setback in Seoul. India's miscalculation on the NSG membership bid paled into insignificance compared to the British Prime Minister's misadventure in holding a referendum on the UK's membership of the European Union. Otherwise there would have been greater criticism of the foreign policy fiasco, which not only resulted in a rebuff to India but also gave a veto to China on India's nuclear credentials and hyphenated India and Pakistan. Moreover, we have elevated NSG membership to such heights that it appears more important and urgent than other items on our wish list such as permanent membership of the UN Security Council, signing of the NPT as a nuclear weapon state, and membership of APEC.

The Seoul experience should be a lesson in multilateral diplomacy for India. First and foremost, credibility is the hallmark of success in the international community. Policy changes should appear slow, deliberate and logical. Sudden shifts and turns are viewed with suspicion. India had a fundamental position that our objective is disarmament and not merely non-proliferation. Not signing the NPT and CTBT arose from the conviction that arms control is not a substitute to disarmament. Distancing ourselves from NPT-centred entities was also part of that philosophy. Rejection of discriminatory regimes and selective controls appeared logical and just. Even after declaring ourselves as a nuclear weapon state, our readiness for nuclear disarmament maintained our credibility.

Our sudden anxiety to join the NSG and other non-proliferation groupings is a departure from the traditional Indian position, particularly since we have not fully utilised the waiver given to us by the NSG. An invitation by the US was not enough to justify our enthusiasm for membership, and canvassing at the highest level in selected countries made matters worse. Having applied for membership only in May this year, we did not allow ourselves time to explain the rationale of our policy change, not only to the NSG members but also the other adherents to the NPT. This explains the hesitation of many friendly countries to support us. Any indication of change in the non-proliferation architecture makes them nervous.

The fact that many Indian initiatives have been successful in the multilateral arena should not lead us into assuming automatic support for our suggestions and requests. Many of our initiatives in the UN in the initial years, such as decolonisation, disarmament, development, human rights and apartheid, were more for the common good rather than for our own sake. Problems arise when we seek advantages and concessions to ourselves, like in the case of Jammu and Kashmir, non-proliferation and Bangladesh or when our positions are perceived as siding with another major power, as in Afghanistan and Cambodia.

Our positions on self-determination and terrorism are not fully appreciated in the international community as yet. It was with patience, persistence and extraordinary diplomatic skills that India had managed to steer clear of embarrassment or rebuff. Approaching multilateralism with an illusion of grandeur or presumption of justice, fair play and reasonableness may be hazardous.

Having a powerful nation to pilot matters of importance to us is helpful, but even the US does not always get its way in the multilateral bodies which require a majority vote or consensus. It loses votes in the UN General Assembly not only on substantive issues but also in elections. Since the real power is in the Security Council, the permanent five manage to wield power there, but wherever votes are of equal value there is no guarantee that they can get support automatically. The votaries of non-proliferation tend to be more loyal than the king and they are aghast that the US appears to be undermining the regime that it had built. In 2008, they went along when the US moved heaven and earth to get India a waiver to secure the nuclear deal, but this time they felt India was overreaching itself. They were not supporting China when they opposed India's admission but merely proclaiming their faith. Brazil, South Africa, Austria and Switzerland are serious nations with extraordinary commitment to the NPT, which they consider to be the cornerstone of international security.

Another lesson India should have known is the undesirability of pursuing too many objectives at the same time. India's claim for a permanent seat on the Security Council as part of the exercise to reflect the realities of global power is well understood, though a global compact to accomplish it is still elusive. Our pressing the point in the appropriate forums is considered legitimate, but any effort to press it to a vote to embarrass and pressurise anyone is bound to fail. At one time, India made an attempt to have a vote in the General Assembly to secure a two-thirds majority just to embarrass the permanent members. But the effort failed when the opposition came not from the permanent members, but from the African Group. The art of persuasion works only when the ground is prepared and there is a degree of satisfaction for all parties involved. Our NSG push violated this sacred principle.

In bilateral relations, the reality of power is what matters and deals can be struck on the basis of give and take. But the dynamics of multilateral diplomacy depend on equations that go beyond the actual size and power of individual countries. Often, clever use of the rules of procedure alone can bestow extraordinary powers on nations. India has no shortage of experts in multilateral diplomacy to handle such matters, but it appears that they have no say in decision-making. They end up getting impossible briefs and misinformation regarding assurances received from the capitals and operate in a vacuum.

India could have pursued membership of the NSG quietly, without making any claims of support from anyone. It appears that there is a feeling in the US circles of getting India entangled in the non-proliferation net instead of leaving it alone to work on the basis of the nuclear deal and the NSG waiver. We should have handled the issue with dignified detachment and waited for a consensus to emerge among the interested countries. If only we had played by the rules of the multilateral game, the Seoul fiasco could have been turned into a victory.'

Like in the Act III of a Shakespearean play, the year 2016 marked a climax in Modi's foreign policy initiatives, following Obama's visit to India, an understanding on India-US cooperation in Asia Pacific, and India becoming a close defence partner of the United States. But its impact on China and Russia and Pakistan, other international developments and certain steps Modi took on account of overconfidence, his tragic flaw, clouds started gathering in the horizon. The advent of President Donald Trump at the end of 2016 changed the whole scene, leading to the proverbial reversals of Act IV.

ACT IV
THE REVERSALS

Coping with the Trump Effect

AS the complications in his foreign policy began to show up, Modi found it necessary to explain the Modi doctrine to the world. For this purpose, *The Modi Doctrine: New Paradigm in India's Foreign Policy* (2016), edited by Anirban Ganguly, a BJP researcher; Vijay Chauthaiwale, coordinator; overseas friends of BJP; and Uttam Kumar, formerly of Banaras Hindu University (BHU), produced a panegyric of Modi.

The three editors themselves could have written the book and given their insights into Modi's foreign policy as its architects. However, they put together a number of credible writers to pen some of the articles. The usual suspects from India, even those who have been sympathetic to the Modi government, were conspicuous by their absence. Satish Chandra, Virendra Gupta and P. Stobdan were the only former diplomats who contributed. It was noteworthy that of the 21 contributors, 12 were foreigners or Persons of Indian Origin living abroad. The external perspectives reflected in the book were a measure of the acceptability of the changes in Indian foreign policy abroad.

Setting aside these unique features, the book had immense value because it revealed the inner workings of the think tank which appeared to provide facts and insights to Modi, though he himself takes the final decisions and articulates them in his characteristic rhetorical style. The purpose of the book was to unveil Modi's objectives, his accomplishments and his plans for the future. The release of the book by the then Minister of External Affairs Sushma Swaraj and the Foreword by the then Finance Minister Arun Jaitley bestowed official blessings on the book.

The theme that threads through every article is the premise that 'India's approach to the world has begun to fundamentally alter, reshape and reposition' on the strength of India's greatness, going back to pre-historic times; the absolute majority for a single party after 30 years; the emergence of a common man, with immense capabilities as the prime minister; and an assertive foreign policy, backed by a strong, growing economy and democracy.

Anirban Ganguly, in the final chapter, states that the supporting pillars of Indian foreign policy are *Samman* (dignity and honour), *Samvad* (engagement and dialogue), *Samridhi* (prosperity), *Suraksha* (security) and *Sanskriti* (culture)—the *Panchamrit* which seems to replace the *Panchsheel*. The writers assert that the foreign policy in the first two years of Modi has been an unqualified success. Failures, such as a troubled neighbourhood, the NSG fiasco and elusive UN reform are turned into challenges yet to be won over by the argument that success has to be earned through hard work. It does not come on a platter and, accordingly, fear of failure should not deter one from striving for success; otherwise it will surely elude us. Modi is prepared to stake his personal reputation when national interests so dictate and he is not afraid to lead from the front.

The editors state, rather dubiously, that 'a striking aspect is that global leaders do not require prior international experience to be one'. Foresight defines a global leader—a clear vision for the country and its people and the ability to build a consensus to achieve the vision. They then go on to summarise each of the 21 articles to support their thesis. This is very helpful, because the reader gets a general idea of the book by reading the chapter entitled 'Modi's foreign policy as problem solving'.

Finding the right partners and understanding and leveraging the priorities of the partners are said to be keys to Modi's success in foreign policy. By pulling in Indian Americans into the forefront, Modi showed US politicians that he held sway over a section of their own political system. The importance of Modi's interaction with 14 Pacific Island countries was perhaps a bit exaggerated. Except for Fiji, which still has a significant population of Indian origin, they are virtual protectorates of Australia and New Zealand and have had little interest in India in the past. To show that it will take more than Modi's vision alone to maintain momentum and that thoughtless bureaucracy could ruin things, one writer points out that a meeting of the Pacific Island countries was held in arid Jaipur, not on the coast.

Having been the Indian envoy to 8 of these 14 countries, I know that their leaders have been taken to Kerala and other coastal states again and again, but our scale of operations and methods of developing maritime resources do not appeal to them. We cannot also match the generosity of Australia and New Zealand in offering projects to them. One has to wait and watch if Modi's intervention will produce any tangible results.

One writer argues that India has not put India's royalty to use to serve foreign policy. He claims that 'there are some doors only royalty can walk through'. Blue blood would be recognised in monarchies even if the Indian royalty has no power anymore. He seems to be unaware that India had recruited several former maharajas into the IFS, causing protocol confusion in some courts. In the UK, the third secretary, a former prince, was ranked above the high commissioner! It is ironic that the writer should advocate the use of princes by a country which prides itself as a democracy, headed by a common man. Modi himself is likely to turn down the suggestion.

China is a recurring theme in virtually every chapter as a rival, as a threat and sometimes as a potential partner. But there is no separate chapter on China, though there are chapters on Sri Lanka, Bangladesh, Nepal, Afghanistan and even Mongolia. China comes up for severe criticism in the chapter on NSG. Satish Chandra argues that the Seoul experience once again demonstrated China's inimical mindset against India.

On many counts, India's credentials for admission to the NSG were excellent, while China was known to be a notorious proliferator. 'Seoul showed up China for what it is—notably a hegemonic, unprincipled and ruthless player, quite prepared to disregard the common good in order to achieve its narrow ends.' Satish Chandra justifies the move for membership of the NSG, but forgets the hesitations of history in the past, not only on NSG, but also on the MTCR, the Wassenaar Arrangement and the Australian Group. The real criticism was about the timing and the manner in which it was pushed, resulting in a victory for China. Needless to say, diplomacy is the art of the possible.

Writing on India-US relations, Lisa Curtis notes rightly that there has been a qualitative improvement in India-US relations since 2014. Among the remaining irritants, she lists the US supply of F-16 to Pakistan and the welcome US accords to China for playing a role in South Asia, including Afghanistan. But the big stories are India becoming a major defence partner of the US and resolving the nuclear liability issue by announcing the commencement of work on six Westinghouse nuclear reactors in India. Curtis has no doubt that India-US cooperation, particularly on security issues, is sure to stay on an upward trajectory. The book has much more on every aspect of India's foreign policy, particularly Modi's skilful use of soft power and the Indian Diaspora to advance the aim of India becoming a global power. That the Modi doctrine has led to Indians across the globe feeling cared for is clearly a strength.

'Re-imagining who is an Indian' is the churning that has happened in the minds of the countrymen, according to the author. The message that the world looks at India not as a recipient or a weak partner any longer, but a leader, and a strong ally is clearly highlighted in the book. The book establishes beyond doubt that India is on its way to be a formidable global power under Modi.

Ramesh Thakur, writing on multilateralism, has argued for India's permanent membership in the UN Security Council not in terms of entitlement, but as a political contest involving building winning coalitions, mobilising sufficient resources and neutralising opposition. But his prescription for the future is provocative and hazardous. He suggests that India and the other candidates should announce non-cooperation with the UN and, if that also fails, should ignore the UN and switch to G-20 and BRICS to pursue their interests. Even more dangerously, he claims that such an agenda is in sync with Modi's style and vision, which is unlikely.

In the final section, 'Thematically Tied to the World', which is a refreshing title in a book on foreign policy, we find interesting lessons adopted from the world by India in economic, strategic, defence, energy, environment and civilizational quest.

The book certainly is a gold mine of the thoughts and ideas of the ruling party on foreign policy. Some of them are well argued and there are signs that Modi has adopted them. Others may be mere kite flying. But it will remain a handbook for those who look for the logic of Modi's foreign policy and for its likely course in the future.

An Arnab Goswami interview in June 2016 was another effort to convince the doubting Thomases about the way Indian foreign policy was going. Modi turned the usually aggressive Arnab Goswami into the very picture of politeness by being charming, patient and reasonable in the first-ever interview given by an Indian prime minister to a private television channel. He made his admirers proud, won friends among sceptics and neutralised many adversaries. No other prime minister after Nehru had bothered to explain his thinking on foreign policy as he did. But as it happens in such frank and forthright discussions, he also exposed the chinks in his armour, including his lack of experience in global affairs and diplomacy.

Perhaps for the first time, he offered an explanation for his hectic travel schedule. After 30 years of weak governments, here was a strong leader with a big majority in India and the world was curious to get to know him. The best thing to do in the circumstances was to speak to them directly. He was not asked why the others did not come rushing to India if they were so keen to know the new Indian leader.

The number of world leaders who came to India after the change of government in 1977 was a record. In fact, Modi was known to the world more than Morarji Desai was when he took over as prime minister. I remember the erstwhile Soviet newspapers, *Pravda* and *Izvestia* took three days to say that someone called Morarji Desai had succeeded Indira Gandhi and the only description that they had of him was that he was a Gandhian, though not a Gandhi!

Modi was known, perhaps for the wrong reasons, and that was why he was keen to talk to everyone personally to establish his credentials. In these days of a communication revolution, was it necessary for him to go to every country?

Mahatma Gandhi had no internet or a twitter account, but the whole world recognised him as the greatest leader of the 20th century. He was also misunderstood and ridiculed, but he did not need to go around the world. With a single sheet newspaper, he created waves around the globe.

Modi gave all credit for his success to his team and said that the team spoke with one voice, unlike in the time of the previous governments. This surprised many as the impression was that he was a one-man army and that the only thing that was expected of his team was to execute orders.

Many had said that the power was concentrated in the PM, particularly in matters of foreign policy and that even the External Affairs Minister was not in the picture. There have been many instances of policy decisions being made without inputs from the Ministry of External Affairs (MEA).In some cases, it was evident that the decisions would have been different if the MEA had intervened. A sense of history was found wanting in foreign policy decisions. Even as the Chief Minister of Gujarat, he used to say that he delegated so much authority that all the district collectors were as powerful as the chief minister. The secretaries in the MEA would have been happier if they were more involved in decision making.

The essence of Modi's foreign policy, as revealed by him, was that he did not want India to stand on the shores of the ocean and count the waves. He wanted India to wade into the ocean and 'ride the waves and decide on our direction, destination and speed'.

According to him, in the past, India had given too much attention to the major powers and neglected the small ones. He wanted to give equal attention and respect to all countries. He gave the example of the Pacific nations, whom he brought together. He confirmed that in the future, it would not be non-alignment, but it would be selective alignments, all at the same time.

But it was not clear what he meant when he said that the bipolar situation was for 'namesake'. Relations should not be just between the governments, but also between people. In this context, he claimed that he had no previous baggage of policy and, therefore, he could be inventive and innovative. He should know of course that India, on the other hand, had a tradition and history and he could not ignore it completely. He said elsewhere that he was actually continuing on the same path established by previous governments.

On China, the PM was very clear that India would continue to pursue its national interests in the dialogue with China and that there would be no compromises. The dialogue should continue even if there were many problems with China. 'We don't have one problem with China, we have a whole lot pending with them.' He did not elaborate or identify the border problem as the most difficult one and did not express any optimism about normalising relations with China. He appeared to hold the view that problems with China should be managed as they would not be solved easily. He started off as PM as a 'Panda lover', but now he appeared to recognise that the relations would be adversarial for a long time.

On the US, the PM was more optimistic. He quoted the US media as having observed that 'the success of Obama's foreign policy had been the warm relationship with India'. He said that the US should not be judged by its support to Pakistan and we should pursue our own strategy to befriend the US. He was happy that the respect shown to India created a hype in the US. In other words, he gave a clear indication that the US should be the first among equals as far as India's friends were concerned. He did not see any dangers in getting too close to the US and was not averse to being an ally.

The prescription for Pakistan was that we should fight poverty together with them and our other neighbours. But he distinguished between those who work on the negotiating table and those who work on the border. The former would be gentle and soft, but those who work at the border would work 'with full strength'.

Pressure on terrorists had increased and the jawans were protecting the borders, risking their lives. 'My country's soldiers have full freedom to answer in whatever manner they have to,' he said. He put the finger on the real problem when he said there were different types of forces operating in Pakistan and that India could deal only with a democratically elected system.

He claimed, however, that his continuous efforts had shown some results in terms of the increasing conviction in other countries that India had good intentions. Although the PM devoted a considerable part of the interview to foreign affairs, the overall picture was sketchy and unclear. He justified his pro-active foreign policy in the context of the changes in the international situation and stressed that India would suffer if the world did not know the new leader of India.

'The world did not know me. It wants to. But if someone wants to know me through the eyes of the media, he would be disillusioned. If this happens, the country will be at a loss. Modi's personality should not be a hindrance for the world to have faith in India.'

The early initiatives for a dialogue, which moved from New Delhi to Russia to Bangkok went in Pakistan's favour as it appeared that a dialogue would begin on Pakistan's terms. At the end of it all, it appeared, as I wrote at that time, that this round was for Pakistan. I wrote on 11 December 2015 as follows:

'In the long and arduous struggle with Pakistan, it is transient victories that matter, not the final result, because no one knows what the ultimate result would be. Considered from such a perspective, one cannot escape the conclusion that Pakistan has won the Paris-Bangkok-Islamabad round. To be able to resume the "composite dialogue" even by another name, "Comprehensive Bilateral Dialogue", without making any progress on the Mumbai attack trials, except a pious assurance of an "early completion of the Mumbai trial" is a dream come true for Pakistan.

Prime Minister Narendra Modi was under international pressure in Paris to relent on his position that terrorism would be the only topic of conversation with Pakistan till the conspirators and perpetrators of the Mumbai attack were brought to book.

The talk of disproportionate use of force from the Indian side and the threat of using tactical nuclear weapons by Pakistan had alarmed the US, the UK and France, who got together to nudge the Indian and Pakistani Prime Ministers to resume the dialogue and that was possible only if India did not insist that the talks would not include Kashmir.

With that concession by India, Pakistan has succeeded in winning the approbation of its Western patrons by appearing to be eminently reasonable. Resumption of the dialogue without any concession on terrorism was their objective. Though it was a sad commentary that the two neighbours had to go to Bangkok to hold the talks, Pakistan promptly seized the opportunity. India's motives in making this concession are far from clear. External Affairs Minister Sushma Swaraj could have visited Islamabad for the Heart of Asia conference without having to make any concession to Pakistan.

Enemies of the United States like Fidel Castro and Yasser Arafat visited New York for UN conferences without budging on their policies to the United States. As for the visit of the Prime Minister for the SAARC conference, this was already announced.

What was then the compulsion for India to rush to comprehensive talks? No one expects that Pakistan will abandon the "core issue" of Kashmir and agree on other matters, just as India cannot be expected to make concessions on Kashmir. The logic of the dialogue is only that even adversaries should remain in contact so that no nuclear weapons are launched on any misunderstanding.

Creating a facade of normalcy while firing continues on the border and terrorists keep infiltrating into India will only hurt India. But it helps Pakistan to get massive assistance from the West in the name of resolving the Afghan situation.

It is not insignificant that there was no decision in Islamabad to hold a Pakistan-India cricket match in Sri Lanka. Some partners of the ruling party are adamant that sporting contacts are undesirable as long as terrorism goes unabated. But how will they accept a comprehensive dialogue, without any concession from Pakistan? Is the cancellation of the cricket match sufficient compensation for them to accept the dialogue?

The fact that the two sides "condemned terrorism and resolved to cooperate to eliminate it" only blunts our pointed accusation that Pakistan is engaged in terrorism across the border, while the terrorism in Pakistan is home grown. The two cannot be equated, as was done in Sharm el Sheikh to the consternation of Indian public opinion.

Trade and commerce are said to be the underlying motive, now that the Prime Ministers on both sides have an inborn trading instinct. But Pakistan has used trade as a weapon in the past and will continue to do so even if it hurts their interests. The compulsions of economic benefits have never been a factor in the India-Pakistan narrative. It can become a factor only if powerful vested interests get into the act. To expect trade to flourish in anticipation of a political dialogue is to allow hope to triumph over experience.

The second announcement of the Prime Minister's participation at the SAARC meeting in Islamabad is also fraught with danger, as I pointed out when the first announcement was made. The future of SAARC is under a cloud, with the deterioration of our relations with Nepal. If the problems with Nepal are not resolved by the time of the SAARC summit, they will dominate the summit to the Prime Minister's embarrassment. Moreover, Pakistan will push for China's admission to SAARC as the host. This was a difficult issue during the Kathmandu summit as all members, except India, were in favour of China's admission. The Prime Minister will face a Hobson's Choice of either acquiescing in China's admission or facing the opprobrium of blocking it. Pakistan must guarantee the avoidance of such a situation before the Prime Minister boards the plane for the Islamabad SAARC summit.

The headline that the ice has been broken between India and Pakistan is a joke, like the claim by a smoker several times that he has stopped smoking. Why do we need to break the ice again and again? If history is any guide, time will not be far before we would need to break the ice again. The resumption of the dialogue will only lead to further recriminations and another freeze, followed by another melting of the ice. A senior Indian negotiator told me in all seriousness once that the good thing about resumption of the dialogue is that we can suspend them when Pakistan launches another terrorist attack!'

The welfare of overseas Indians was the fourth pillar of Modiplomacy after development, security and the neighbourhood. If there was one issue on which all political parties agreed, it was the imperative to include overseas Indians in India's economic development and to take care of their needs and aspirations. Successive governments have been vying with each other to give more and more concessions to them as acknowledgment of their contribution by way of remittances, investment, lobbying for India, promoting Indian culture abroad and for building a good image of India by their intelligence and industry.

India was initially sensitive to the view that championing the cause of overseas Indians might offend the host countries, who should be fully responsible for their welfare and security. The Indian community and our diplomatic missions interacted on national days or other important occasions, but diaspora diplomacy was low key.

Rajiv Gandhi was the first Prime Minister who changed the diaspora policy by inviting Indians abroad, regardless of their nationality, to participate in nation-building, much like the overseas Chinese communities. In return, he promised them opportunities to work with India, like in the celebrated case of Sam Pitroda, who was entrusted with the task of modernising telecommunications in India. The response was not ecstatic, but many volunteered to help out in various ways. However, this brought to focus the many inadequacies of the Indian system for the diaspora to collaborate with India or to invest in the country. Grievances like red tape, multiple clearances, and distrust of government in fulfilling promises were addressed through hesitant reforms and promotional measures.

The first test of the new diaspora policy came in 1987 when Sitiveni Rabuka ousted a Fiji Indian majority government in Fiji and reduced them to second-class citizens. Rajiv Gandhi, in a major departure from established policy, protested vehemently, imposed trade sanctions against Fiji, got it expelled from the Commonwealth and raised the issue at the United Nations. This bewildered those Fiji Indians who did not want to disturb the race relations in Fiji, but energised the Indian diaspora, generating faith in them that India would not be a silent witness, as it was in the past, to discrimination, racism and disenfranchisement of Indians abroad. The Indian position was instrumental in democracy and racial harmony returning to Fiji after 10 years.

After India and the overseas Indians rediscovered each other under Rajiv Gandhi, there came a host of measures such as a separate Ministry of Overseas Indian Affairs, the Person of Indian Origin (PIO) Card, Pravasi Bharatiya Divas, Pravasi Bharatiya Samman, Overseas Citizen of India Card, NRI funds and voting rights for Indian citizens abroad, some from the United Progressive Alliance and some from the National Democratic Alliance governments. The response from the diaspora was diverse, as these affected different categories of Indians in different ways. For the Indian nationals in the Gulf and elsewhere, welfare measures and resettlement facilities were more important, while the prosperous communities in the West, who were clamouring for dual citizenship, felt short-changed. But, on the whole, they were energised into espousing Indian causes in the US. Of course, their support to Indian interests was not automatic and they often urged India to modify its policies to suit American sensitivities. Indian-Americans contributed little by way of remittances or investments, but the establishment of the India Caucus in the House of Representatives and turning around doubting legislators into voting for the India-US nuclear deal were major accomplishments.

Modi made the diaspora a centrepiece of his foreign policy and, during his foreign visits, addressed mammoth meetings of the community to project India's priorities and needs. But he did not address any of their demands or announce any new plans for removing their grievances such as travel issues and protection of their properties in India. If anything, the merger of the Ministry of Overseas Indian Affairs with the Ministry of External Affairs, though pragmatic, has been construed as a negative step. The irregularity of diaspora conferences and awards has also caused some concern in the diaspora.

Together with the new hopes and expectations raised by the government, there are new fears and concerns among and about the overseas communities. The volatility in West Asia, together with the fall in oil prices, has caused fears of a massive return of Indian nationals, curtailing remittances and making demands on the job market. In Kerala, for instance, workers from other states have bridged the demand-supply gap in various sectors. The Gulf countries will require foreign workers for some more time, but India's relations with many of them remain in the employer-employee mode. Of course, it was heartening to see Saudi Arabia resolve a serious issue relating to starvation among Indian workers, but we should be ready for the eventuality of Indian workers returning, though a massive 'Indexit' is unlikely.

A recent phenomenon is that of 'discovering' Indians wherever there is a crisis. India does not have any precise data on the number of Indians in different parts of the world. The amount of risks that Indians are capable of taking to get medical education, for instance, is phenomenal. Whether it is in Ukraine, Yemen or Syria, Indians are discovered eking out an existence in difficult circumstances. General V.K. Singh (retd), Minister of State for External Affairs, became virtually the Chief Repatriation Officer, flying into hotspots with chartered flights to rescue Indians and bring them home. He was often bewildered when many Indians refused to use the facility for return and insisted on staying on in difficult situations either to seek alternative jobs or to settle their claims. Back home, disquiet has been expressed that public money is being spent on bringing people who have gone on their own for their benefit.

Even more serious is the suspicion that some Indians are travelling to the Islamic State areas either to join the jihad or to settle there in what is considered a Promised Land. Adventurism of this kind needs to be stopped. We used to take pride in the fact that Indians never joined terrorist organisations, but the latest trends are very disturbing.

The dilemma for India is whether movements of Indians abroad for education or employment should be curbed. This will be against the spirit of freedom; but there should be at least an accurate count of Indians in different countries and projections should be made of future prospects. States must be prepared with plans for rehabilitation of Indians, with the possibility of offering the same kind of jobs they were doing abroad. Asking them to turn into entrepreneurs overnight would be counterproductive. There should also be a clear division of labour between the Central and the State governments in crisis situations.

The Indian diaspora is more prosperous than before and its involvement in India's development is increasing. Indians overseas are conscious of their opportunities in India. At the same time, new fears about scaled-up return of Indians or their involvement in global terrorism are raising their heads. Firefighting is not enough. We should have a comprehensive plan involving both the Centre and States to invest remittances intelligently and to find alternative ways of livelihood for those who return.

The complex international situation and diverse problems of the Indian diaspora and their different political affiliations were not conducive for the kind of relationship that Modi had envisaged. A certain amount of disillusionment set in as a result. But whenever he went to new countries, he did not neglect to give them attention. But there was a marked lack of enthusiasm in the crowds as the novelty wore off.

For instance, though Modi's visit to the UAE was an unqualified success from the point of bilateral relations, there was considerable disappointment over the lack of attention given to the Indian workers, most of them Indian nationals. Ever since the announcement of his visit to the UAE, speculation was rife about some major plans and programmes that he would announce in Dubai for the welfare of the Indian workers there.

All eyes were on the mammoth gathering at the Cricket Stadium in Dubai, where he addressed the Indian community. Although there was no indication that any such grand plans were on their way, Indian community groups and the media produced their own list of measures that would transform the plight of Indian workers. Most important of them was an understanding on slowing down of localisation of jobs, resettlement of returnees in India, air travel facilities and voting rights. No such dramatic announcements were made, but the Prime Minister declared a new strategic relationship between the two countries, which, it was presumed, would have a salutary effect on the life of Indians in the UAE. Modi used his electrifying speech to present his own report card on his achievements in the last one year to the 50,000-strong NRI audience.

At the very end of his speech, he dealt with the 'small problems' of the Indian workers and announced various portals to deal with their grievances. But these measures did not seem to satisfy those who had expected the Prime Minister to find solutions for their problems. That the Prime Minister generally focused on broad policy issues and not on matters of detail left them bewildered. His silence on voting rights of Indians abroad also disappointed many.

The biggest applause went to the announcement that the crown prince of Abu Dhabi had allotted a piece of land for a Hindu temple. Modi himself suggested a standing ovation for the crown prince to express gratitude. His very warm references to the reception he received and the announcement of Rs 4.5 lakh crore of UAE investment must have gladdened their hearts.

The support of the UAE for India's permanent membership of the UN Security Council was projected as a major gesture of solidarity. But the main body of the speech, which was a catalogue of his achievements in foreign policy, could not excite his listeners. They may have seen it as a campaign speech with eyes on the forthcoming elections in some states.

The support extended to India by the UAE on terrorism was a major theme in the speech, and Modi did not miss the opportunity to take a few digs at Pakistan without naming it. His pointed reference to 'no good Taliban and bad Taliban' was particularly significant, as the UAE had once recognised the Taliban government in Afghanistan. The problem of defining terrorism at the UN hinges on the claim that freedom fighters should be exempted from charges of terrorism and this has a bearing on Pakistan's position on terrorism in Kashmir.

The fact that the UAE supported India on our proposal for a Comprehensive Convention on Terrorism was a welcome step in this context. Modi proved the point about borderless terrorism by citing the terrorist attack in Bangkok he had just heard about. He said the world had recognised that terrorism was no more a law and order problem and that it was a global phenomenon that should be tackled by international cooperation.

India's improved rating by the World Bank and others and 48 per cent increase in foreign direct investment were pointed out as singular achievements. Modi dwelt at length on the improvement of relations with neighbours and hinted at moving forward with SAARC without Pakistan, which was blocking cooperation and integration. He gave the details of the new understanding with Nepal, Bangladesh, Sri Lanka and the Maldives in a bid to isolate Pakistan. He also mentioned the agreement with the Nagas. He made a pointed reference to the indispensability of dialogue to resolve problems, whether inside India or among countries.

Many references to the contributions of the Indians in the Gulf to the development of the UAE and enhanced pride of India raised the hope that Modi would deal with specific problems of the workers in the Gulf, particularly after he visited a labour camp. He waxed eloquent on the support extended by the Indians in the Gulf, who held out a helpful umbrella at the time of need and cheered the election victory of the BJP.

The recollection of the contribution made by the Indians in the Gulf to the fund launched by Atal Bihari Vajpayee, following the nuclear tests of 1998 was particularly heart-warming. It was noted at that time that the bulk of the deposits came from Indians in the Gulf and not from the richer Indians in the US and Europe.

But Modi chose to leave the solution of the day-to-day problems to the embassy and the consulate with an assurance that the grievances could be transmitted to the government through the various platforms, which have been established. He gave the embassy 30 days to rectify the problems of the e-Migrant portal and also promised more schools. Though the Community Welfare Fund and Consular Camps for the Indians outside major towns are not new, the mention of these by the PM was significant. The message was that the government would be sensitive and responsive to the needs of the Indian workers.

No doubt, Modi reached out to the Indian community in various ways, just as he reached a new understanding with the rulers of the UAE. His visit to a labour camp and the grand mosque in Abu Dhabi symbolised his approach. He stressed how he had rectified the negligence of the past by travelling to Dubai to acknowledge the contribution of Indians and to raise the relationship with the UAE. The expectation is that the new relationship with the UAE will lead to the betterment of the Indians, now that the UAE has a stake in India's stability and prosperity.

Modi's Dubai speech was heavy on his own national and international agenda, but it had the right mix of sentiment for the UAE and the Indian community. It met the twin objectives of making the UAE a strategic partner and endearing himself to the Indians in the Gulf. Modi's oratorical skills were once again on display, but doubts were expressed about the follow-up action required to fulfil the promises.

Next to bilateral initiatives, fight against terrorism was the major plank of the Modi Government on the international platform. Addressing the UN General Assembly in September 2016, the Minister of External Affairs, Sushma Swaraj suggested, for the first time, that Pakistan should be isolated for not joining the fight against international terrorism. This was more an emotional and rhetorical call than a thought-out proposal for action by the other member States. Isolation of any member State by the others is an action taken only in exceptional circumstances as every State has the right to pursue its own policy, with the option of not joining any international arrangement. Isolation of Pakistan, on account of not joining the consensus even if there was one, was not a practical proposition.

In reality, the Prime Minister admitted that the Indian proposal for a Comprehensive Convention on Terrorism had not gained traction. It was stuck on the question of the definition of terrorism because one man's terrorist was often another man's freedom fighter. In the absence of a consensus on this issue, there was no ground for isolating Pakistan. On the other hand, Pakistan repeatedly claimed that it was a victim of terrorism and that it was willing to fight terror. It was even a partner of the United States in the war against terror at least in name.

The history of the United Nations shows that some kind of isolation was imposed only on South Africa on account of apartheid. India was the first country to raise the issue of apartheid and it took us many years to persuade other countries to impose sanctions. Many had argued for many years that apartheid was an internal matter of South Africa even after the liberation struggle assumed the proportions of a civil war. An arms embargo and sanctions came much later.

Isolation of South Africa was never complete even after a majority of States wanted South Africa to be isolated. Several neighbours of South Africa, even while supporting the sanctions in principle, continued to have trade and other dealings with the apartheid regime for the sake of survival. South Africa, even with a despicable regime, was necessary for them.

In the case of Israel, there was a near universal consensus that it was guilty of defying the United Nations by occupying Palestinian territory and there was a body of resolutions, demanding that Israel should withdraw to its 1967 borders. The Israeli settlements on Palestinian territories were universally condemned, but no isolation was possible even when violence broke out in Gaza. No sanctions were possible except those imposed by individual countries. After the normalisation of relations by Egypt following the Camp David Accords, Israel became more and more acceptable even without any change in policy on its part. The call to isolate Pakistan on the ground of sponsoring and supporting terrorism, particularly when the UN had not even defined terrorism, was a wild goose chase.

For India, a country that has worked in multilateral fora for nearly 70 years on a global agenda, subsuming its interests in pursuit of the global good, the recent tendency to focus on a single issue like terrorism did not seem appropriate. Such an approach only confirmed the suspicion that it was using terrorism as a convenient weapon to battle Pakistan diplomatically. Like Queen Gertrude says in Hamlet, people have begun to say: 'The lady doth protest too much, methinks.'

One point on which the world ridiculed Pakistan in the past was that it could not think beyond Kashmir, whatever the forum and the topic for discussion. India is today on its way to opening itself to similar criticism—that it is stuck in the terrorism groove. India's warnings about terrorism in and around South Asia fell on deaf ears for more than 20 years, but the revelation that the 9/11 attacks were the handiwork of terrorists with similar affiliation to those who were attacking India changed the whole situation. Now there is no doubt that the 'mother ship of terrorism' is Pakistan. No one disputes the attributes we have given to Pakistan in this context. But for India to pursue isolation of Pakistan on this count at every forum and to make it a litmus test of every country's friendship to India does more harm than good. Every speech of the Prime Minister, regardless of the venue and the topic of discussion, was a ringing denunciation of cross-border terrorism.

The BRICS Goa summit was turned into a battle of wits between India and its guests as to how far the group could go in identifying itself with India in isolating Pakistan. Moreover, India made no secret of its motivation and made it clear to its guests that the way to India's heart was by targeting Pakistan. Given the fact that no one wants to create enemies in such diplomatic conclaves, many of them, particularly the Chinese, may have felt uncomfortable to be caught in an awkward situation. Eventually, China acted as Pakistan's proxy in the discussions in Goa.

The outcome of the Goa meetings could have been projected as a diplomatic victory for India if the expectations were not pitched so high by the Prime Minister himself. What we have is a condemnation of terrorism in all its manifestations, a consensus position of the UN itself, without a definition of terrorism, which has eluded the international community even after 9/11. The global concern over the growth of the Islamic State (IS) appeared to take precedence over the special situation in South Asia as the IS is now 'spread over' more than 30 countries and others dread its expansion. India should take the opportunity to speak strongly against the IS and project cross-border terrorism as another manifestation of the same problem.

Building a broader constituency against terrorism is more beneficial than focussing on its own specific situation. By narrowing down exclusively to the action India expects from the international community to meet its concerns, such as declaring Pakistan as a terrorist state, may not have the desired effect.

A single dignified and forceful presentation by India to multilateral fora, leaving it to the member countries to tackle the issue effectively, would have been more appropriate. Anticipating the possible outcome and calibrating India's requests accordingly should have been the strategy to be adopted. Otherwise, the wide gap between India's assertions and the language of the outcome will be visible to all. Together with India's application for membership of the NSG and aspiration to permanent membership of the UN Security Council, the country appears to be knocking at too many doors instead of offering global solutions to global problems. India modified its position of 'eligibility' for permanent membership to its 'right'. Such assertions will have no impact on others unless its demand is projected as part of the need to correct the imbalance in a crucial world body.

India confining itself to the terrorism groove showed lack of direction when it had altered the dynamics of its relations with Pakistan by carrying out surgical strikes. Having taken precipitate action, India should move in a predetermined course of action. The old pattern of terrorist attack by Pakistan, angry verbal reaction by India and resumption of dialogue does not make sense anymore. If such a course has not been prepared, this is the time to frame such a course of action. This could consist of informing the international community of the state of play, combatting terrorism on the ground with measured use of force, and dealing with the internal situation in Jammu and Kashmir with a view to eliminating internal support to cross-border terrorism. Other options available to India such as amendment of the Indus Waters Treaty, trade sanctions, and so on should also have been considered. Efforts to isolate Pakistan as part of the strategy contradicted India's established position against internationalising the Kashmir issue.

The clear lesson to be learnt from recent experience is that the world at large does not see terrorism in Jammu and Kashmir as part of the global terrorism which threatens international peace and security. The recognition by the UN that Kashmir is a disputed territory influences the policy of most nations, including those who are friendly with India. A broader framework for the terrorism debate shows a way out for those who support India without wanting to get embroiled in a dispute.

India's pursuit of the Comprehensive Convention on International Terrorism that was tabled in the UN General Assembly in 1996 has very little chance of success. It was seen at that time as an anti-Pakistan measure. The convention received some attention by the legal committee of the UN in the wake of the 9/11 attacks, but it got stuck in the old argument that one man's terrorist was another's freedom fighter.

India's advocacy of nuclear disarmament is an excellent example of the country subsuming its interest in the desire of the global community for a nuclear weapon-free world. It was only when the Nuclear Non-Proliferation Treaty regime became discriminatory that India stepped out of it and took a firm decision not to sign the treaty. On the question of fissionable material, India stands ready to join the negotiations on the Fissionable Material Cut-off Treaty rather than plough a lonely furrow. India harmonised its position with that of the developing countries in environmental negotiations to protect its interests and succeeded up to the point of formulating the Kyoto Protocol. It ill behoves a country like India with a long record of using its membership of the UN for the common good to fall in one groove, however important that issue may be. Multilateralism accepts constant reiterations of national positions, but to forge a consensus, the positions should be integrated with common concerns to the extent possible.

The new partnership with the US made Modi neglect the constituency of Non-Aligned and G-77 countries, in which we had a leadership role. He did not attend the summit of the NAM held in Venezuela in 2016. A summit of the NAM without the Indian Prime Minister is like Hamlet without the Prince of Denmark and that is what was enacted in Venezuela. The only other time when an Indian Prime Minister stayed home was in 1979, when the historic Havana summit took place. Prime Minister Charan Singh's absence, however, had nothing to do with NAM; this time, the absence of Prime Minister Narendra Modi had a political message.

Sources close to the Prime Minister took pains to explain that his absence was deliberate as he did not find NAM to be important enough for him to spend a couple of days in distant Venezuela. Therefore, the explanation given by the Head of the Indian delegation, Vice President Hamid Ansari, that the summit was not a conference of Prime Ministers and, therefore, Indian participation was adequate, did not carry conviction.

Non-alignment has not been in the vocabulary of Prime Minister Modi. He has been on a quest for selective alignments to suit his needs for India's development and security. His advisers have now begun to rationalise India's distancing from NAM. One argument is that NAM did not have any binding principles and that it was a marriage of convenience among disparate countries. This argument arises from the narrow, literary interpretation of non-alignment. Many commentators had felt, right from the beginning, that the word 'non-alignment' conveyed the wrong notion that it was not aligning with the power blocs and that the be-all and end-all of non-alignment was to remain unaligned. But the quintessence of non-alignment was freedom of judgment and action and it remained valid, whether there was one bloc or two. Seen in that context, non-military alliances can also be within the ambit of non-alignment, which was subsequently characterised as 'strategic autonomy'. In other words, India does not have to denounce non-alignment to follow any foreign policy it chooses to follow.

Another argument being heard is that NAM countries did not come to our help on any of the critical occasions when India needed solidarity, such as the Chinese aggression in 1962 or the Bangladesh war in 1971. Even in the latest struggle against terror, NAM has not come to assist India in any way. But the whole philosophy of NAM is that it remains united on larger global issues, even if it does not side with a member on a specific issue. India itself has followed this approach, whenever the members had problems with others either inside or outside the movement. NAM positions have always been the reflection of the lowest common denominator in any given situation.

That NAM has no ideal or ideology as a glue is a wrong assumption. Though the criteria for NAM membership are general, anti-colonialism, anti-imperialism and anti-racism were essential attributes of NAM countries. There was a consensus on nuclear disarmament also till India broke ranks by keeping out of the NPT. The diversity reflected in both Singapore and Cuba being NAM members has been its strength. Therefore, Egypt signing the Camp David Accords with Israel in 1978 or India signing the Treaty of Peace, Friendship and Cooperation with the Soviet Union in 1971 did not result in any disruption of membership.

All said and done, the golden age in India's foreign policy was in the first 15 years after Independence, when NAM provided a constituency for India because of our non-violent victory over the British and the leadership it provided to the newly independent countries. Our problems were different from the small and impoverished nations that thronged the movement, but Jawaharlal Nehru's vision and statesmanship inspired them. We did not seek to resolve our problems through the machinery of dispute resolution in NAM, but actively assisted those who sought such assistance. India led the NAM effort to resolve the Iran-Iraq dispute.

As expected, political issues continued to engage NAM and we benefitted from its activism occasionally. In fact, it was through NAM that we operated to counter the efforts to expand the UN Security Council by including just Germany and Japan as permanent members. NAM submitted its own proposal and ensured that no quick fix was permitted.

The question we need to ask is whether our continued involvement with NAM would stand in the way of our 21st century ambitions. The very informal nature of NAM permits members to operate individually. It also has the facility of members reserving their positions, as we did on the non-proliferation positions of NAM. Our new nearness to the US is not a red rag in NAM and our ability to be helpful in formulating US policies gives us an advantage. No NAM country may agree to isolate Pakistan, but the NAM forum will be an effective instrument to project our anti-terrorist sentiments.

NAM is particularly important in elections at the UN, including the possible identification of new permanent members of the Security Council. The NAM position may not be decisive, but in the normal process of consultations, every grouping will get its own weight age and it is convenient to have a lobby behind us. NAM today, like the Commonwealth has always been, is a heritage we need not discard.

The decision to say farewell to NAM is very much in keeping with the new transactional nature of the foreign policy Modi had developed. NAM was a part of our larger vision for the world, but today it is seen as inconsequential to our present preoccupations. This transformation will not be lost on the world community.

The period following Modi's visit to Washington in June 2016 marked the highest level to which the India-US roller coaster rose and the outlook was splendid. The India-US collaboration in the Asia Pacific, close defence co-operation and the ongoing cooperation in several fields gathered momentum. Although the candidature of Donald Trump gained traction, it was generally presumed that Hillary Clinton would win and the new administration would continue the policies of the previous administration, particularly in the case of India and China.

India expected to have its comfort zone in the Asia Pacific further strengthened. Modi made no effort to contact Trump or his campaign team, though the Embassy in Washington maintained regular contacts. A contingency plan for a possible Trump administration was not prepared because of the apparent certitude of a victory for Hillary Clinton that was shared by most in the media, think tanks and other influential circles. Republican Party itself was not comfortable with the ways of Trump and the general expectation was that his candidature would fizzle out one way or another. The US saw the most contentious campaign in history, but there were signs of a Trump victory by September 2016.

Sensing that India was totally unprepared for a Trump victory, on 20 September 2016, I wrote a piece with the title, 'Donald Trump—A Contrarian View':

'India has an old love affair with the Democrats in the United States, but the Republican Presidents and legislators have done more for India-US relations than Democrats in recent years. John F. Kennedy and Bill Clinton and their wives conquered hearts in India, but they did not transform the relationship as the younger George Bush did. Mr Clinton initiated the process of normalisation with India, but came down on India like a ton of bricks when it tested nuclear weapons in 1998.

In the days following the tests and sanctions, many close Democrat friends of India, even the Chairman and members of the India caucus in the Congress, deserted us, except for Congressman Frank Pallone. The State Department was not on talking terms with us. It was a statement by former Secretary of State Henry Kissinger that he could understand India's concerns as it was in a "tough neighbourhood" that changed the bleak atmosphere for India in Washington. Again, it was Senator Sam Brownback, a Republican, who whittled away the sanctions against India over a period of time.

Though Democratic presidential candidate Hillary Clinton was once referred to as "the Senator from Punjab" by her detractors, there is no evidence of her having gone out of her way to favour India. She has maintained a friendly face towards India, but her concerns about China and Pakistan were all too evident during her term as Secretary of State. As President, she is likely to continue the ambivalence.

Barack Obama started off as a hot favourite in India, but appeared disillusioned after his visit in 2010, when he failed to win the nuclear and the fighter aircraft contracts. His initial opposition to the nuclear deal did not stand in the way of its implementation, but he extracted a price for every step he took with Narendra Modi to take the relationship to greater heights. Despite all his camaraderie with the Indian Prime Minister, he spared no occasion to lecture India on the merits of religious tolerance and nuclear fidelity. Many tricky issues remain even as we call ourselves a major defence partner of the US.

Republican presidential candidate Donald Trump remains an enigma wrapped in mystery, with his confusing pronouncements on domestic and foreign policy. He has been accused of having neo-fascist tendencies. But his positions are evolving. He seems to have abandoned the idea of banning Muslim immigration, building a wall between the US and Mexico and stopping all migration and outsourcing. He has realised the value of the North Atlantic Treaty Organisation, even though he still believes that the partners should pay for the services they receive. But he is capable of thinking out of the box and this may well be the reason why he is still neck and neck in the race with Ms Clinton today.

Terrorism is the recurring theme in every speech that Mr Modi makes and that is a measure of India's most important preoccupation today. Mr Trump's agenda is identical and India can rely on him to fight terrorism in all its forms, whether it is the Islamic State, al-Qaeda, Taliban or the Pakistan-sponsored outfits. "Pakistan is probably the most dangerous country in the world today. The only country that can check Pakistan is India," he said in September 2015. No Democratic President, not even Ms Clinton, will take such an unequivocal position on Pakistan and terrorism.

As a businessman, Mr Trump has been an admirer of India to the extent of encouraging investment in India. Two Trump Towers are in the making in Mumbai and Pune in partnership with Indian entrepreneurs. He has gone on record as saying that after the installation of the Modi government, India has become a "top place" for investment. In January 2016, Mr Trump complimented India for "doing great" and expressed surprise that nobody was talking about it. Since he puts his money where his mouth is, as President, Mr Trump is likely to embrace India. As a businessman President who has pledged to bring prosperity to the US, he may find a valuable partner in Mr Modi.

Mr Trump's admiration for Russian President Vladimir Putin and his championship of Brexit may well be signs of his wanting to be different from others. But neither of these, even if taken to their logical conclusion, will hurt India's interests. On China, Mr Trump has been ambivalent. His main criticism about China is on trade and currency matters. In fact, his anticipated "trade war" with China could wipe out $420 billion off China's exports, according to Kevin Lai, a Hong Kong economist. Mr Trump has also had some good words to say about China, but his distrust of Beijing is obvious and he is not likely to act against our interests. The Democratic optimism about China being a responsible nation that can be entrusted with looking after stability in South Asia is not likely to be shared by Mr Trump.

In the middle of September, barely two months before the polls, Ms Clinton may have a slight edge over Mr Trump but the matter is not settled as yet. Mr Trump has begun to lead in critical "battleground states" like Ohio and Florida, where Ms Clinton was leading till recently. If the Americans take a leap into the dark on account of their frustrations about the economy, terrorism and China, as the British did in the case of Brexit, we may end up with Mr Trump as President. India has fewer reasons to be uncomfortable about such an eventuality than generally feared.'

My article did not change opinion in India, but it turned out to be prophetic in certain ways. A highly respected senior colleague and Sree, my son in New York, admonished me for sticking my neck out.

8 November 2016 turned out to be the day on which a *deus ex machine* appeared that changed Modi's fortunes both in external and internal affairs. Even as the news of a Trump victory was streaming into the Asianet News studio, where I was giving a commentary on the results, I noticed that Modi was making what appeared to be an important announcement. We continued with the news from the United States, but calls began to flow into the studio asking us to cover demonetisation, just announced by the PM. When the anchor asked me for my comment, I could only say something about my experience of demonetisation in Burma in the 1980s. But it was very clear that Modi would encounter two of his biggest challenges, very much like a Shakespearean hero. The stage was set for the final Act of the Modi drama.

My quick assessment of the victory of Donald Trump was as follows on 10 November 2016.

> 'Wishful thinking at best and conspiracy at worst prevented an accurate assessment of Donald Trump's chances to win the presidency of the United States. The mainstream media in the United States and elsewhere, several political leaders around the globe and almost all pollsters concluded that the experienced and well-known Hillary Clinton would prevail over a man who knew nothing about things other than business and tax evasion.
>
> On top of it, his suitability to become even a supermarket manager was challenged on account of his questionable moral character, neo-fascist tendencies and hatred of sections of the world population. I expressed a contrarian view last September, not to praise Trump, but to look for straws of hope in the event of his becoming president. After stating that we should be prepared for a Trump presidency, I had said "India has fewer reasons to be uncomfortable about such an eventuality than generally feared".
>
> After Trump's stunning and convincing victory, fear was being expressed that he would lead his country to isolation, war and injustice to the poor.
>
> His campaign speeches were being quoted to suggest that his presidency would be an apocalypse. His acceptance speech should remove some fears as he said he would be the president of all the American people and a friend of all countries.
>
> We should respect the democratic choice made by the American people and give Trump a chance to prove worthy of the trust. Trump has a tendency to make an impact by saying the damnedest of things in the belief that any publicity is good as long as his name is spelt right. He had already backed out of his vow to stop the migration of Muslims and to stop spending money on NATO. If he has come this far, he should have the wisdom to win friends and influence people for the sake of his country, which he has promised to make great again. If he picks the right advisers and proceeds with caution, he may become a good president.

As for the India-US relationship, it has been like a roller coaster ride, not because of the personalities involved, but because of geopolitical reasons and the positions taken by either country at different times. The bipartisan support was its mainstay. But the fact remains that the Republicans have tended to be more helpful to India in the past. In the days following the nuclear tests of 1998, President Clinton and many close Democrat friends of India, even the Chairman and members of the India caucus in Congress, deserted us.

The State Department was not on talking terms with us. It was a statement by former Secretary of State Henry Kissinger that he could understand India's concerns as it was in a "tough neighbourhood" that changed the bleak atmosphere for India in Washington.

Many tricky issues remain even as we call ourselves a major defence partner of the US. Obama's support for India's permanent membership of the UN Security Council and for membership of the NSG turned out to be hollow. Donald Trump is notoriously unpredictable, but his evolving positions may align with some of our concerns.

Trump's admiration for Russian President Vladimir Putin and his championship of Brexit may well be signs of his wanting to be different from others. But neither of these, even if taken to their logical conclusion, will hurt India's interests.

The people of the United States have leapt into the dark by electing Trump as president on account of the deep frustration over the establishment represented by Clinton. Trumpism, marked by "nativism" was found attractive not only by the whites, but also the minorities, including Hispanics, whom Trump had criticised.

His declaration that he is a great fan of India and the Indian Prime Minister during the campaign need not be taken at face value, but there is no indication so far that he will be unfriendly to India.'

The mood in the world was one of extreme concern that Trump might lead the world to a Third World War. There were wide protests before and after the swearing-in with the intention of upstaging his election. It took some time for countries, including India, to make tentative steps towards working with Trump as President.

The arrival of Donald Trump on the world scene has transformed international relations beyond recognition and his impact will be of great significance on Modi's foreign policy moves. The success or otherwise of Modi's foreign policy will largely depend on the equation he is likely to strike with Trump. Given Trump's mercurial character, there is no guarantee that he will build on the foundations laid by Modi and Obama.

Modi's sterling achievement in his first three years was the way he brought India-US relations from the rock bottom of the roller coaster to its pinnacle. Setting aside issues like the denial of a US visa to himself and the Devyani Khobragade incident, Modi went right ahead to strengthen the strategic relationship and to expand it further into closer cooperation in the Asia Pacific and to close defence cooperation.

He sought to cut the Gordian knot of the liability law issue to enhance nuclear cooperation in accordance with the historic nuclear deal, which the BJP had opposed and countered with the liability law. During his fourth visit to the US, he announced in the US Congress in 2016 that henceforth the world would hear a new symphony in India-US relationship. Obama echoed the same sentiments and began co-designing and co-producing advanced military equipment with India. Obama called Modi a man of action and the latter came close to being named *Time*'s Man of the Year.

The arrival of the *deus ex machina*, literally a god from the machine, was as dramatic, unexpected and inevitable as it used to happen in the Elizabethan theatre. The BJP camp, which had counted on Obama's reincarnation in female form, was as surprised by the advent of Trump as the majority of psephologists. They started counting their blessings in terms of his hatred of Islamic terrorism, allergy towards China, inclination towards Russia, love of business and affinity to his Hindu fundraisers.

It was hoped that his migration policies would not come in the way of the deployment of our IT personnel in the US in large numbers. A Trump-Modi meeting was anticipated to establish a new equation between the two men, who had appeared to share decisiveness, rightist policies, business mindedness and courage, to carry the new symphony forward. But the freeze that descended on the international scene had its impact on India. Except for a phone call and meetings at lower levels, there was no sign of extensive and intensive interaction between the two countries. Nor was there a date for their meeting in sight. As Trump began to move on to the international scene, many myths were shattered. Russia became a dreaded ghost in a scandal, which could lead to a first step towards impeachment. The North Korean threat to blow up the world transformed China from an adversary and a currency manipulator to a partner.

Trump gave a message of peace to the Muslim world, not from Cairo, as Obama did, but from the land of the Holy Mosques itself. Islamic terrorism was downgraded to Islamist extremism. Not a word was spoken in public about human rights issues. Migration control began to affect Indian IT personnel.

The method in the madness of the election campaign gradually emerged. US foreign policy appeared to return to its traditional moorings. The expectation today is not that Trump would bring in new dynamism, but that the traditional comfort level between India and the US would be maintained. The best hope is that at their first meeting, Modi and Trump would strike an equation.

The terrible mess that our neighbourhood became at the beginning of the fourth year of the Modi government may have nothing to do with the Trump phenomenon. But the hard-line stand that China and Pakistan took with India may be the result of confidence on their part that neither the US nor Russia would go out of their way to side with India. India also became tough with them as evidenced by the worsening situation on the Pakistan border and the Indian boycott of the Chinese One Belt One Road (OBOR) Summit. Modi's vision of cooperation with neighbours lie shattered as China has considerably enhanced its influence over them. His effort to build a SAARC without Pakistan might end up in a SAARC without India under China's tutelage.

The recent launch of a satellite for use by South Asian countries other than Pakistan was a diplomatic coup, but there was fear that it might become a white elephant, with the countries in the region not having the technology or the ground facilities to make use of the satellite. Moreover, some of them already have arrangements with China or some of the European countries for use of satellites. Whether ISRO will be able to replace them is a matter to be seen. The height of irony will be if these countries get Chinese money to build ground facilities to use the Indian satellite.

A legal victory in the International Court of Justice, new surgical strikes and increased tension have added a new dimension to India-Pakistan relations. A silver lining in the region is the PM's visit to Sri Lanka during which there were signs of Sri Lanka's disillusionment with China.

In the fourth year, the Modi government appeared formidable internally, having overcome the hazards of demonetisation, but it looked vulnerable on the foreign policy front. Too many imponderables made it difficult for India to steer clear of the turbulence on the international scene.

When the first meeting between Trump and Modi was announced in June 2017, there was considerable scepticism on both sides. Expectations for the meeting were so low that many India-watchers in Washington said Modi's best-case scenario might be simply reminding Trump that their countries share numerous interests, especially in combating so-called radical Islamic terror. 'Or, better still, the two might connect on a personal level, possibly preventing further public outbursts of derision from Trump', said the *Washington Post*. 'They could either hit it off amazingly or fall out completely', said Rajiv Kumar, an economist and author of the book *Modi and His Challenges*. 'They're both strong personalities, and both of them have a rather exalted opinion of themselves.'

But the visit went off much better than expected in form and substance and there were even moments of cordiality. The swift and decisive victory he had in the White House was much against the views articulated by the sceptics, doubting Thomases and prophets of doom.

No other visitor to President Trump's White House had gone back home unscathed because of Trump's unpredictability and idiosyncrasies. Modi not only had a red carpet rolled out for him on the White House lawn, but also had Mrs Melania Trump waiting with her husband for his arrival. As soon as he arrived, Modi started a pleasant conversation with the Trumps like a long-lost friend before he was ushered in. By the time he came out after nearly five hours, he had a one-to-one conversation with the President, a delegation-level meeting, a reception, a dinner, a tour of the residential areas of the White House and a joint statement of a kind none of his predecessors ever had. It was almost a dream come true for him and India. He also managed to hug the unsuspecting President not once, but twice.

The reason for this happy turn of events was not a sudden change of heart of the mercurial Trump or Modi's irresistible charisma, but a cold calculation that there was scope for a cool trade-off between his desire to nail Pakistan and China and Trump's wish to make America great again through creation of jobs.

Modi knew that the way to Trump's heart was through a few arms deals and quietly placed an order for $2 billion worth of drones and made it known that F-16s would be co-produced by the Tatas and that Spicejet was in the process of buying more than a hundred Boeing planes. Trump quickly realised that what he was getting was hard cash and jobs while what he had to offer in exchange was mere words, which would make no difference on the ground. So, he tested the waters with categorising the Hizbul Mujahideen chief as a global terrorist, much to the ecstasy of the Indian press as well as Modi himself.

Further concessions were made by listing Pakistani terrorist outfits together with IS and Al Qaeda, which should be combatted jointly by India and the US. They urged that Pakistani soil should not be used for launching terrorist attacks and that the culprits of the attacks in Mumbai, Pathankot and Uri should be brought to book. It cost nothing for Trump to do this, as there was no guarantee that any joint operations would be launched. But for Modi, it was a triumph, never savoured by any Indian Prime Minister before him. He declared that one man's 'Make in India' was another man's 'Make America Great Again'.

The sound of firing from the India-Pakistan border and the noise of a scuffle between Indian and Chinese soldiers in the Himalayan heights reverberated in the ornate halls of the White House to help the great India-America trade-off. Clearly, the bilateral mechanism established for combating terrorism was pregnant with possibilities, which included sharing of intelligence, training and actual engagement in the event of a threat in either of the two countries. The practical application of the principles established was expected to go a long way in deterring potential terrorists, particularly radical Islamic terrorists.

On the China front, what Modi was demanding was not any concrete action, but a formulation of words that would gladden Indian hearts, without even mentioning China by name. The two leaders simply agreed to take further measures to strengthen their partnership in the Asia-Pacific region in the hope of intimidating China. They expressed concern about rising tensions over maritime territorial disputes and affirmed the importance of safeguarding maritime security and ensuring freedom of navigation and over flight throughout the region, especially in the South China Sea, the whole of which is claimed by China.

The leaders called on all parties to avoid the use, or threat of use, of force in advancing their claims. They urged the concerned parties to pursue resolution of their territorial and maritime disputes through all peaceful means, in accordance with universally recognised principles of international law, including the United Nations Convention on the Law of the Sea. None of these would make any difference to China or rule out separate deals between China and the United States!

On realising that there has been no nuclear trade between India and the US ever since the nuclear deal was sealed and delivered in 2008, the US and India reaffirmed their commitment to implement fully the US-India civil nuclear cooperation agreement and even established a Contact Group on advancing the implementation of civil nuclear energy cooperation in order to realise early their shared goal of delivering electricity from US-built nuclear power plants in India. This would only amount to holding a dialogue to discuss all implementation issues, including but not limited to administrative issues, liability, technical issues, and licensing to facilitate the establishment of nuclear parks, including power plants with Westinghouse, a company which had declared bankruptcy, and GE-Hitachi technology.

Though one of them had withdrawn from the Paris Agreement and the other had signed it reluctantly, the leaders declared that they are committed to working towards the success of the Paris Agreement, including the creation of a new global agreement on climate change. India's opposition to renegotiating the Paris Agreement did not deter Modi from calling for a fresh agreement on climate change.

In apparent criticism of China's Belt and Road Initiative, the President and Prime Minister emphasised the need to accelerate infrastructure connectivity and economic development corridors for regional economic integration linking South, Southeast, and Central Asia. The President reiterated that the United States, through its New Silk Road and India-Pacific Economic Corridor, is promoting the linkage of India to its neighbours and the wider region to enable a freer flow of commerce and energy. India had boycotted the OBOR summit while the US had attended it at a fairly high level.

More seriously, the leaders asserted the importance of a sustainable, inclusive, sovereign, and democratic political order in Afghanistan, and committed to continue close consultations and cooperation in support of Afghanistan's future. They also urged North Korea to take concrete actions toward denuclearisation and other goals, as well as to comply fully with all its international obligations, including all relevant UN Security Council resolutions, and to fulfil its commitments under the 2005 Joint Statement of the Six-Party Talks. Surprisingly, the President reaffirmed his support for a reformed UN Security Council with India as a permanent member. Trump and even his Permanent Representative to the UN did not have much faith in the UN itself. The so-called 'reaffirmation' was apparently meant to make India happy, not to propose a reform of the Security Council.

Sadly, all these accomplishments in Washington did not gladden Modi's opponents, who pointed out that the Joint Statement did not have any reference to the H1-B visa, which faced extinction under Mr Trump. Apparently, Trump had given a strong message to the Indian side that he was not flexible on this issue and no purpose would be served by discussing it. Moreover, this is within the purview of the US Congress and the administration would not be able to provide any relief. But when Foreign Secretary S Jaishankar was asked about this omission, he said that he did not expect any adverse action as the Joint Statement said elsewhere that cooperation between India and the US in the digital world was important and that the contribution of the Indian community was of great importance. The Indian and American IT companies, however, continued to worry that any new restriction would turn out to be expensive for them.

There is a certain inevitability about the success of summits, as even the most disappointing outcomes can be projected as a resounding success. But Modi and Trump could claim that they came, they saw and conquered each other.

Although Modi's visit to Washington was a success, uncertainty and unpredictability prevailed and there was no guarantee that the trajectory of the relationship would be promising. India did not seem to be on Trump's radar for the present, except when he addressed migration issues. He did not think that India could help him to resolve the big issues on his plate like Korea or Iran. The flux in international relations did not seem to favour a significant improvement in relations. It was clear that much would depend on the evolution of the US-China-Russia relations and the new configurations in West Asia.

India's relations with the US cast a shadow on relations with Russia, which moved closer to Pakistan with arms supplies and joint military exercises. The revival of the Quadrilateral (the US, India, Japan and Australia) deepened Chinese suspicions and led to hardening of positions on NSG membership, the UN terrorist list and the Dalai Lama. Doklam took us close to a conflict with China and dragged Bhutan into the border dispute between India and China. Donald Trump was totally silent on this brush with conflict in the Himalayas. Bhutan itself seemed to waver in its loyalty to India as it did not seem to justify the Indian action in Doklam.

Doklam was a part of the process of teaching India a lesson set in motion by China in 1962. If the original lesson was that India should not aspire to leadership in Asia, the lesson of Doklam was that India should not stand in the way of Chinese supremacy of the world by aligning itself with the US, Japan and Australia. India should also accept the global dispensation that China has designed, and play second fiddle to it. Any sign of defiance will be resented and another lesson administered.

Back in 1962, India's 'guilt' was that it had acquired a global status that had appeared formidable. India's independence was a matter of pride for the colonial people around the world and the decolonisation initiative taken by India in the United Nations led to rapid freedom for many of them. They thronged to a new movement, which defied both capitalism and communism. India's agenda for disarmament and equitable development was embraced by the developing world. Together with India's vision of Afro-Asian solidarity, the stature of India appeared to be a future threat to China's secret ambition to dominate the world.

China had its own grievances against India that its claims on the border were rejected by India and that the Dalai Lama was given refuge in India. But the Chinese aggression of 1962, the unilateral withdrawal and the subsequent formalisation of the claims on Indian territory were motivated more by Chinese global designs rather than by the desire to resolve the issues at hand. What we see today is nothing but an extension of a plan hatched by China in 1962 or even earlier.

China's actions throughout half a century were malevolent to the extreme, without any silver lining. Pakistan was seen as the enemy's enemy and adopted as an all-weather friend. Come dictatorship or democracy, Pakistan remained the focus of China's policy in South Asia and beyond. Apart from serving China's interests, Pakistan grew bold enough to challenge India at every forum and to launch terrorism and even war.

With the rapid progress that China achieved by opening up its market to capitalism and foreign investment, its ambitions grew higher and as it grew into the second most powerful economy and technological hub, it kept an eye on India's own growth and did everything possible to counter Indian interests. Even on those issues in the multilateral fora, where Indian and Chinese interests coincided, like trade and environment, China did not hesitate to let us down and strike deals with others, as it happened in the case of climate change in Copenhagen in 2007 and in Paris in 2015.

The strategy adopted by China was to keep India guessing on its intentions on the border, even after signing a treaty to maintain peace and tranquillity on the border, by moving Chinese troops deep into

Indian territory beyond the Line of Actual Control. The timings of these moves were chosen to coincide with significant events involving China and India. The 'most unkindest' cut of all was the Chinese intrusion at the very moment when President Xi Jinping was sitting on a swing with Prime Minister Narendra Modi on his visit to Ahmedabad. Protests were made when the Indian Prime Minister visited Arunachal Pradesh and they reached a feverish pitch when the Dalai Lama visited Tawang. The introduction of staple visas for the residents of Kashmir was bad enough, but when it was applied to a General who was posted to Jammu and Kashmir was a clear provocation. In their records, China even reduced the length of the border between India and China to exclude the border in the Kashmir sector.

More recently, China opposed India's entry to the NSG even though it had agreed to the waiver of its provisions at the time of the negotiations on the India-US nuclear deal. The Prime Minister's fervent personal efforts to break the impasse were flatly rejected. China also vetoed the inclusion of an acknowledged terrorist on the UN list without any reason.

The Chinese initiative, the 'One Belt One Road' (OBOR) was an open admission of its ambition to dominate the globe with an unparalleled communications network. When country after country fell prey to the Chinese machinations by joining the project, India saw it as a debt trap and imposition of Chinese priorities for development on others. Moreover, the Pakistan segment of the OBOR passed through Pakistan Occupied Kashmir (POK), challenging openly India's sovereignty. Although hints were given that India might consider participating in the conference hosted by China if only the Pakistan segment was excluded from OBOR, China insisted on going ahead with the project as originally designed. India's absence from the conference became a provocation for aggravating Chinese animosity.

The Doklam crisis may well have been the cumulative effect of the events of the last half a century. Unlike the previous intrusions, the event was staged at the India-Bhutan-China tri-junction, the status of which was supposed to be safeguarded by both China and Bhutan till the three countries were ready to settle it. The Chinese argument that India had no locus standi on the issue is laughable because the India-Bhutan treaty specifically gives India the responsibility to assist Bhutan in its defence of its territorial integrity. A special feature of the stand-off in Doklam is the refusal of China to enter into any negotiations till the unconditional withdrawal of the Indian soldiers. Entering direct negotiations with Bhutan, securing the establishment of a Chinese embassy in Bhutan and gradually weaning it away from India are clear objectives of China. Bhutan is the last pearl that China is seeking to add to the string designed to choke India.

Though a confrontation was avoided after a series of threats, it was clear that it was India which budged and accepted a simultaneous withdrawal, which was not entirely mutual. The rumours still persist about construction activity by the Chinese. Doklam crisis is likely to have grave consequences for India-China relations. China will move from the present phase of asserting itself on important issues to an open confrontation to browbeat India into accepting China's dominance. India will face the Hobson's choice between openly confronting China or acquiescing in the Chinese world view and acting in consonance with it. By choosing the first option, which is most likely, India will find obstacles in the way, leading to demand from peaceniks in India and abroad to come to terms with China. If Trump's US turns a blind eye and Japan also begins to toe the Chinese line, India's cup of woe will be filled to the brim.

Another conceivable scenario is for India to forge a coalition, which distances itself from China and the US and builds relations with both the US and China like what we did during the Cold War between the US and the Soviet Union. But that is conditional upon an open rivalry between the US and China, leading both to seek friends. Whatever policy we may adopt, the challenge of China will be India's preoccupation for another half a century.

In sum, PM Modi had to contend with a number of issues as he entered his fifth year. He was not to be blamed for it, but in a sense, much of the work done in the first three years lay wasted because of the changes in the global situation. A new three-cornered Cold War had already begun among the US, China and Russia with no clarity on who their allies are. Trump has alienated NATO and many old allies of the US have now close relations with Beijing. The trade war between the US and China threatened to cause a global recession. Russia, after raising hopes for a new detente, has become an adversary to the US. Though India is closer to the US than the other two, we need to find new equations with all the three. The recent informal 'agendaless' summits with China and Russia were part of an effort to remove the perception that India's relations with both these countries had deteriorated. With France and Germany, India has developed mutually beneficial relations.

The new transactional foreign policy that PM Modi had developed had distanced India from the developing countries' fraternity like the NAM and the Group of 77. These constituencies were useful to deal with issues on which we could make common cause with the developing countries. China has maintained its solidarity with the developing world and used that profile to get their support and even to exploit them economically. Non-alignment does not inhibit linkages with other countries and we get a convenient platform.

One region in which India made headway in the fourth year of PM Modi's tenure is West Asia, particularly Israel, Saudi Arabia and the United Arab Emirates. The traditional relationship with Iran is intact, though not flourishing because of the US pressure. With our deep interests in the region, the new partnerships have strengthened our energy security and employment possibilities.

India had good relations with Israel for a long time, particularly in the post-Cold War world. Israel was the key to good relations with the United States during the second term of President Bill Clinton. But Modi was the first Prime Minister of India to de-hyphenate Israel and the Arab world. India became confident of engaging the two without hyphenating them, an art that Israel had developed to separate India from its Palestine policy. I had noticed during my early UN days that Israel never confronted India even when we spoke more strongly than the Arabs about their misdeeds. Ambassador Bloom of Israel, who used to speak mercilessly against anyone who spoke against Israel spared the Indian representative each time. Initially Modi thought that he should dilute India's support for Palestine in order to get closer to Israel and remained silent on an attack in Gaza. But it turned out that Israel did not care about the words used by India in the Parliament or in the UN as long as the cooperation in important sectors got strengthened. For Prime Minister Netanyahu, his journey to India was to build relations with a powerful friend, not to change India's policy towards Palestine.

Before focusing on Israel, Modi had assiduously cultivated other regional players like Saudi Arabia, Qatar and Iran and reassured them that engagement with Israel would not be at their cost. Modi became the first Indian Prime Minister to visit the Occupied Territories and the visit was intentionally made by helicopter from Amman, Jordan, rather than link it with a visit to Tel Aviv. Prior to visiting Ramallah,

Modi met King Abdullah of Jordan and discussed the peace prospects following the announcement by the US President, Donald Trump, to recognise Jerusalem as the capital of Israel. Modi completely transformed the Indian position on the Middle East with these clever manoeuvres. Consequently, India's relations with Israel have progressed without any irritation on the side of the Arab countries. But Modi was cautious enough not to use his influence in the region to meddle in Middle East politics. He was aware of the risks involved in trying to revive the Middle East peace process even with a balanced relationship with Israel and the Arabs. Even US Presidents have been reluctant to engage in the Middle East except through quiet diplomacy as Donald Trump appears to be doing through his son-in-law.

Modi appeared to be torn between his anxiety to forge close relations with Myanmar and the need to preserve its traditional stand of permitting refugees to enter the country. From the days when Bengali Muslims are believed to have migrated to Rakhine state of Burma in the 19th century, India seemed to waver between security concerns and humanitarian considerations in dealing with them. For years, they have been fleeing to Bangladesh, India, Thailand and Indonesia and also perishing on the high seas, barely noticed. Persecution of minorities is not unheard of in the world, particularly South Asia. Myanmar has a number of stateless persons, including Indians, who have not been given nationality. Very few Hindus have survived in Pakistan and even Shias have been attacked there. Further afield, both Jews and Palestinians have been persecuted for centuries.

Myanmar is known for 'a million mutinies' within the country and no particular attention has been given to the other minorities being put down by military might. After the Cold War, the emergence of racist trends and the ethnic cleansing in several countries have been treated differently by the international community.

It is, therefore, inexplicable that, on this issue, the UN Security Council has issued a consensus statement, condemning the violence in Myanmar's Rakhine state that has led more than 370,000 Rohingya Muslims to flee to neighbouring Bangladesh, and calling for immediate steps to end the violence. It was the first time that the UN Security Council issued a statement in nine eventful years on the situation in Myanmar. The Council expressed concern at reports of excessive violence during security operations by Myanmar and called for a de-escalation of the situation, re-establishment of law and order, protection of civilians and a resolution of the refugee problem. The Security Council welcomed Bangladesh's efforts to help the refugees as well as support from the UN and other international agencies.

India's sudden turnaround on the Rohingyas issue during Prime Minister Narendra Modi's visit to Myanmar (on 5 September 2017), on his way back from China after the BRICS meeting, took the world by surprise. This was obviously a hasty decision to get close to Myanmar, without thinking of its ramifications. India had been allowing Rohingyas to enter India as refugees for several years, but suddenly Modi characterised them as a threat to national security.

Although India had not signed the UN Refugees Convention, it had taken on the obligations of a signatory by way of allowing refugees to enter, looking after them in cooperation with the UN and sending them back only when the situation in their country became normal. The Bangladesh war was fought to create conditions for a million refugees to return. But in the case of the Rohingyas, Modi expressed concern over 'extremist violence' in Rakhine, without mentioning Rohingyas by name and announced that, on this issue, India stood with Myanmar in fighting terrorism. He made no mention of the alleged persecution of the Rohingyas. Nor did he give any credit to countries like Bangladesh for the burden borne on account of the influx of refugees.

'We hope that all stakeholders together can find a way out in which unity and territorial integrity of Myanmar is respected', Modi said in a joint statement with State Counsellor Aung San Suu Kyi in Nay Pyi Taw, Myanmar's capital. Suu Kyi thanked India for taking a strong stand on the 'terror threat' faced by her country. She said that India and Myanmar jointly can ensure that terrorism is not allowed to take root on their soil or in neighbouring countries. The strategy was to win over Myanmar at a time when it was under international pressure over the Rohingya crisis.

India and China found themselves on the same page as champions of the Myanmar regime. But Bangladesh complained that India had not balanced condemnation of terrorism by acknowledging the pressure on neighbouring countries on account of refugees being forced out in large numbers. India quickly issued another statement that 'India remains deeply concerned about the situation in Rakhine State in Myanmar and outflow of refugees from that region. At the same time, India maintained that the Rohingya refugees in India will be expelled, whether they had UN documents or not. The reason for India's tough position on Rohingyas is being unofficially explained as a response to the information received that the Arakan Rohingya Salvation Army, which staged an attack on the army of Myanmar in August, was led by someone trained in Pakistan as a terrorist. What was till recently a pure humanitarian matter was now being influenced by considerations of national security. 'We cannot rule out the possibility of a security threat', said Home Minister Rajnath Singh. To take care of the humanitarian aspect, India sent a consignment of food and other materials to Bangladesh.

India's unprecedented decision to expel Rohingya refugees

prompted the UN High Commissioner of Human Rights, Prince Zeid bin Ra'ad of Jordan, to use unusually harsh words against India: 'I deplore current measures in India to deport Rohingya refugees at a time of such violence against them in their country… India cannot carry out collective expulsions, or return people to a place where they risk torture or other serious violence.' India naturally reacted strongly to the statement as the UN had no business to force the hand of a member country on the refugee issue. But the action taken by the Security Council has caused some embarrassment to India. Doubts were expressed in India and abroad whether the proposed action was on account of Modi's agenda.

The unconditional support India has extended to Suu Kyi, together with the assurances of expeditious implementation of projects in Myanmar, have strengthened the relationship with Myanmar. But any stern action against the Rohingyas will dent India's image abroad and draw protest from within the country. The way out is to root out the terrorists, if any, and allow the others to remain in India, like before, as refugees. In handling the Rohingya issue, Modi made an error of judgment in the eyes of the world. The reputation of Aung San Suu Kyi also plummeted on this account.

Another challenge to India was President Trump's revolutionary attitude to the United Nations. He said in his address to the General Assembly of the United Nations in 2018, 'We believe that when nations respect the rights of their neighbours, and defend the interests of their people, they can better work together to secure the blessings of safety, prosperity, and peace. Each of us here today is the emissary of a distinct culture, a rich history, and a people bound together by ties of memory, tradition, and the values that make our homelands like nowhere else on Earth. That is why America will always choose independence and cooperation over global governance, control, and domination. I honour the right of every nation in this room to pursue its own customs, beliefs, and traditions. The United States will not tell you how to live or work or worship. We only ask that you honour our sovereignty in return.'

For President Trump, the UN is merely a forum to listen to him in awe and admire his accomplishments without challenging him in any way. He withdrew from the UN bodies, which had painstakingly worked out consensus positions to serve the cause of peace like the Human Rights Council, which the US itself had proposed, UNESCO, the Paris Agreement and the Iran nuclear deal, proclaiming loudly that he would go his own way, using his power to isolate nations through sanctions, trade war or war itself.

He asserted, 'America is governed by Americans. We reject the ideology of globalism, and we embrace the doctrine of patriotism'. Nothing could be farther from the thoughts of the founding fathers of the UN when they founded the UN to save the succeeding generations from the scourge of war. He wishes to turn the UN from a body designed to ensure international peace and security on the basis of a common commitment into a 'coalition of the willing' to support US interests. The US would work with the UN when it suits them or act on their own, when necessary.

For President Trump, the reform of the United Nations consists largely of reducing the US commitment to it, such as reducing its contribution to the peacekeeping budget to 25 percent and shifting more of US funding from assessed contributions to voluntary so that they can choose who to support. For the sake of form, of course, he declared, 'Only when each of us does our part and contributes our share can we realize the UN's highest aspirations. We must pursue peace without fear, hope without despair, and security without apology'.

India was the first country that President Trump chose to mention approvingly in his speech, but it was hardly a compliment. About a country, emerging as a global power and aspiring to be a permanent member of the Security Council and a close defence partner of the US, he said condescendingly, 'There is India, a free society of over a billion people, successfully lifting countless millions out of poverty and into the middle class'. No mention was made of the common values, which made India and the US natural allies and strategic partners and India's role in the growth of technology in the US.

The way the President made use of the opportunity of the US Presidency for the month of September 2018 to preside over the Council for a day was nothing but an affront to the traditions of the Security Council. The UN Secretary General and his staff must have worked hard to find a formula for the President to hold forth from the chair of the Security Council against those who he did not approve of and to encourage those who worked with him. The agenda chosen was non-proliferation of weapons of mass destruction, as his primary target was Iran. The worst end of the stick was reserved for China, which was accused, surprisingly, of interfering in the forthcoming elections to the Congress in the US. He attacked Russia for making a mess of Syria, but praised it for not bombing out the Idlib province. He had very kind words about President Kim Jong-un, whom he had threatened to destroy earlier, but pledged to suffocate Iran till it abandoned its nuclear ambitions. It was a monologue which even America's closest allies could not endorse, but that did not matter to him. He was exercising his sovereignty, which the other nations had a duty to protect and defend. He had no proposal to make for nuclear disarmament or any kind of offer to make to the world. President Trump virtually redefined multilateralism as an option of the weak nations. The powerful nations would simply dictate to the world to go by their patriotic demands.

Modi had set his heart on securing a permanent membership for India in the UN Security Council and had changed the Indian narrative on the issue by asserting that India had the 'right' to be a permanent member rather than having the qualifications for it as his predecessors had claimed. The discussions on the issue had meandered on for years and many formulae were put forward, but none which could elicit the support of two-thirds majority of the General Assembly and the five permanent members of the Security Council. After Donald Trump downgraded the United Nations itself among the priorities of the United States, no progress was made on this front.

UN reform is a continuous process, dictated by changes in the international situation. The composition, agenda and working methods of the UN have undergone many changes in the 66 years of its existence. The Charter has been resilient enough to let the UN change with the times even without any amendment to its provisions. But the effort, launched since the end of the cold war, to seek an expansion of the permanent membership of the Security Council, is nothing short of a demand for a revolution. The proponents of change are challenging the very foundation of an institution, born out of a world war, the winners of which gave themselves the responsibility of maintaining world peace and security by assuming extraordinary powers.

Five countries are permanently placed at the core of the UN Security Council, which is the heart of the global security system. Paul Kennedy said in *The Parliament of Man:*

'Upon what they do, or decide not to do, and upon what they agree to, or veto, lies the fate of efforts to achieve peace through international covenants. Even more amazing and disturbing is that any single one of the Permanent Five, were its national government determined upon it, can paralyze Security Council action; moreover, it would be fully within its Charter right to do so. Some states are more equal than others.'

The UN Charter, which was crafted by them, has been embraced voluntarily by 193 nations. That there has not been a world war since and that the UN has served as a stabilising factor in the world is the strongest argument for continuing the status quo. But the contrary argument is stronger, because the global equations have changed so much in the last 66 years that it is imperative that the UN must reflect those changes to maintain its representative character and moral strength. The struggle is on between those who wish to perpetuate their privileged positions and the forces of change that cannot but win. But no one can predict the time and nature of revolutions. They have their own logic and time.

The question today is not whether change is needed, but whether a real change can be brought about by the provisions of the very Charter that established the institution. If history is any guide, major changes take place when the time is ripe, in unexpected ways, regardless of the strength of those who seek change and those who resist. The provisions of the law that seek to protect the establishment will be thrown to the winds and the old system will yield place to the new. We have many examples in history of those who conceded change lasted longer than those who resisted the forces of change.

India was among those who lit the first spark of inevitable change, back in 1979, at the height of the cold war, when an item entitled 'Equitable representation on and increase in the membership of the Security Council' was inscribed on the agenda of the General Assembly. The demand was to add a few more non-permanent members, on the simple logic that the ratio between the strength of the General Assembly and that of the Security Council should be maintained; that the exponential increase in the membership of the

UN should be reflected in the size of the Security Council. This principle was, in fact, followed in 1965 when the number of non-permanent members was raised from six to 10. Implicit in the proposal was the issue of under-representation of developing and non-aligned countries in the Security Council.

The reaction from the permanent members was instant. In an unprecedented show of solidarity against the move, they argued that expansion of the Security Council would undermine its efficiency, integrity and credibility. In the face of stiff opposition, the sponsors agreed that the agenda item would be considered, but no action would be taken. Action was postponed year after year, with a nominal and sterile debate till the end of the cold war.

The game changed in the early 1990s, when the idea of adding new permanent members was brought up by Brazil. India, as the main sponsor of the original agenda item, initiated the exercise of ascertaining the views of the members and setting up a mechanism to study the proposals and to reach consensus. An Open-ended Working Group of the General Assembly was established. Though India was entitled to chair the Group, it decided not to take it, as it was one of the declared candidates. The permanent members led by the US offered a quick-fix after initial hesitation and proposed the addition of Japan and Germany as permanent members on the ground that they were the highest contributors to the UN budget after the US. 'We enthusiastically support the addition of Germany and Japan as permanent members', was the refrain of the US representative at that time. The objective of the proposal was to alleviate the peacekeeping and budget assessments of the permanent members. But the addition of Germany and Japan would have only aggravated the lack of balance in the Council. India's claim was not even acknowledged. The US also favoured a marginal increase in the non-permanent membership. If India had not stopped the quick-fix and continued to insist on comprehensive reform with the support of the non-aligned group, the door for expansion would have been closed after inducting Japan and Germany at that time. India demolished the payment argument by stating that permanent membership should not be up for sale. The author, then Deputy Permanent Representative of India at the UN, told the Working Group in February 1995:

> 'Contribution to the UN should not be measured in terms of money. We do not agree with the view expressed by a delegation that permanent membership is a privilege that can be purchased. Financial contributions are determined on the basis of "capacity to pay" and those who pay their assessments, however small, are no whit less qualified for privilege than the major contributors.'

As a lethargic debate went on in the Working Group for years, national positions evolved and loyalties changed, but it became clear that the expansion of the Security Council could not be easily accomplished. The formation of an interest group, under the leadership of Pakistan and Italy, called the 'Coffee Club' and later 'Uniting for Consensus', which opposed any expansion of the permanent membership, made the situation more chaotic. India itself advanced its position from seeking to establish criteria, such as population, seminal contribution to the UN, participation in peacekeeping operations, etc. to staking a claim and began campaigning bilaterally in capitals. Over the years, India's claim became strong and it came to be universally recognised that if a single developing country were to become a permanent member, that would be India.

One adverse consequence of the debate was, however, that the discussions highlighted that a vast majority of member states had not served even once on the Security Council, while countries like India, Japan, Pakistan and Egypt had served several times. This led to India's long absence from the Council from 1993 to 2010 after having been elected as a non-permanent member seven times in the earlier period. After India's bid for a non-permanent seat was thwarted by Japan, India decided not to contest against any of the countries which had announced candidature. In 2010, the withdrawal of the declared candidate, Kazakhstan, in India's favour led to the election of India as a non-permanent member. As the only candidate from the Asian Group, India won 187 out of the 192 possible votes.

Ismail Razali, the Malaysian President of the General Assembly in 1997, introduced a framework resolution to amend the Charter in several steps: first, the General Assembly would adopt a framework resolution to increase the size of the Security Council; second, the Assembly would vote for five candidates for the new permanent seats without veto, as follows: two from the industrialised states, and one each from the developing countries of Africa, Asia and Latin America; third, two-thirds of the entire General Assembly would have to approve the amendment; fourth, two-thirds of all the member states, including the five original permanent members, would have to ratify the amendment; and finally, 10 years after ratification, the UN would convene a review conference. The Razali formula was novel in the sense that it did not require two-thirds approval of the entire General Assembly during the first two steps, only two-thirds of the members present and voting. By circumventing Article 108 in the earliest and most problematic stages (agreeing to reform and selecting the new permanent members), the Razali Plan was a good compromise, but it was never put to a vote; if it had been, it would not have passed due to opposition from the African states.

Efforts made outside the Working Group were also fruitless. After the deliberations of a High Level Group, Secretary General Kofi Annan proposed two plans: Plan A, proposing creation of six permanent and three non-permanent seats; and Plan B, proposing eight new seats for four years subject to renewal and one non-permanent seat. He stated:

> 'I urge Member States to consider the two options, models A and B, proposed in that report (see box), or any other viable proposals in terms of size and balance that have emerged on the basis of either model. Member States should agree to take a decision on this important issue before the summit in September 2005. It would be very preferable for Member States to take this vital decision by consensus, but if they are unable to reach consensus this must not become an excuse for postponing action.'

Although the Secretary General included both the plans, Plan B had greater acceptability in the group and could well be resurrected at a later date as an eventual compromise. It was at the insistence of General Satish Nambiar, the Indian member of the group, that Plan A was included. Initially, an effort was made by some of the members, including some representing P-5 countries, to have only Plan B as the recommendation of the group. General Nambiar expressed his disagreement with the formulation and informed the Chairman of the group that he would not be able to support such a recommendation. As a consequence of this, and because some of the other members would not accept Plan A, the final report included both the plans. General Nambiar received the support of the representatives of Brazil, Japan, Tanzania and Ghana as well as two members representing P-5 countries.

Another exercise undertaken by India, Brazil, Germany and Japan (G-4) in July 2005 established a certain framework for expansion of the Security Council. G-4 had proposed that the General Assembly should adopt a resolution calling for an increase of six permanent members and four non-permanent members on the Security Council. It committed G-4 to seeking six permanent seats, increasing the size of the Council from 15 to 25. The six new permanent members would be two each from Asia and Africa, one from Latin America/ Caribbean and one from West Europe and other states. G-4 also toned down the demand for veto by conceding that they were willing to be just permanent members 'with or without veto'. The resolution, which had 23 sponsors, was not put to a vote on account of African objections. Among other things, the African Group was not in favour of not demanding the veto.

India had never been in the forefront of the move for abolition of the veto as it had benefitted from the Soviet veto at certain crucial moments, though it went along with the consensus within the Non-Aligned Movement in favour of its abolition. The original proposal for an expansion of permanent membership was on the basis that the new members would have the same privileges and obligations as the original permanent members. But it has become abundantly clear that there will be no expansion if the veto is insisted upon. Apart from the permanent members, a vast majority of the general membership may also not favour the veto for new members as they had pressed for abolition of the veto. As a Canadian representative put it, 'Five vetoes already impaired the good functioning of the Council. How would adding five more help, and who would it help?' For this reason, India went along with an idea of postponing the issue for 15 years. This was in recognition of the fact that the new permanent members would not have the veto in any event.

The General Assembly mandated intergovernmental negotiations on reform in 2008 when the Working Group failed to reach any agreement. The negotiations were meant to suggest a 'timeline perspective' to agree on reform in two stages on the basis of a draft text. But the participants were unable to shorten the compilation text, listing the position of all member states. The President of the General Assembly convened a new forum, 'Group of Friends on Security Council Reform', in 2011 to facilitate a compromise.

A French proposal for an intermediate solution that could provide a new category of members with a longer mandate than that of the members currently elected is under consideration. This proposal is similar to Plan B of Kofi Annan's proposal, except that on completion of the intermediate period, a review would be made to convert these new seats into permanent seats.

In 2011, G-4 canvassed support for a simple resolution to decide that both permanent and non-permanent membership will be expanded. This was a clever way to see whether the idea of expansion of permanent membership could be endorsed with the required two-thirds majority of the General Assembly. But according to the latest reports, the G-4 has decided not to table it, as it attracted the support of only about 80 countries. The P-5 countries, some of which had not yet agreed to an expansion of the permanent membership, may have worked behind the scenes to thwart this move.

The story of India's quest for a permanent seat on the Security Council was alternately joy and despair. The reason for joy was that the need for expansion had been recognised by the entire membership and there was also recognition that if the permanent membership was ever expanded, India would be the first developing country to find a place in it. For the rest, there are almost as many views as there are members of the UN about the size, composition and rights and responsibilities of the members of the Security Council.

The framers of the UN Charter did not intend that it should be amended easily. Article 108 of the Charter stipulates that any amendment should be adopted by a vote of two-thirds of the members of the General Assembly and ratified by two-thirds of the members, including all the permanent members of the Security Council. The alternate route prescribed in Article 109 is through a General Conference, but the majority required is equally stringent. But that has not prevented the UN from transforming itself to deal with new issues and new circumstances. Today's preoccupations of the UN like peacekeeping, human rights, environment, climate change, etc. were not anticipated in the Charter. The flexibility and resilience of the Charter have been tested again and again and nothing in the Charter has prevented the UN from taking on new responsibilities and obligations. Charter amendments have not been initiated even to remove anachronisms like the enemy countries clause (Article 107) and the changed name of one of the permanent members. The most crucial article of the Charter on the veto itself has been changed in practice as abstention by a permanent member is considered a concurring vote under Article 27.

Proposals for reform, like the working methods of the Council introduced in the Working Group from time to time, are mere diversionary tactics as these could be adopted without any amendment to the Charter. Boutros Ghali's reforms under 'Agenda for Peace' were dealt with by a resolution of the General Assembly. But when it comes to an expansion of the Security Council, the only way is to bring a Charter amendment. This explains why the only amendment of the Charter was made in 1965 to raise the number of non-permanent members from six to 10 when the strength of the General Assembly increased. The different groups of countries and entrenched interests are in no mood to repeat the exercise, particularly if the permanent membership should be touched.

The P-5, for instance, consider that they only stand to lose by adding new permanent members with veto. They have made it clear that there is no question of veto being extended to the new permanent members, even though some of them tactically accept the African demand for veto. Even the UK, France and Russia, who have extended support to India and others, have not taken any action to bring about changes. One thing that France and the UK dread is the suggestion that the EU should have only one representative, while it already has two inside and another at the door. They are not willing to float a formula for expansion even to set the ball rolling. The same is the case with many others, who have pledged support to India and other candidates. In many cases, such support is an easy gesture to win goodwill. No group, outside the G-4, is actively campaigning for a formula. The African group differs significantly from G-4 because of their insistence on the veto and an additional non-permanent member. Moreover, the idea of the African group is to rotate two permanent memberships within the group, itself a contradiction. At the minimum, Africa will have to choose one among their members as a permanent member for the reform process to begin. The Uniting for Consensus group wants to add only 10 new non-permanent members. This is an attractive proposition for a large number of small states, whose chances of serving on the Council will increase, while they have nothing to gain by adding new permanent members. In other words, the G-4 proposal for six new permanent members and four non-permanent members cannot as yet win a two-thirds majority in the General Assembly, not to speak of the support of the P-5.

The US, which had supported Japan and Germany in the early 1990s, now favours 'two or so' new permanent members, including Japan and 'two or three' non-permanent members, making an addition of only five to the Security Council. Such a formula is a non-starter. The support extended to India by President Obama during his visit to India is in the form of a wish without a commitment to bring it about. His words were: 'In the years ahead, I look forward to a reformed Security Council that includes India as a permanent member.' Though this is a significant departure from the previous US position, it is not enough for the US to extend support to India; it should shape a formula, which is acceptable to the membership.

Its reservation over Germany and Brazil will itself deprive it of being decisive on the issue of expansion.

We did not need Wikileaks to find the reasons for the United States' reluctance to bring about an expansion of the Council. But we now have in black-and-white what we knew from the beginning. The US Ambassador said in a cable in December 2007:

> 'We believe expansion of the Council along the lines of the models currently discussed will dilute US influence in the body.... On most important issues of the day – Sanctions, Human Rights, Middle East, etc. – Brazil, India and most African states are currently far less sympathetic to our views than our European allies.'

The US delegation at the UN seems to have only a watching brief till intervention becomes necessary to prevent an expansion that will not serve US interests. There is expectation, however, that President Obama might declare openness to a modest expansion of the Security Council at the next session of the General Assembly. But a special report of the Council on Foreign Relations (CFR), which has urged the President to do so, makes the expansion contingent on demonstration of the qualifications of permanent membership. The position of the aspirants on non-proliferation, climate change and human rights will be subject to scrutiny.

A CFR report, by Stewart M. Patrick, Senior Fellow and Director of the International Institutions and Global Governance Program at the CFR, has strongly argued the Indian case for permanent membership, as follows:

> The rationale of India's candidacy is obvious. The world's largest democracy with more than 1.2 billion people, India has a dynamic, fast growing economy, the world's fifth largest navy, and an impressive army with a distinguished role in international peacekeeping. India is increasingly at the forefront of efforts to police the global commons and combat transnational terrorism and, although not a member of

the Nuclear Non-proliferation Treaty regime, has established a strong record over the past decade in combating nuclear proliferation. India, simply put, has the assets to become a bulwark of world order.

Patrick adds that the United States has geopolitical interest in expanding the UNSC's permanent membership. 'The time for a global dominant state to cede some power to rising ones is when it can still dictate the terms of the shift,' he says. The United States can help relieve its strained resources by sharing some of the privileges and burdens of global leadership. Patrick has recommended establishing criteria for new permanent members so that they accept not only the privileges, but the weighty obligations of membership. However, the US Administration does not seem to have accepted the logic as yet.

China is opposed explicitly to Japan and implicitly to India, though it pays lip service to developing countries' representation on the Council. China's statement that it expects India to play an important role in the UN is not an endorsement of permanent membership for India in the Security Council.

It will be difficult to accomplish the fundamental change India is seeking by way of the procedure laid down for change. G-20 was formed when G-8 could not resolve the unprecedented economic crisis; a similar situation may arise when the P-5 find it difficult to maintain international peace and security without additional permanent members and thus force their hands to accept change. Such an ominous future was predicted by the President of the General Assembly, when he said on 16 May 2011, 'Unless we find the determination to advance on the issue, the UN will lose its credibility. Our organisation will be marginalised and important issues will be discussed in other forums and groupings, which are perceived to be more efficient and more representative of the new realities of the day.' Such a situation may arise sooner than later, and that gives India reason for joy even in the midst of despair.

The UN needs reform not to make one country or the other happy, but to make itself more relevant, credible and effective in the world and it will be ready for a revolution sooner rather than later. A time will come when global governance will not be possible without the participation of countries like Germany, Japan, India, Brazil and South Africa in the Security Council. When that happens, the provisions of the Charter will not stand in the way of restructuring the UN just as they did not stand in the way of expanding the agenda or ignoring anachronistic ideas and institutions. Fundamental changes cannot come like raindrops, they come like avalanches. The amendments route will, at best, create a third category of members with long or permanent terms in the Council, but without being equal to the original permanent members. What the UN requires is not a fix, but a fundamental change to reflect the realities of the present century.

Modi has not been active on this issue, but a permanent membership for India in the Security Council remains a clear objective for him, in keeping with his grandiose vision of India's role in the new global order. But he realises that major increases in the economic and military power of India is essential to be on the prestigious horseshoe table in the Security Council chamber. That makes his effort to make India a trillion dollar economy, a well-equipped military power and an influential member of the international community all the more urgent.

ACT V
THE DENOUEMENT

Readjustment of Modi's Foreign Policy

THE denouement of the Modi drama began by the middle of 2018, when the Trump Presidency began to unravel and Modi realised that he could not rely on the United States to guarantee security and development for India. The tendency of Trump to withdraw from the global arena became clear as he proceeded to disown several international agreements and denounce multilateralism itself. He sought to destroy the simple premise on which the UN was founded that by joining the world body, every country will be surrendering a little bit of its sovereignty for the common good of the world. A time had come at the end of the Cold War, when a Secretary General suggested that the time of absolute sovereignty of nations had passed and that nations should work more and more in the interest of the global commons. The member states did not subscribe to the idea fully, but promised to work towards less stress on sovereignty, but more on universality. President Trump went to the other extreme and said that every country should act in its own interests.

For most of the world, 2018 was an annus horribilis. Though

nothing catastrophic happened and no major war broke out, most developments around the globe did not augur well for the world. A tectonic shift in the world situation was in the offing, with no guarantee at all that the world would be better in 2019 than in 2018. The trade war between the US and China marked the beginning of the end of regulated and fair trade. The callous way in which the climate change negotiators handled their agenda in Katowice raised doubts about the future of the planet itself.

Never in history has a democratically elected leader done so much harm to the world as Donald Trump has done in two years. Short of ordering launching of nuclear missiles, he has done everything to destroy peace and stability. The whole global architecture built by the US itself after the Second World War lies shattered, with the US withdrawing from various bodies and treaties and disavowing globalism and multilateralism.

The Singapore summit between President Trump and President Kim Jong-un was the most spectacular peace initiative of the year. It was preceded by much sabre rattling by both sides, but it appeared that Trump had a method in his madness. North Korea ceased nuclear testing and even claimed that some of its nuclear facilities were destroyed even before the summit. The agreement reached in Singapore appeared significant in the sense that both sides agreed to denuclearisation of Korea, though with different interpretations of the concept. By meeting face to face with an American President and being praised by him, Kim Jong-un achieved something which his predecessors had failed to do. The cold peace on the Korean Peninsula and the tentative move towards normalisation between the two Koreas was a silver lining of 2018. But an explosion cannot be ruled out on account of mutual accusations of betrayal.

The turmoil in Europe, created partly by Trump, aggravated in the year with grave implications for the future. The refugee crisis triggered many political changes in Europe, including Brexit, which was in shambles at the end of the year. The revolt in the ruling party in Britain threatened Theresa May's Prime Ministership and raised the possibility of reversing Brexit itself. The 'Yellow Vests' in France undermined President Emmanuel Macron, even though he conceded the demands of the protesters. A popular hero became a villain overnight. The revolt raised the question whether democratically elected governments could pursue their agendas simply because they have a majority. Macron's pro-rich policies became suspect even though he had relented on many of his policy objectives, designed mainly to generate wealth and to protect the environment. The movement spread to neighbouring countries, prompting countries as far as Egypt to ban the sales of yellow vests. The fall of Angela Merkel, though slow and painless, was another sign of the turbulent times.

The most explosive move by Trump was the declaration of Jerusalem as the capital of Israel and the shifting of the US Embassy there. But the relative calm with which the international community reacted to the move showed that disruptive moves in frozen situations could lead to solutions eventually. The changed situation in Saudi Arabia and other countries, which had become more tolerant of Israel left the Palestinians with no option except protests and mobilisation of international support. War was no more an option in the Middle East.

The US reaction, particularly of Trump, to the foulest murder in history, that of Jamal Khashoggi in the Saudi Consulate in Istanbul, was also a sign of the times. As far as Trump was concerned, after the biggest arms contract signed by Saudi Arabia, brutal crimes and violation of human rights were of no concern. The 'Davos in the desert' moves on even with other countries as oil is considered thicker than blood. With the President's son-in-law as his best friend, Mohammed bin Salman has nothing to fear.

Among all the agreements that Trump has pulled out, the most significant were the Iran nuclear deal and the Paris Agreement on climate change. But a catastrophe was immediately avoided because the other parties to the Iran deal did not follow suit and Iran reacted with uncharacteristic restraint. But, in the long term, the US withdrawal from these agreements will impact international peace and security and the future of the planet. Having undermined NATO, US cannot rely on its European allies to serve the interests of the US.

The biggest beneficiaries of the Trumpian gymnastics were China's Xi Jinping and Russia's Vladimir Putin, who emerged strong and stable during the year. The pressure on China in the Indo-Pacific is much less today, now that the Quadrilateral has receded. China has also found spaces in Europe and elsewhere to put their foot in. Putin has a love and hate relationship with Trump and his capacity to change the fortunes of the US has been established. Though there is no automaticity of support from any of the allies of the three major powers, they can count on the support of several countries on an issue by issue basis. Unlike Trump, Xi and Putin do not have to face elections or impeachment in the near future.

Modi began to readjust his foreign policy after the advent of Trump as nobody was certain what his next tweet will proclaim. Trump has not said or done anything against India except to demand reciprocity in trade and to reduce the intake of Indians with H1B visa. In fact, in the case of Iran and Russia, the US has exempted India from the policy of using sanctions to fight political battles. The new symphony that PM Modi promised in the US Congress has not materialised because of the unpredictability of the US leadership. He has, therefore, sought to reset relations with China and Russia through his visits to Wuhan and Sochi. Putin is pleased that he sold the missile defence system to India and China has benefitted from India's political and economic concessions without insisting on reciprocity. Modi may be seeking to establish some equidistance from the three big powers to seek a fourth pole in a multipolar world. With his poor performance in the five state elections and the unpredictability of the results of the general elections, Modi was in a desperate hurry to declare success in his assertive diplomacy.

Till today, we do not know what PM Modi discussed with Xi Jinping and Vladimir Putin, but we have been told that the relations have been reset.

We have no evidence from China to show that anything has changed, even though India had made several gestures in preparation for Wuhan. Soon after Wuhan, in an unfriendly step, China set up an alternative to SAARC, by creating the China South Asia Cooperation Forum and India quietly participated in the initial meeting. No news came also about any new understanding on the contentious issue of violation of Indian integrity by the China Pakistan Economic Corridor as part of the Belt and Road Initiative of China. Prime Minister Modi, on the other hand, was excessively cautious about China in his address in the Shangri-La Dialogue.

The one case which became a publicity disaster for President Donald Trump was his meeting with President Vladimir Putin of Russia for more than two hours in Helsinki, without Sherpas, at a particularly delicate moment in the US-Russia relations. Trump's obsequious behaviour with Putin at a press conference soon after the summit brought him to the brink of impeachment. Trump said that they talked only about sweet nothings like lovers would do, but Putin listed several issues on which he secured approval for the status quo in his favour. There were no record takers or recordings and the only people present other than the principals were the interpreters. Since interpreters are sworn to secrecy and will not share their notes with anyone, there is talk of subpoenaing them to get to the truth. If only Trump and Putin had their aides with them, Trump would not have been accused of becoming Putin's lapdog or worse. But then summits without Sherpas have become not only fashionable, but also indispensable to resolve intractable issues. Modi might be subjected to questioning in the case of Wuhan and Sochi.

In the case of Russia, there have been reports of progress on certain nuclear matters and arms deals. The Sochi meeting was an effort to shore up an old relationship at a time when global ties were being disrupted and the rumblings of it were being heard even about India-Russia bilateral relations. The Indian statement on Sochi spoke of the special and privileged strategic partnership between the two countries, signifying its uniqueness as a special category among scores of strategic partnerships. But there was no evidence of any new initiatives and the impression created was that India was on a tightrope-walk between the US and Russia. The corrective that Modi had sought was accomplished only partly. The purchase of S-400 missile defence system and the US waiver of sanctions to facilitate it were Modi's victories in the Fifth Act.

The first important strategic dialogue between the Minister of External Affairs Sushma Swaraj and the Minister of Defence Nirmala Sitharaman and Secretary of State Michael R. Pompeo and Secretary of Defence James N. Mattis in the newly inaugurated 2+2 format ended in New Delhi with emphasis on continuity in defence cooperation, sidestepping the thorny issues of India's relations with Russia, China and Iran, which the US side had wished to raise.

The signing of a Communications Compatibility and Security Agreement (COMCASA) that was negotiated over a long period of time as part of strengthening India's status of a major defence partner of the United States served to stress continuity in the relationship, despite the wish list carried by the US delegation to dictate terms to India on some fundamental aspects of India's foreign policy.

Showing COMCASA as a major outcome of the dialogue is misleading because we have been resisting it and also the other fundamental agreements the US had been asking us to sign as a major defence partner. The Manmohan Singh government had serious reservations about them. The US wish list may have been discussed, but the Joint Statement skirts those issues and stresses mutual cooperation, particularly in defence and in combating terror. The only hint of difference came when the US Defence Secretary made it a point to mention that the question of India's acquisition of S-400 missile defence system from Russia was not settled. It goes to the credit of both countries that the atmosphere of the dialogue was not vitiated by contentious issues.

The dialogue has been described in the Joint Statement as a 'reflection of the shared commitment by Prime Minister Modi and President Trump to provide a positive, forward-looking vision for the India-US strategic partnership and to promote synergy in their diplomatic and security efforts'. Moreover, it recognises that the two countries are strategic partners, major and independent stakeholders in world affairs and are committed to work together on regional and global issues, including in bilateral, trilateral and quadrilateral formats.

Apart from signing the COMCASA, India and the US have created a new tri-services exercise and agreed to further increase personnel exchanges between the two militaries and defence organisations. They have also agreed to strengthen cooperation between the US Naval Forces Central Command and the Indian Navy, underscoring the importance of deepening their maritime cooperation in the western Indian Ocean.

The 2+2 dialogue reaffirmed the consensus on terrorism reached in Washington last year without diluting the clear denunciation of cross-border terrorism from Pakistan, though Pompeo had just visited Pakistan to greet the new Prime Minister. The reiteration of denial of anti-terror funding to Pakistan was also music to Indian ears.

The Wuhan Summit and Prime Minister Modi's presentation at the Shangri-La dialogue on 1 June 2018 had indicated a dilution of the US embrace in the Indo-Pacific region and the same is reflected in the rather tame paragraph in the Joint Statement on the cooperation between the two countries. The formulation is guarded when it states: 'Both sides committed to work together and in concert with other partners toward advancing a free, open, and inclusive Indo-Pacific region, based on recognition of ASEAN centrality and on respect for sovereignty, territorial integrity, rule of law, good governance, free and fair trade, and freedom of navigation and overflight.' There is no mention of the Quadrilateral either, except as a forum for cooperation.

The shared commitment to a united, sovereign, democratic, inclusive, stable, prosperous and peaceful Afghanistan and support for a peace and reconciliation process and India's role in Afghanistan's development does not reveal any forward movement. The statement on North Korea is routine, but the reference to those countries that supported North Korea in its nuclear activities recognises Indian concerns. The support to India's admission to the NSG has no operational element in it.

The demand for balancing trade, a favourite point of President Trump, is hidden in a seemingly innocuous section on trade. A sense of resignation is evident in the section on the civil nuclear energy partnership and the projected establishment of six nuclear power plants in India. The various hurdles to nuclear trade between the US and India, such as the Liability Act, have not been mentioned.

India appears to have stood its ground on strategic autonomy by resisting US pressure on Russia, China and Iran, but succumbed to the temptation to walk into a tighter embrace in defence cooperation, a high priority of the Trump administration.

However, given President Trump's determination to reshape the world according to his own lights, the reprieve may well be temporary. The ministers have done their best in papering over differences, but a tweet from Trump will blow the papering and reveal difficult options for India. What we seem to be doing is to look beyond President Trump and safeguard the established avenues of cooperation for consolidation of the relationship at a future date.

The Afghanistan situation posed another challenge to Modi at the end of his term and the dilemmas in Afghanistan became more evident. He appeared helpless in making a choice. President Donald Trump announced dramatically that he was withdrawing half the American forces in Afghanistan and the US had entered into direct negotiations with the Taliban. Russia also started its own peace initiatives in which India participated at the unofficial level. The change of position of the US is quite likely to lead to the formation of a government in Afghanistan and if India kept away from the peace process, it could be isolated. On the other hand, it is tough for India to enter into direct negotiations with Taliban, which is still a terrorist organisation. But the US and others, including circles within India, are urging India to open a dialogue with the Taliban. The risk of India losing all the investments in Afghanistan and the pressure of terrorism are real if Taliban comes to power and the US withdraws by declaring victory. President Trump has mocked India's work in Afghanistan as building libraries, amounting only to a week's US investments in Afghanistan. The end of war on terror by the US will also encourage Pakistan to increase terrorism in Jammu and Kashmir.

It remains to be seen how India handles the new situation as legitimising a terrorist organisation is anathema to India. There have been reports that Taliban has also made moves to engage India, while negotiating a settlement with the United States. The time has come for India to decide whether to move with the times or remain adamant about not engaging Taliban directly. Support for the settlement in Afghanistan without direct negotiations with Taliban may be the option that India eventually adopts. A Taliban takeover in Afghanistan will be a setback for India, which Modi will be unable to prevent.

Non-Aligned Movement (NAM) is anathema today even to those who helped shape it and revelled in it for years. India was one of its leaders, if not the leader. India had a stake in its integrity and India toiled tirelessly to keep it on the middle road, not to be hijacked by Cuba to the left or Singapore to the right. We fought to keep Egypt within it when every Arab country wanted it to be ousted in 1979 after the Camp David agreements. Indira Gandhi risked a bear hug from Fidel Castro as she took the NAM gavel to save it from the uncertain leadership of Iraq. Had it not been for India, NAM would have been wound up at a ministerial meeting in Ghana in 1991 soon after the collapse of the Berlin Wall. It was characterised as the 'last gasp of the old style radicals'.

India argued vehemently against those who felt that NAM had outlived its utility. Since the essence of nonalignment was freedom of thought and action, India insisted that it was valid whether there was one bloc or no bloc. Even while building alliances with others, we availed of the NAM umbrella to promote our national strategies when it suited us. The very lack of homogeneity and unity in NAM enhanced its utility for us. One forum where we effectively used the NAM constituency was the Working Group on UN Reform, where we blocked an effort by the US and others to add Germany and

Japan as permanent members and close the doors for further expansion.

An effort was made in 2012 to craft a 'Nonalignment 2.0' in the context of the new global situation, India's growing importance and the rivalry between the US and China. The report moved the concept of nonalignment away from its origins. It reiterated that India needed to move quickly to extend its global role and influence. But the authors said India's big challenge would be to aim at not just being powerful but to set new standards for what the powerful must do. India's legitimacy in the world will come from its ability to stand for the highest human and universal values, and at the global level, 'India must remain true to its aspiration of creating a new and alternative universality'.

In a situation where the world is no longer bifurcated between two dominant powers, non-alignment today will require managing complicated coalitions and opportunities in an environment that is not structurally settled, the report said. The policy of 'strategic autonomy' recommended that India should not take sides in the rivalry between China and the US. The report emphasised that for its strategic and foreign policy to be successful, India must sustain domestic economic growth, social inclusion and democracy.

Coming as it did in the wake of a strategic partnership with the US, a revival of NAM, even with caveats of various kinds, did not seem to appeal either to the Manmohan Singh government or the opposition Bharatiya Janata Party. For Prime Minister Narendra Modi too, NAM was nothing but a relic of the Nehruvian past and it did not form part of his vocabulary. As he pursued his priorities of development, security, neighbourhood and the diaspora, maintaining a constituency of the poor nations of the world had no place. In his transactional foreign policy, it is easier to act alone rather than as the spokesperson of a group. It was no wonder, therefore, that he did not find it necessary to attend the NAM Summit in Venezuela in 2016. India, which conceived and nursed the concept, was ready to cast it into the dustbin of history. We began a journey from the leadership of the super poor to become a super power.

Into the second half of his term, Mr Modi's balance sheet shows an altogether different scenario. As a close defence partner of the US and a member of the 'Quadrilateral', India is right in the US camp. As the baton of the orchestra passed into the hands of a wayward conductor, the new symphony in India-US relations promised in 2016 has not quite materialised. Both China and Russia, which have been identified as adversaries in the US world view, have their problems with India. Doklam and the Maldives have shown that China is in no mood for a compromise. In fact, China has attributed the increase of its defence budget to the formation of the Quadrilateral, which is being seen as a direct threat to China.

An obvious way is to revive NAM by breathing new life into it and making it fit to deal with the new norm. But it has baggage, which may be difficult to unload. A movement conceived in the context of a bipolar world may not suit a tripolar world, which could become a multipolar world. A partnership of near equals like India, Brazil and South Africa (IBSA) with similar interests without any ideological conflict is probably the best model to follow. Something on the lines of the G-15 organised by India and like-minded countries some years ago could be put together with the objective of dealing with the kind of issues identified by Modi at Davos—climate change, terrorism and protectionism. The members may have links with the US, China and Russia, but should be able to work together without the undue influence of the three.

Modi is not someone who will hesitate to think out of the box to achieve his objectives. Given the present impasse in international relations with little leeway for game-changing initiatives, India will do well to move away from being a camp follower of one of the emerging poles to create our own fourth pole. Though Modi did not go so far, when he began resetting India's relations in the Fifth Act, he recognised Nehru's vision of the world and made some tentative moves to get closer to smaller countries, particularly in South-East Asia. He realised that new equations should be sought with smaller powers with a view to get them closer to India. In his recent actions and utterances, PM Modi appeared to be moving away from purely transactional relationships and looking for relations based on affinities and past relationships. He also appeared to move towards linkages with smaller countries in the East on the basis of strategic autonomy, a basic principle of India's non-aligned past.

PM Modi's keynote address at the Shangri-La Dialogue on 1 June 2018 gave the clearest articulation of his new thinking. His praise for Singapore itself was a pointer. 'This great nation shows us that when the oceans are open, the seas are secure, countries are connected, the rule of law prevails and the region is stable, nations, small and large, prosper as sovereign countries. Free and fearless in their choices', he said. 'Singapore also shows that when nations stand on the side of principles, not behind one power or the other, they earn the respect of the world and a voice in international affairs', he went on to say. Doesn't this sound as though Singapore is a model he would like to emulate?

PM Modi had no great respect for history and precedents and his initial approach was to think out of the box and overcome what he disapprovingly called 'hesitations of history'. But from the very first day when he met the leaders of South Asia, he began to realise that 70 years of history could not be wished away. A gift of a saree for PM Nawaz Sharif's mother or a visit to attend his grandson's wedding did not help to bring about a thaw in India's relationship with Pakistan. He learnt very fast that the old issues persisted, regardless of his good intention to resolve them.

US-India Joint Strategic Vision for the Asia-Pacific and Indian Ocean Region developed by President Obama and PM Modi in January 2015 was clearly an arrangement for regional security in the Asia-Pacific vis-a-vis China, which was followed by the Quadrilateral, a grouping of the US, India, Japan and Australia. Characterising these new linkages as having overcome the hesitations of history, he claimed that it had deepened the relationship with the West. But he stressed that 'an important pillar of this partnership is our shared vision of an open, stable, secure and prosperous Indo-Pacific Region'. He also spoke with equal warmth about expanding cooperation with China, including trade. 'We have displayed maturity and wisdom in managing issues and ensuring a peaceful border', he said.

The 'agendaless' summits with China and Russia were clearly in the context of broadening and diversifying India's foreign policy. This was affirmed by PM Modi: 'In April, a two-day informal summit with President Xi helped us cement our understanding that strong and stable relations between our two nations are an important factor for global peace and progress. I firmly believe that Asia and the world will have a better future when India and China work together in trust and confidence, sensitive to each other's interests.' Those words were reminiscent of Nehru's 'India-China *bhai bhai*' approach in the 1950s.

PM Modi's warm reference to his visits to Indonesia and Malaysia were also significant. He said that India-Indonesia relations were upgraded to a Comprehensive Strategic Partnership. Among other shared interests, a common vision for maritime cooperation in the Indo-Pacific was mentioned. For PM Modi, who has imposed an expiry date on politicians, meeting face to face with the 92-year-old PM Mahathir Mohamad must have been an eye-opener.

In the middle of Modi's struggle to build his legacy in foreign policy, his controversial deal to purchase 36 Rafale fighter jets from a French company became one of the biggest controversies he faced. There was no sign of the storm abating even as the dates of the elections of 2019 were announced. The Rafale (literally meaning 'gust of wind', and 'burst of fire' in a more military sense) is a twin-engine, canard-delta wing, multirole fighter aircraft designed and built by the French aircraft manufacturer, Dassault Rafale. The Modi government signed an inter-governmental deal with France in 2016 for the sale of 36 Rafale medium multi-role combat aircraft (MMRCA) in flyaway condition. The deal was worth 7.87 billion euros (Rs 59,000 crore at 2016's conversion rate).

The Manmohan Singh government had earmarked 10 billion dollars (Rs 68,000 crore) for the deal in 2007. Under that deal, 126 jets were to be acquired. Eighteen of these were to be imported in fly-away condition. Hindustan Aeronautics Ltd (HAL) was supposed to manufacture the remaining 108 jets with assistance from Dassault Aviation. The offsets clause of the agreement allows for economic growth of the country in the process of completing the deal. While some offset clauses may ask for investments, others may impose terms like on boarding of local suppliers in the process. The key objectives of offsets are to leverage capital acquisitions to develop national defence R&D and encourage the aerospace and internal security sectors. Under the Modi government's Rafale deal, French aircraft-maker Dassault and its partners, engine-maker Safran and radar-maker Thales, are to source Rs 30,000 crore worth of purchases from India's local industry. The deal's offsets of approximately Rs 30,000 crore were the largest since the policy was introduced in 2005.

In March 2018, the French government submitted a list of 72 offset partners for the Rafale deal to the Indian government during President Macron's official visit, showcasing its commitment to the government's flagship 'Make in India' programme. Dassault says it chose Anil Ambani-owned Reliance Defence Limited as an offset partner as per the defence ministry's offset policy.

On 27 October 2017, Anil Ambani and Dassault CEO Eric Trappier laid the foundation stone for a facility to produce parts of the Falcon business jets under Dassault Reliance Aerospace Limited (DRAL), a 51:49 joint venture between Dassault and Reliance Defence. The DRAL JV could account for between 15 and 17 per cent of Dassault's share of the offset pie or roughly between Rs 1,260 and Rs 1,428 crore.

It has been alleged that Anil Ambani's defence company was favoured over the government-owned HAL. Even more questionable is the fact that a government-owned firm was sidelined to pick Reliance—a company that doesn't have any experience in making defence equipment. What is more, Ambani's defence company was registered only 12 days before the Prime Minister announced the 36 aircraft deal in Paris in April 2015. The timing adds to former French President Francois Hollande's revelation: 'It is the Indian government which proposed this group and Dassault who negotiated with Ambani. We did not have a choice, we took the interlocutor who was given to us.'

Also adding to the allegations of crony capitalism is the fact that the deal with Dassault Aviation came as a lifeline for Reliance Defence, a firm struggling to pay its land dues. In addition, Anil Ambani's Reliance Entertainment financed a film starring French actress Julie Gayet, Francois Hollande's partner. The fact that the film was being financed by an industrialist who stood to gain from the Rafale deal, even if as an offset partner, has added to the controversy.

At the centre of the entire controversy are allegations that the Modi government paid a higher price for the 36 Rafale fighter jets than what the UPA had agreed to pay for 126 Rafale jets in 2012. The government refused to divulge the pricing details citing confidentiality clauses in the inter-governmental agreement with France. There were no middlemen in what was a deal between the Governments of India and France, but in the presence of businessman Anil Ambani as a defence offsets partner in the deal, the Opposition saw evidence of crony capitalism. On the other hand, the government denied all wrongdoings, but declined to reveal facts such as the price of the jets and the nature of the equipment on the grounds of national security.

The Rafale controversy was only of marginal importance to foreign policy, but it became Modi's biggest challenge because the Congress Party, led by Rahul Gandhi, took up the case with the slogan, 'the guard is the thief' and secret documents were leaked to the press to show the inconsistency of the government story. The jury is still out as to whether Modi is guilty on the Rafale deal. But the general sense is that something is rotten in the state of Denmark.

The Pakistani terror attack in Pulwama on 14 February 2019 was a blessing in disguise for Modi as it changed the whole scene as the opposition had to rally round him because of the nature of the attack, the subsequent bombing by India of the terrorist camps deep inside Pakistan and the counter attack by Pakistan in which we lost a plane and a pilot was taken prisoner. Though there were neither winners nor losers in the short conflict, Modi came out as a courageous Prime Minister, who risked a nuclear war not only to avenge terrorist action, but also pledged to root out corruption. The international community virtually handed over the leadership of the fight against terror in the region to India.

The tragedy and the futility of the war apart, the balance sheet is important for the strategists and thinkers. It is a matter of comfort that the events did not spiral into a full-scale war. Modi took advantage of the situation by taking full credit for meeting the threat effectively. The call for revenge and stern action electrified the nation, but the capture of our pilot dented national pride to a great extent. The feeling remains that the cycle of violence has not been broken and matters can flare up any time with another terrorist attack.

Truth is the first casualty in every war, as in accounts of peace negotiations. The narrator always wins against his opponent. Nobody is good at counting when it comes to war and the Pulwama was no exception. The number of casualties on Valentine's Day varied from 36 to 44, but it was cruelly rounded off to forty. The terrorists killed in the Indian attack was in the range of 1 to 300, but the Air Force, we were told, was not in the business of counting dead bodies and it was the job of the Ministry of External Affairs (MEA), something unheard of before. I thought the job of the MEA was to prevent war, not to count the dead bodies. In the event of war, the MEA merely gave the figures given by the Ministry of Defence to friends and foes. As for aircraft, India lost a MIG-21, while Pakistan lost an F-16. India also lost a helicopter somewhere, but not in action. Another MIG-21 crashed after the war as 'flying coffins' do.

After the numbers game that remained unresolved, the question arose as to who won the war. Of course, according to us India did, as we lost fewer men and planes. We gave a fitting reply to Pakistan and the one pilot taken into custody by Pakistan was received as a hero on the Wagah border. Pakistan said it won because they killed BSF men, shot down an Indian pilot, killed many on the Indian side of the border and launched a peace initiative by returning the pilot. The world thought it was a 'draw' between the cricketing and nuclear-armed neighbours and asked everybody to stay quiet.

Speculation was that Pakistan planned everything to ensure that PM Modi does not win the election. It seems to have had the opposite effect. He fought F-16 with MIG-21 and showed his mettle. He did not even ask for the return of Wing Commander Abhinandan Varthaman. He went around electioneering with the pictures of Pulwama martyrs as backdrops. Everything was left to the brave soldiers, he said. Rafale appeared to disappear as an election issue. He claimed to have the nation's business at hand and the opposition did not even have the Parliament to disrupt.

As for Imran Khan, the return of Abhinandan was a backspin which sent the opponents into a tizzy. At least some in India thought he was gracious in defeat and victory. 'It is just not cricket' is what would be said in English if anything unfair or unjust is done by a person, who is otherwise fair and honest, as cricket is supposedly a gentleman's game. Having to say so to a world-famous captain of a leading cricketing country is paradoxical and even painful. But that is what we have to say to Imran Khan in the aftermath of the Valentine's Day gift he presented to India this year. Even if we concede that he is only the Prime Minister of Pakistan, who does not necessarily know all that his country does, he cannot escape the responsibility for providing a mask to the Pakistan Army to engage in unlawful activities and to wage aggression after India retaliated to the terrorist attack.

There was some expectation that Imran Khan would be different from other Pakistan leaders because of his basic decency and popularity in India. But those who know how he became Prime Minister will understand that he did not have much of a choice. When he first tried to assume power as a messiah of change and peace, he did not make any headway and it was the compromise he made with the deep state in Pakistan that made him the Prime Minister.

It is India which remains Khan's biggest foreign policy challenge. He cannot move an inch on the Kashmir issue as the Army is dependent on it for its very existence. Terrorism is the alternative to war for them. The entire world is aghast at the thought of a nuclear war between two nuclear-armed neighbours and, therefore, war is not an option.

Reaching out to New Delhi is a path fraught with risk for civilian leaders in Pakistan, where foreign and defence policies are dominated by the powerful military. Many analysts believe that it was former PM Nawaz Sharif's strong advocacy for better India ties that earned him the wrath of the military. It had also prompted vociferous criticism from Khan, who accused Sharif of trying to please India at the expense of Pakistan's interests. For these reasons, the prediction was that India-Pakistan relations will deteriorate under Khan's watch. The present indications are that the prediction will come true.

'I was a little saddened by the way the Indian media portrayed me, as if I'm a villain in a Bollywood film', the new PM acknowledged in his victory speech. But in an apparent about-turn after his poll victory, Khan has advocated peace as the only way forward. 'Pakistan and India must dialogue and resolve their conflicts including Kashmir ... and start trading', he tweeted once.

Imran Khan's posture after the terror attack was predictable. He stated that Pakistan would retaliate with full force if India launched an attack and did exactly that when he ordered an air attack on Indian military installations. However, given his penchant for 'googlies' he surprised everyone by readily returning Abhinandan Varthaman, with a declaration that he had done it for the sake of peace. At the same time, he continued to bombard our borders and ordered no respite to terrorism. It would have been a great gesture if he had announced that he would stop the support to terrorists on Pakistan soil, as his predecessor had promised. Khan did not get any credit for releasing Abhinandan because it was attributed to the pressure exerted on him by the US, Saudi Arabia and China. President Trump had let the cat out of the bag when he announced that he was expecting some good news minutes before the news of the release hit the news waves. India took the position that Pakistan had no choice but to release the prisoner of war as we released the huge number of POWs in 1972. India did not even thank the Pakistan Government for the release of Abhinandan. But the fact is that public opinion in India was grateful to Imran Khan for the gesture, as they had expected worse from him.

The curious thing about the whole episode was that a resolution was submitted to the Pakistan Parliament, recommending Imran Khan for the Nobel Prize for Peace for de-escalating tension with India, even when intensified firing was continuing on the border. Self-serving recommendations for the Nobel Prize for Peace are common in election days. The nominees may never get the Nobel Prize, but the candidates concerned may get some extra votes!

If only Imran Khan had the authority and if he was not indebted to the Army and the fundamentalists, Khan would have emerged as a peacemaker. But the best we could hope for is a pre-Valentine's Day situation, at least till the elections in India were over. In the meantime, the voice of human grief cries out as the legendary Malayalam poet Ayyappa Paniker wrote in *Kurukshethram*: 'Give us our happiness, O Lord, Give us our happiness'.

Never had the concepts of war, peace and diplomacy been so entangled as it happened in the India-Pakistan situation in February 2019. The war against terrorism is underway and Pakistan is determined to fight India, but at the same time, they are waving a fake olive branch to take the credit for peace-making. India did not see any merit in the offer and ignored it. Prime Minister Narendra

Modi went about his business of running the country and entered his election campaign. Those who engaged in high-level diplomatic efforts believed that they established peace by pressurising Pakistan to release Abhinandan Varthaman, an issue which was handled exclusively by the Indian Air Force. No politician of any kind was allowed to meddle in the matter. PM Modi did not even mention the issue till Abhinandan was released for fear that Pakistan will claim a quid pro quo for his release. In the meantime, fighting on the border continued with loss of lives, even as we watched scenes of a proud India receiving its brave son. Amidst all these, External Affairs Minister Sushma Swaraj was seen explaining the evils of terror to the Organisation of Islamic Cooperation (OIC).

This mindboggling situation seemed to defy all theories of war on terror, peace-making and diplomatic practice. We seemed to be rewriting the rules in these areas. With the United States retreating from the war on terror they initiated, India has inherited the mantle of the global terror warrior state. This explains the near universal expression of support to India's battle against terror, though there is no clear definition of terror. One country's terrorists are another country's freedom fighters even today. Gone are the days when there was a near consensus in the wake of 9/11 that there are no good or bad terrorists. The US, which declared the war on terror in Afghanistan, was engaged in negotiations to hand over power to a Taliban-dominated government, after declaring that terrorism in Afghanistan was no more a threat to the United States. The US will realise sooner than later that the remaining heads of the terror monster will rise again with greater lethal capability, provided by new technology. If President Donald Trump had reviewed his decision to withdraw from Afghanistan, it would have been an appropriate response to the terrorist attack in Jammu and Kashmir. Leaving India holding the can of fight against terrorism would not work without additional resources. India took on a new role without the whole-hearted support of the international community, which is divided on the definition of terrorism.

In normal circumstances, the parties to any conflict will give attention to any sign of the possibility of peace. Any little sign of peace will be explored to ensure that the war does not go out of control. It was in this belief that Prime Minister Imran Khan decided to release Abhinandan and to express readiness to a dialogue. India's decision to ignore these peace moves arose from its conviction that Khan was merely shielding the Pakistan Army to continue its attack. If Khan's announcement was prompted by world leaders like President Trump, they are likely to be annoyed by the Indian decision and dilute their support for India. PM Modi could well have spoken to Khan and given the standard assurance that the matter would be considered. We could also have begun a conversation between the local commanders to eliminate the tension on the border. Wars are meant to ensure peace, not to perpetuate conflict. PM Modi's bitterness over the rejection of his peace initiatives in his early years as PM is understandable, but it is important not to lose sight of peace. We should stick to our established policy of no dialogue till the elimination of terrorism, but we should constantly look for signs of change in Pakistan. An appearance of seeking peace constantly should be an ingredient of war.

Diplomacy ends when the war starts. India did an excellent job on the diplomatic front, having briefed foreign governments at different levels and given credible evidence of Pakistani involvement in the terror attacks of 14 February. As a result, a clear message went to Pakistan that India had the support of the international community. But this support can be sustained only if the diplomatic efforts continue. The widespread reports in the Western press seem to suggest that our claim about having dismantled the terrorist outfits inside

Pakistan is exaggerated. No proof has yet been given of the extent of the damage inflicted. The rejection of the peace initiative from Pakistan also needs to be explained.

The present chaotic situation in which war, peace and diplomacy appear to be hampering each other is not helpful. These have to be disentangled and each should be pursued in parallel. The system of all decision-making being concentrated in one person makes for consistency, but involvement of other actors at different levels helps when several issues have to be addressed simultaneously. The electioneering in the middle of all this created the impression that all matters were being politicised.

The spectacle of External Affairs Minister Sushma Swaraj at the OIC in the midst of tall and hefty Islamic leaders added a touch of irony to the whole situation. OIC has been the most ardent supporter of Pakistan on Kashmiri militancy. Even our best friends in the OIC would join in the consensus on Kashmir resolutions put up by Pakistan and tell us privately that they did not endorse those resolutions. Would there be a change to this sad state of affairs? Most probably not, unless we appear to be flexible about some concerns of Pakistan. Some attention has to be paid to this in the midst of our many preoccupations. PM Narendra Modi has many loose ends to tie as his first term hurtles to a denouement. His political future may depend on how deftly and swiftly he handles war, peace and diplomacy at times of conflict.

A tactic Modi adopted was to build national security as the main plank to seek a mandate to lead India for the next five years. The 'Chowkidar' theme became the catch phrase this year just as 'Chaiwallah' became decisive five years ago. Interestingly, both these phrases were invented and popularised by the opposition to discredit Modi. He declared that it was his foreign policy that led to the release of Wing Commander Abhinandan Varthaman by Pakistan, attributing the pressure on Pakistan from India and abroad to his robust diplomatic and security policies. He further reinforced that claim by 'Mission Shakti', a bold move in the face of it being considered a violation of the model code of conduct, which was in place. The congratulations extended by Rahul Gandhi to the Defence Research and Development Organisation (DRDO) and the decision of the Election Commission that the announcement was not a violation of the code have vindicated the move.

Following PM's own announcement that India had shot down a live satellite in space and had become the fourth country to do so, the Ministry of External Affairs announced that the purpose of the test was to verify that India has the capability to safeguard its space assets. The test was significant because India had 'tested and successfully demonstrated its capability to interdict and intercept a satellite in outer space based on complete indigenous technology'. India used one of its own existing satellites operating in the lower orbit for the mission, the statement said. As for the timing, it said that the test was done after acquiring the 'required degree of confidence to ensure its success'.

As the curtain fell on the Fifth Act of the Modi saga, he appeared unfazed about issues such as demonetisation and Rafale, which had hurt him most. The events in the last Act had made him strong domestically as well as internationally. The measures he had taken to cope with the new international situation and the bold steps he had taken against Pakistan made him formidable and together with his welfare measures for the poor, led to his triumphant victory in the elections. Like the wedding bells in Shakespearean comedies, the end of his first term was a time for jubilant celebrations.

Epilogue
Towards a Fourth Pole in the Emerging Multipolar World

THE deafening applause for a Shakespearean hero is normally when the curtain falls on the Fifth Act, but in the case of Modi, the mood was sombre at that time because of the uncertainty of the results of the election which followed. Many commentaries in India and abroad projected the situation as tough and predicted a possible hung Parliament. Many Prime Ministerial candidates emerged and Modi's campaign itself appeared to be a fight for survival. There were many issues, but the only real issue was whether Modi would have another five years to rule India. A western magazine characterised him as a 'Divider-in-Chief' in an issue, which also carried a catalogue of his achievements. A question was asked whether India could endure another five years of a Narendra Modi government.

The dramatic victory of BJP and its allies was clearly Modi's triumph, but his entire record was re-examined to find the secret of his success. Finally, there was near consensus that the major factors were his foreign and security policies and mundane matters like drinking water, cooking gas and toilets. The patriotic fervour aroused by the Balakot attack in reply for terrorism in Pulwama and the wide international support Modi received in getting Wing Commander Abhinandan Varthaman released and getting Masood Azhar declared an international terrorist after years of Chinese resistance were clearly factors in Modi's victory. Modi quickly identified his 'tragic flaw' when he added 'trust of all' to 'being with all' and 'development of all' as his mottos.

The five years of Prime Minister Narendra Modi's foreign policy began and ended with India's neighbourhood. The assemblage of South Asian heads on the day of his swearing-in ceremony was as dramatic as the attack on Balakot towards the end of his first term in office. The period covered the whole spectrum from peacemaking and the promise of economic growth of the whole region through cooperation to a military conflict with Pakistan. The 'Neighbours First' policy, which sought to overcome the hesitations of history was haunted by the compulsions of history and geography and remained elusive. He confronted more or less the same problems faced by his predecessors and he had to tackle them with firmness and flexibility with mixed results. The greatest irony was that the very organization, which was founded to increase economic cooperation, the South Asian Association for Regional Cooperation (SAARC) became moribund because of the worsening of relations with Pakistan, and the bilateral relations with the other countries also fluctuated during the period. Instead of regional cooperation leading to better relations with the outside world, Modi claimed that the success of his foreign policy elsewhere helped him to win the battles with Pakistan both on the border and the UN Security Council.

Modi's biggest challenge was China, which was at the root of every issue he faced in external relations, including the neighbourhood, which was deeply influenced by China emerging as an alternative to India as a regional power, capable of providing economic and political support to the countries in South Asia. China's Belt and Road Initiative (BRI) offered an attraction for them to build their infrastructure and their development plans became an instrument of China's expansionism. Modi maintained a continuous dialogue with China and did his best not to provoke it, but China did not help to resolve any of the old problems and added new ones involving serious threat to India's security and sovereignty like Doklam and the BRI through the Pakistan Occupied Kashmir. The border discussions made no breakthrough and China created obstacles to India's minor aspirations like the membership of the NSG and the listing of Masood Azhar as a global terrorist, not to speak of India's candidature for permanent membership of the UN Security Council.

The greatest success of Modi was the 'new symphony' he choreographed with the United States from 2014 to 2016, taking India closest to the United States as a 'close defence partner' of the US as part of the Make in India programme, including co-designing and co-manufacturing of defence equipment. He signed defence agreements with the United States, which his predecessors had hesitated to do. The second visit of any US President to India in 2015 resulted in a historic agreement on cooperation between the two countries in the Asia-Pacific. The 'Quadrilateral' for cooperation among the US, India, Japan and Australia began to take shape. Investments grew and it appeared that India-US relations would reach unprecedented levels. Both China and Russia watched these developments with concern and began showing signs of diversifying their relations in South Asia.

But like the 'deus ex machina', a totally unexpected person or event that descends on the path of Shakespearean heroes, the advent of President Donald Trump altered the course of India-US relations. It appeared initially that Trump would be a valuable partner in our fight against terrorism, in balancing China and in building trade and economic growth, but his isolationist 'America First' approach and dislike of globalism made the trajectory of bilateral relations unpredictable and rough. Trump did not go against India's interests in any significant way, but his immigration and trade policies caused concern in India. In other words, the major investment that Modi made in cultivating President Obama and laying the foundations of a significant partnership with the US as a pivot to India's foreign policy did not create the intended benefits. Trump's policy of withdrawing assistance to Pakistan for failing to fight terrorism was a blessing, but his dependence on Pakistan to find a compromise arrangement in Afghanistan, together with Taliban and to withdraw his troops from Afghanistan was a setback for India. At the time of Doklam and other instances of China's adversarial approach to India, Trump's silence was eloquent. Modi came to the inevitable conclusion, therefore, that he could not rely on the US as a strong partner in the circumstances, but remained engaged with the US on the basis of the existing arrangements for cooperation.

India has long dreamt of becoming a fourth pole in an emerging global order. The time has come for us to pursue this dream, now that the world is in a flux and the three existing poles are not able to cover the entire globe.

India, having experimented with embracing the United States till 2017, feels it necessary to find an alternative and neither China nor Russia holds any attraction for us.

India too has no constituency of its own, either in our neighbourhood or elsewhere, as the glue of non-alignment has withered away. The emergence of Narendra Modi as the leader of the biggest democracy presents an opportunity for India to build a string of friendships with common aspirations for beneficial cooperation.

Even in the absence of overwhelming economic and military power, India may be able to build an affinity with a variety of countries across continents and ideological affinities. Countries like Japan, Germany, Australia, Brazil, South Africa, Indonesia, Malaysia, UAE, Saudi Arabia and Israel come to mind.

One positive development in this context is the overwhelming support India has received from the international community for Modi's relentless fight against terrorism, exemplified in the intervention by Trump to de-escalate the situation on the South Asian subcontinent and the listing of Masood Azhar as a global terrorist.

We have done so without deploying our army abroad or launching a hunt for terrorists around the world. The United Nations, which has been unable to define terrorism so far because of it being confused with freedom struggles, has come out clearly against terrorism.

There was no international criticism of the attack on Balakot. If India's efforts to save the world from the scourge of terrorism succeed, India will earn a special place in the global community.

Modi's initial forays into foreign policy had the flavour of 'Aswamedha Yagas' launched by ancient kings to conquer the world. He overcame the hesitations of history and explored unconventional ways to win friends and influence people.

But soon enough, he was faced with the realities of history and geography, which prompted him to proceed with caution. But his definition of national interests and pursuing them with vigour gave him the image of a man of action and the powerful leader of a potential great power.

A good relation with the United States was at the centre of his global vision and brought in a new symphony in India-US relations. But the advent of President Donald Trump altered the global situation and prompted him to reset relations with the major powers and to seek alternate ways to attain his goals.

The second term, which was, among other things, a reward for Modi's world view and foreign policy has provided him and India with an opportunity to consolidate the gains of the past, apply the necessary correctives and move forward.

Our immediate concern is to build an alternative to SAARC as a regional organisation for economic cooperation. India has embraced the Bay of Bengal Initiative for Multi-Sectoral Technical and Economic Cooperation (BIMSTEC) as an alternative.

The Bay of Bengal could become the key economic connection between East and South Asia and a potential zone for Asian economic growth. An overarching priority for the BIMSTEC member states would, therefore, be to further strengthen the regional integration process.

Today, BIMSTEC is celebrating 20 years of its establishment. In these two decades, BIMSTEC has progressed in regional cooperation and integration front, whereas, at the same time, it has faced several new challenges.

Infusing BIMSTEC with a political cohesiveness and economic clout is an onerous responsibility for India. At the same time, we need to cast our net wider to larger concentric circles to South East Asia and beyond to build a constituency, which has faith in India's policies. Our ability to help and hurt should be highlighted by a string of projects in which each of them has a stake. Economic cooperation and investments must grow and the Make in India initiative has to be vigorously pursued. For this, we need to project our requirements as part of the global agenda and not as transactional deals.

Our quest for a permanent seat on the horse shoe table of the Security Council has no chance of success as the vast majority of the members of the United Nations would rather abolish the veto than give veto to new members. The permanent members will naturally resist sharing their privileged position with others.

Reflecting the change in the power structure of the world is not the sole responsibility of India. When that realisation comes, as it must, India will not be excluded. We may do well to appear to be patient and realistic on this issue. We should, however, insist on membership of bodies like APEC. The exclusion of India from APEC is a relic of an era when the Indian economy was considered illiberal.

The strong second mandate has given Modi a stature similar to those of Xi Jinping and Vladimir Putin in terms of stability and that too through the ballot box. The Western prejudices articulated close to the elections against Modi must evaporate with the massive mandate.

Trump has already indicated his willingness to work closely with Modi. These advantages, together with Modi's penchant for international affairs, a congenial economic climate and a broad consensus inside the country in his favour, should give his foreign policy a new thrust and vigour.

Modi is faced with a number of tough foreign policy challenges in his second term. The US has indicated that it would be willing to work with Modi on the basis of the foundation laid by the previous Presidents of the United States and that it would continue its strong partnership with India. At the same time, on issues like trade, immigration and defence cooperation, Donald Trump's views would prevail. The dangers of a tight embrace with the United States were all too evident in Modi's first term. China has made no concessions on any of the problems that have plagued bilateral relations since the sixties. Russia's steadfastness also cannot be taken for granted. Steering clear of these inherent hazards even while cooperating with them and finding a niche for India in the emerging multipolar world should be the objective of Modiplomacy 2.0.

From the Journals

*M*odiplomacy is not a research work, but an impressionistic narrative of current history. It has, therefore, no footnotes or glossary. But that does not mean that it has been written without reading what others have written. I believe that, on an average, every writer has to read at least a thousand words by others before writing a hundred words. This is not to plagiarise or even to borrow ideas from others, but to be as original as possible in the light of what has already been written.

I am indebted to a large number of writers, whose articles and books I have read in my quest for the essence of Prime Minister Narendra Modi's foreign policy and his practicing style. His own speeches and writings have been my basic material. I have not had the opportunity to interview anyone specifically for this book. But by reading those whose erudition and expertise I respect, I have been able to fine-tune my narrative and judgment. But the primary responsibility for the contents is entirely mine.

My publisher had kindly assigned to me a young research scholar, Lekshmi Parmeswaran, to assist me in my work. She was profuse in bringing to my attention a large number of essays by prominent writers, clubbing them together topic wise and time wise. This was of immense help. Among those writers, there was a clear division between pro-Modi and anti-Modi sentiments, while my approach was to make an objective assessment, based on my experience of policymaking and implementation for nearly four decades. In the process, I may have focused on certain areas, in which I had direct experience like the US, the UN, the neighbourhood, Europe and the diaspora. There are obviously gaps, when it comes to the issues I never dealt with.

The section, 'From the Journals' consists of the summaries of the more important of the essays Lekshmi compiled to bridge some of the gaps in the narrative. Instead of referring to them in footnotes, we decided to reproduce them in the book for the benefit of the readers. We express our appreciation to each of the writers and their publishers for their contribution.

T.P. Sreenivasan

INDIA-PAKISTAN RELATIONS

Auditing Modi's Pak policy

K.C. Singh, The Tribune, 4 Jan 2018

- The answer is the game is not about trust, it is about managing a difficult relationship where trust will follow engagement and not the other way around.
- Thus began a cycle of episodic Pakistan engagement, followed by quick regression to confrontation and jingoism. Redlines to judge Pakistani behaviour were brought to the very fences of army camps.
- A leitmotif in Modi's electioneering has been the use of images and rhetoric of a muscular and nationalistic foreign policy into domestic electoral fodder.

PM Narendra Modi has made Pakistan pay more for terrorism

Aarti Tikoo Singh, Economic Times, 16 February 2018

- For the first time since 2012, India and Pakistan resumed foreign secretary level talks in 2015, which were followed by Prime Ministerial diplomatic talks in Ufa. The initial bonhomie between India and Pakistan began dissipating after the terror strikes, first on Gurdaspur police station in July 2015 and later on Pathankot Air Force base in January 2016.
- The net result of all track I or track II diplomacy in the last three decades therefore has been a constant—cross border terrorism with the exception of 1999 Kargil war. Pakistan is convinced that its sub-conventional approach will deliver victory in Kashmir just as it did in Afghanistan.
- Therefore, talks or no talks, India has and will continue to receive only terror from Pakistan until Kashmir is "resolved". And even if Kashmir were settled, Pakistan's paranoia about India, which it considers an existential threat since the creation of Bangladesh in 1971, it will remain adversarial towards India

and open new fronts of proxy war as it did after its Khalistani terrorist movement was defeated in Punjab.

- In the absence of a détente, India has escalated the cost for Pakistan's cross-border terror—pressure from the Trump administration to act against Kashmir-centric terror groups and their leaders, NIA investigations in terror funding of Kashmiri separatists, intensified counter-insurgency operations in Kashmir and cross-LoC limited strikes. These measures will be followed by talks at some point but for now without a Mikhail Gorbachev in Pakistan, and a tangible détente encouraged by Pakistan.

How successful has India's Pakistan policy been?

Jungjoo Gernail, DailyO, 3 May 2018

- The reality being—failure of India policy, which tragically translates to failure of Pakistan's current national identity, because Pakistan's identity is built upon antagonism towards Hindu/India, and therefore if Pakistan has to win, India must lose.
- As a student and observer of South Asia peace and security studies, it's apparent to me that India has no end state defined for Pakistan, expect one—that of defending India in all possible ways—by fighting or by appeasement or managing status quo.
- What followed is even more naïve and, in my opinion, borderline imprudent, especially coming from tenured hands of Ajit Doval—the famed or infamous and notorious (from the vantage point of Pakistan) national security advisor who also has extensive field experience in covert operations.
- Surely, one thing works in Modi's favour is his ability to face reality and realign. India has since, drifted back into "terror has to stop" mode, with greater focus on international isolation for Pakistan, aligning US-Afghanistan to India's policy and continuing to chip away Pakistan fauj's grip over its subject by covert actions inside Pakistan and overt action on the Line of Control.
- In my opinion, the only success India deserves credit for since PM Modi, is raising the cost of terror for Pakistan, and below are three key results:
  1) Pakistan-sponsored terror attacks are restrained to Army camps (unlike in the past where civilians were prime targets).
  2) Terror attack target and penetration limited to border areas (unlike in the past where terrorists reached major Indian cities and towns).
  3) Improved terrorist kill rate to total deaths in terror incidents.

- Significantly, the cost of poor policy and lack of will to pursue an end state by India affects not just India, but Kashmiris on both sides and even Pakistanis who are trapped in the vicious psychosis of "nazaria-e-pakistan".

Modi's Kashmir policy is playing right into the hands of Pakistan's ISI

Prem Shankar Jha, The Wire, 22 July 2018

- ISI's ambition to wrest Kashmir from India had dwindled during the years of peace and reconciliation that had followed Atal Bihari Vajpayee's historic 2004 meeting with Musharraf. They dwindled further when, in 2012, the Pakistan army command officially revised its threat perception and stated that this lay mainly to its west and not its east.
- Its ambitions were revived when the surreptitious hanging of Afzal Guru by Delhi in February 2013 caused a spike in the number of young men joining the armed militancy, just as the hanging of Maqbool Butt had done in 1986.
- But it was Modi's policies, of humiliating the Hurriyat, spurning Nawaz Sharif's overtures for peace, destroying the People's Democratic Party by entering into an alliance with it that it had no intention of respecting, ignoring and trivialising the remaining mainstream parties in the Valley, putting ever moderate nationalist leader in Kashmir—from Mirwaiz Umar Farouq, Yasin Malik and Ali Shah Geelani, to Shabbir Shah, Naeem Khan and Shahid-ul-slam—into jail or under house arrest, and adopting a "ten for one" policy of retaliation for firing across the Line of Control that claimed the better part of 832 civilian lives in Pakistan-occupied Kashmir that sent the ISI and the Pakistan army onto a full offensive in Kashmir.
- From the ISI's point of view, therefore, the Modi government was a gift from heaven. The very last thing it wanted was for anything to impede India's accelerating descent into self-destruction in Kashmir. Asad Durrani, a former director general of the ISI and convinced "peacenik", summed this up at a recent book launch in Delhi. When asked what the ISI would do next, he said, "Nothing. You have done everything it wanted."
- The message they sent was unambiguous: terrorists, and their puppet masters, could kill a man but not the ideals he embodied.

The problem with Narendra Modi's Pakistan policy is not ideology—but hubris and incompetence

Manoj Joshi, Scroll.in, 22 September 2018

- India's tough response after Pathankot, which included denouncing Pakistan in international forums and capitals and responding to border skirmishes with disproportionate force clearly did not achieve the desired goal and led to great hardship of the people living near the border. Neither did it lead to any appreciable reduction in Pakistan's cross border attacks. The most recent being the attack on Sunjwan camp in February 2018, leading to the deaths of five army personnel.

- In fact, this writer's own belief is that talks are good, and we must be prepared for the Pakistani deep state (read the Army) to seek to disrupt them.
- What we need are nerves and stamina for the long haul. India does no favour to Pakistan by talking to them. These talks need to be part of our own strategy of flexible containment or engagement whose goal is not to defeat Pakistan, nor embrace it—but to manage it in a manner that ensures that it does not derail us from our primary national goal—transforming the economic life of our country and its hundreds of millions of dirt-poor people.

INDIA-US RELATIONS UNDER TRUMP

How Modi and Trump can bring a new dimension to India-US Relations
Arun M. Kumar, HuffPost, 22 June 2017

- The US-India relationship carries great political and economic significance in the current geopolitical and security context. The US and India share concerns on global terrorism, but on economic globalisation, their impulses differ as India has been a beneficiary of globalisation.
- The Trump administration has been focused on large deal announcements on one hand and trade deficits on the other. It must take into account the disinclination of Indian leaders to view the relationship on a transactional basis.
- States in the US have been crucibles of innovation and industry. Indian states with dynamic leadership have shown the ability to attain double digit rates of growth.
- A business forum with American and Indian states will go a long way in creating the next paradigm of growth for the US-India relationship and will be aligned with the themes and priorities of both leaders.

Why the US and India need to have each other's backs
Nirupama Rao and Richard Verma, Fortune, 26 June 2017

- Shared values that used to draw the two nations together are yet to be reaffirmed by the new White House; the US role in Asia is less assertive, leaving India to recalibrate and hedge against a reduced US presence; and America's withdrawal from the Paris climate agreement is set to kill a burgeoning area of cooperation. Further, economic irritants such as the immigration of Indian tech workers to the US, limits on market access for US goods and services in India, and disputes over the adequacy of Indian intellectual property protections have resurfaced and threaten to infect the broader relationship.

- The significant advances in the complexity of US and Indian military exercises, intelligence sharing, defence sales, and co-production opportunities, as well as counterterrorism cooperation, point to a deepening of the strategic partnership. Last year, more Indian students studied in the US than ever before, more visas were issued by both countries than at any point in their histories, and two-way trade numbers were the highest ever. And even when the governments falter, the three million Indian Americans serve as a natural bridge, pulling the countries even closer together.

- For his part, Modi should aim to dispel the anxiety about globalisation and its impact on American workers by emphasising the significance of Indian investments in the US and affirming the role these investments can play in boosting American job creation.

- Finally, as the world's two largest democracies, India and the US have a deep stake in strengthening the vibrancy of their own democratic systems as models to secure equality, freedom, and tolerance.

- The importance of the US-India partnership is only growing. Modi was right: This is an indispensable partnership and the two are natural allies. That is why no differences or disagreements should impede the two leaders from keeping their eyes on the future and the interests they have in shared success.

Don't underestimate India's cunning Narendra Modi

Harry G. Broadman, Forbes, 30 June 2017

- In fact, the bear hug shocked the US President, ironically in the same way are people whose hands Trump initially shakes in conventional fashion but are then pulled into Trump's clutches up close and personal. Modi gave Trump a taste of his own medicine.

- And, then Modi caught Trump even more off guard in their substantive discussions by deliberately not tabling at all the issue of moves by the US to clamp down on H1 visas, which control the flow of Indian (and other foreign) workers for jobs with firms on US soil. Nor did Modi raise his displeasure with the US administration's backing out of the Paris global warming accord. Trump and his team—ready to pounce on Modi at his very mention of these issues—were left scratching their heads.

- Instead, it allowed Modi to create an environment for his non-governmental meetings with US businesses and investors—usually the most important part of state visits anyhow—where the currently strong performance of the Indian economy could speak for itself.
- But there is also the likelihood that Modi's reform program, and even more importantly the confidence his reform energy inspires, are increasingly becoming fundamental drivers of India's growth today. And unlike growth generated by changes in commodity prices, the types of reforms being undertaken by the Modi team and planned for down the road are destined to make lasting, rather than transitory, changes in the microeconomic structure of the Indian economy.
- For years, this is exactly what the doctor has been ordering for India. Yet few Prime Ministers before Modi were ever as cunning and effective in focusing on and achieving some modicum of success at these types of reforms.
- In this context, it's curious that The Economist has been critical of Modi, calling him more of an 'administrator' than a 'reformer'. For those of us who have slogged on the ground investing in and driving improvements in business governance, growth and innovation in emerging markets for decades, the British newspaper comes off as naïve, at best deliberately posing a strawman argument for effect. Like Modi seems to be, one needs both a reformer and an administrator at the very top.
- Not only has the ascendency of Modi's governing prowess (what The Economist would call his 'administrator role') and his reforms helped to boost India's GDP growth in part (recall the notion of a 'lag' mentioned above), but they've also begun to help produce sizeable increases of inflows of foreign direct investment (FDI) to India—often seen as the 'put-your-money-where-your-mouth-is" vote of confidence in both an economy and its policy leadership. Here the change for India has been startling, even when compared to China.

India's new 'Modi doctrine' straddles the US-China divide

Yuji Kuronuma, Nikkei Asian Review, 10 July 2018

- Military watchers were surprised earlier this month when the Chinese People's Liberation Army sent a 10-member, high-level delegation to New Delhi. The officials went for talks "to promote strategic trust and mutually beneficial cooperation between the two militaries," according to Luo Zhaohui, China's ambassador to India.

- The thaw began in earnest in the morning of April 28. Modi and Chinese President Xi Jinping took a quiet lakeside walk in the Chinese city of Wuhan. "[I] came to know about the PLA's Doklam build-up very late," Xi told Modi, according to sources from both governments. The Chinese military had been constructing a road near the border, which prompted the standoff.

- The world began to grasp the significance of the shift on June 1, when the Asia Security Summit rolled around. "Asia and the world will have a better future when India and China work together in trust and confidence, sensitive to each other's interests," Modi said in a keynote speech at the meeting in Singapore, also known as the Shangri-La Dialogue.

- The annual Malabar Naval Exercise, held off Guam in mid-June, underscored the divisions within the Quad. A US aircraft carrier, Indian stealth corvettes and a Japanese helicopter carrier took part, but Australia sent no vessels because India opposed its participation.

- At least, Modi appears to be returning his diplomatic posture to neutral. This is in line with India's traditional stance dating back to Jawaharlal Nehru, the first Indian prime minister.

- But there is more to Modi's strategy than maintaining equal distance from two global powers. He seems to want India to be an active participant in both the US- and China-led camps.

- "What is new about [Modi's recent diplomatic approach] is inclusiveness," said Srikanth Kondapalli, a professor at Jawaharlal Nehru University. He said it means "India is willing to accept the Chinese role in the Indo-Pacific."

- Modi's "inclusiveness" extends not only to the US and China but also to Southeast Asian countries. He is treating them as partners in shaping the Indo-Pacific order.

- To summarise Modi's audacious balancing act: He is participating in Western efforts to check Chinese power, while agreeing with Xi on the need to avoid stepping on each other's toes. At the same time, he is keen to establish Southeast Asia as a third countervailing force. And he wants to keep India at an equal, close distance from all three camps.

- Modi, who makes little secret of his ambition to leave a legacy greater than Nehru's, seems to see diplomacy as another way to win hearts and minds.

- Yet, the prime minister is gambling with a protean diplomatic strategy that features simultaneous, deep involvement with two antagonistic powers. And there is no guarantee that cooperation with Southeast Asia will produce a sufficiently powerful third pole.

India is getting cold feet about Trump's America
Atman Trivedi, Aparna Pande, Foreign Policy, 30 August 2018

- Despite efforts by Mattis and others to impose a strategic direction and invest in strengthening ties, there are plenty of fresh doubts in New Delhi. In the short term, that unease has been stirred by Trump's economic nationalism and the White House's unreliability. But something more significant—the longer-term direction of US foreign policy—may be making India cautious.
- Some still harbour suspicions about closer ties and view Washington as unreliable. The Trump administration's erratic behaviour may be inducing latent tendencies to resurface.
- Trump's trade rhetoric, tightened H-1B visa rules for high-skilled workers, metals tariffs (imposed on spurious national security grounds), and the threatened removal of developing-country trade benefits portend a rough patch, whether or not ongoing negotiations produce a ceasefire.
- That has quietly raised plenty of fears in New Delhi beyond just trade. To their west, Indian diplomats struggle to rule out a self-confident president who is overlooking Pakistan's military-intelligence complex and relying instead on the earnestly spoken words of a new civilian leadership. Some worry that Trump's desire for a quick, domestically saleable exit from Afghanistan, based on negotiations with the Taliban, could result in Delhi being asked to reduce ties with Kabul.
- To its east, India must adjust to the White House's ever-changing China policy. Today, the president is lobbing verbal grenades at China. Tomorrow, some Indian analysts fear, he could be working for a far different endgame: a "G-2" alliance to carve up the region with Asia's ultimate deal-maker, Chinese President Xi Jinping.
- Not surprisingly, India is starting to respond to all the uncertainty by rebalancing its strategic portfolio, showing the early signs of someone living in a tough neighbourhood who's not sure who has their back. As a post-colonial, developing nation, India has always been most comfortable in a multipolar world, where it isn't forced to choose between great powers. Trump has made it easy for India to slip back into the habit, learned in the Cold War days, of pandering to as many sides as possible.

- At Asia's signature annual security dialogue this June, Modi delivered a carefully measured keynote speech that took pains not to cross Asia's other giant and featured the milquetoast lexicon of nonalignment alongside more forward-leaning messages. In recent months, India has also sought to reassure an old ally and long-time defence supplier, Russia, that closer US ties don't signal abandonment of Moscow.
- Delhi has also appeared reluctant to stoke perceptions of a formal military alliance—especially when everyone's full commitment is in question. This preference for strategic autonomy continued this month with India reportedly opting out of a joint project launched by other Quad partners to present high-quality infrastructure alternatives to China's Belt and Road Initiative.
- Add in new concerted Indian efforts to expand diplomacy with European powers such as France and underscore Southeast Asia's importance to the region, and it all begins to form the outlines of a classic hedging strategy, reflecting the pursuit of maximum options with minimum restrictions.
- India is fundamentally different from traditional allies for whom the United States was and is the key security provider. India doesn't want to depend on security guarantees, but a more confident and independent India that enjoys strong relationships with leading countries helps US interests in preserving Asia's balance and freedom, even if the United States takes a step back from the region over the long term.
- US-India ties are likely to grow more complicated, but any realignment in Delhi may yet offer a satisfactory—if not thrilling—outcome, buying time until the United States gets its house in order.

INDIA'S NEIGHBOURHOOD POLICY

India is on the defensive in its neighborhood

Dhruva Jaishankar, The Washington Post, 21 September 2016

- But as India and the world continue to grapple with Pakistan's support for Islamist militant groups, another story is unfolding in the region: India is rediscovering the rest of its neighborhood.
- India's aggressive engagement with its neighbors over the past two years has been motivated by two interrelated concerns. One is the rising tide of nationalism, which often manifests itself as anti-Indianism in many of these countries.
- Additionally, every country in India's periphery (with the exception of landlocked Bhutan) is seeing the growing economic and political influence of

China, now unquestionably South Asia's second power. Pakistan and Bangladesh are the two largest recipients of Chinese arms.

- For India's smaller neighbors, playing the China card is a tempting way to counter perceived Indian regional hegemony.
- India's neighborhood engagement has not been restricted to trade, aid and migration. New Delhi has also been taking a stronger position on its neighbors' long-term political trajectories.
- Of course, India has often had to compromise, taking into account tactical considerations and short-term interests. While welcoming Myanmar's democratic transition, India has been noticeably silent on the fate of the Rohingya, an ethnic group that the Myanmar government discriminates against and refuses to acknowledge as citizens. In Bangladesh, India stood behind Hasina despite flawed elections in 2014 that were boycotted by the main opposition party. And in the Maldives, India has had to do deals with the government of Yameen Abdul Gayoom, even as India pressures it to democratise.
- For the foreseeable future, India will be playing aggressive defense in its own back yard.

From Rajiv to Modi, coercion replaced by cooperation

Constantino Xavier, Carnegie India, 28 July 2017

- Exactly 30 years ago today, on July 29, 1987, prime minister Rajiv Gandhi flew into Colombo to sign the "Indo-Sri Lanka Agreement to Establish Peace and Normalcy in Sri Lanka," creating an Indian military mission to enforce a cease-fire, disarm Tamil insurgents and implement constitutional amendments to end the island's conflict.
- In practice, however, beyond nice intentions and speeches, July 29 marked the end of a long strategy of Indian coercion that conditioned Sri Lankan sovereignty. This had become apparent to Colombo when, two months earlier, the Indian Air Force violated the island's air space to drop 23 tonnes of humanitarian relief on Jaffna, where Tamil insurgents resisted a Sri Lankan Army offensive.
- Such past demonstrations of hegemonic power are in stark contrast with India's current approach to Sri Lanka, focusing on cooperation rather than coercion. For example, in late May, exactly 30 years after the Sri Lankan Navy impeded an Indian flotilla with humanitarian assistance for the beleaguered Tamils, Colombo welcomed three Indian Navy vessels (INS Shardul, Kirch and Jalashwa) as first responders to assist in relief operations after the island's devastating floods.

- The positive momentum is the result of a shift in India's strategy towards its smaller neighbouring states. While, in the past, New Delhi insisted on prerogatives such as the right of first refusal, it is now focused on expanding its capacity of first delivery. Denial and exclusivity are no longer options for India in the region. In a world of greater economic interdependence, and where China offers an attractive alternative, New Delhi realises that it must step up its game and focus on developing resources to deliver first, more and better. This is the cardinal objective of Prime Minister Modi's "neighbourhood first" policy and is nowhere more apparent than in Sri Lanka.

- While India's current approach is focused on connectivity and friendly delivery, one should not forget that its geostrategic and democratic concerns about Sri Lanka can often induct a sudden policy shift. Cooperation across the Palk Straits may be the flavour of the day, but coercion is still a tool in New Delhi's regional toolkit.

A 'Neighbourhood First' foreign policy has little value for India
Kanwal Sibal, Hindustan Times, 15 December 2017

- All big countries have, in reality, problems with their smaller neighbours because the disparity in size and power create insecurities in them, not to mention loss of identity as in the case of India's neighbours who share with us ethnic, linguistic, cultural, civilisational and even religious commonalities. To balance the bigger neighbour, outside powers are cultivated, which in our case is principally China, though in the past the United States has played this role.

- The conclusion to be drawn from this is not that India is necessarily mismanaging its relations with neighbours, but that they too, enticed by China, are mishandling their ties with India. They know India's limitations in imposing its will on sovereign countries in today's world. Reciprocity is the governing principle of diplomacy. While a bigger country may not seek strict reciprocity, it cannot sacrifice national interest simply for the sake of generosity. Our neighbours cultivate China at India's cost even though generosity is by no means the guiding principle of Beijing's foreign policy, whereas display of power, meting out punishment and asserting sovereign rights unilaterally are the hall marks of its increasingly nationalistic external conduct.

- 'Neighbourhood First' cannot be the basis of foreign policy, especially at a time when the world's most powerful country believes in 'America First'. India needs investments and access to technology.

- None of these pressing needs can be fulfilled by our neighbours. And so, while it is a bonus to have friendly neighbourhood ties, it is not a prerequisite for India's progress and the achievement of its aspirations.

"Neighbourhood First" should begin at the border

K. Yhome, Observer Research Foundation, 12 January 2018

- The simple logic that drives smaller neighbours is how to maximise benefits from the two rising Asian giants. For its own rise, India is aware of the need to take along its neighbours. How much of that convinces its smaller neighbours is not clear. Delhi needs to create a narrative that reassures its smaller neighbours that it wants to contribute to their rise as well. Hence, a neighbourhood policy driven solely by a China-centric approach may partially serve India's long-term interests as it may overlook the genuine needs of the smaller neighbours.
- A few recent developments indicate how India's strategic concerns and the yearnings of its smaller neighbours are at odds with each other. The tumultuous victory of the Left alliance in Nepal that fought the elections promising development to the electorates with an underlying message that roads would open up Nepal, and importantly, alternative to India, paid off. On coming to power, the seemingly pro-India government under President Maithripala Sirisena threatened to review Chinese infrastructure projects awarded under the previous administration of Sri Lanka. Nevertheless, it ended up handing over a 99-year lease on Hambantota port to a Chinese company. Despite the cooling of ties, the Maldivian government under President Abdulla Yameen stressed the "India First" policy in its external engagements. This policy did not stop it from signing a free trade agreement with China.
- India-Bangladesh ties have witnessed a growing trajectory in recent past under Prime Minister Sheikh Hasina government. During the same period, Dhaka's economic and defence ties with Beijing have also scaled up which included economic deals worth several billions and purchase of two submarines from China.
- The Doklam crisis further strengthened Bhutan's relationship with India. Bhutan was also the only neighbour that stayed away from the Chinese Belt and Road Initiative (BRI) along with India. The biggest challenge of India's "neighbourhood first" policy remains in dealing with Pakistan and the growing nexus between Islamabad and Beijing.
- A common factor in all these developments is, even as India's smaller neighbours have emphasised 'India First' policy or a 'balanced relationship' with India and China, like a number of nations in other parts of the world, none wants

to forego the economic benefits of a rising China. For India, this is a double-edged challenge as it not only constricts its role in the development of its neighbourhood but also gives the smaller neighbours the China-card as a source of assertion while dealing with Delhi.

- Managing assertiveness of smaller neighbours on the one hand, and dealing with China's rise, on the other, will be a major foreign policy challenge for India in the coming days and months

- Moreover, rather than playing one political player against the other in domestic politics of smaller neighbours with the hope of finding a friendly regime, a prudent strategy would be to respond to the growing aspirations of the smaller neighbours by focusing on leveraging India's strengths, most visible at the borders where development and security interests are interlinked. Re-integration with the smaller neighbours needs to begin at the borders.

Coming to terms with China: Modi's foreign policy initiatives in our neighbourhood

Col R Hariharan, South Asia Analysis Group, 26 April 2018

- PM Modi's relationship building initiatives with other countries are applied at three geo-strategic levels—neighbourhood, regional and global. They are not mutually exclusive and need to be considered holistically.

- At the strategic level, he is dehyphenating India's relations with other countries in keeping with the dynamics of strategic power play to come to terms with China's efforts to create a new world order.

- India's national security responsibilities have also increased, in keeping with its increasing international foot print, resulting at times in competing interests with China.

- PM Modi's initiatives have addressed some of these glitches affecting the neighbours with mixed results. To a large extent, during the last three years India has managed to improve its relations with neighbours (barring Pakistan) to retain its status as their key partner. However, India is still slow on delivering upon its promises, thanks to its internal "democratic" political decision-making process and limitations of bureaucracy to think out of the box. Of course, the same weaknesses apply to India's neighbours in making good of India's readiness to help.

- However, the two countries differ in their aspirations. India's efforts in this region aim to protect its interest, rather than neutralise China's entry.

Reviving 'Neighbourhood First'

Rakesh Sood, The Hindu, 9 May 2018

- Even Prime Minister Narendra Modi's critics acknowledge his uncanny ability to take bold decisions and this reflects in his foreign policy initiatives. Interestingly, he is also demonstrating an ability to undertake course corrections.

- The informal summit at Wuhan, China, last month and a visit to Nepal this month reflect a change aimed at reviving the 'neighbourhood first' policy announced in 2014. The big challenge, however, will be providing a sense of direction to the policy on Pakistan which has oscillated between 'jhappi' and 'katti'.

- Mr. Modi had received Chinese President Xi Jinping in September 2014 in Gujarat reflecting his personalised diplomacy even though the ongoing stand-off in Chumar in eastern Ladakh cast a shadow on the visit. The personalised diplomacy was reciprocated the following year when Mr. Modi visited China and Mr. Xi received him in Xian, but its limits soon became apparent.

- Both leaders soon realised the risks of the downward spiral of confrontation and were pragmatic enough to understand the need to restore a degree of balance to the relationship.

- A similar exercise appears to be under way with Nepal. Mr. Modi's visit in 2014 had generated considerable goodwill but subsequent decisions queered the pitch. India's public display of unhappiness with Nepal's new Constitution and support for the Madhesi cause created ill-will.

- Clearly, Delhi was disappointed with the election outcome but decided that the relationship with Nepal was too important to let past misunderstandings fester. A new beginning was necessary.

- Undoubtedly, the fact that he begins his visit to Nepal by landing in Janakpur, capital of the sole Madhesh-ruled province will give comfort to the Madhesi community, but Mr. Modi realises that his challenge is to repair ties with the wider Nepali community.

- The resumption of the stalled Track II Neemrana Dialogue last month in Islamabad indicates that a shift may be likely. Pakistan realises that the time frame for a shift is limited before India goes into election mode.

- A change in the Pakistan policy may well be the reset to enable Mr. Modi to reclaim his 'neighbourhood first' policy.

Evaluating India's new Neighbourhood Policy

Duryodhan Nahak, Mainstream Weekly, 25 September 2018

- It is to be noted that till recently, there has not been any major change particularly in the matter of India's neighbourhood policy. In other words, irrespective of regimes, India was not lacking in a grand strategy in dealing with the major compelling issues. Even non-Congress governments were following the path paved by earlier leaders with little alteration.

- The composite dialogue process with Pakistan which was initiated by Prime Minister Gujral, re-initiated by A.B. Vajpayee and carried forward by Manmohan Singh.

- It is rightly stated friends can be changed but countries have to co-exist with their neighbours. The sorry state of affairs is that now India is tilted towards the US and European powers at the expense of neighbours. This does not augur well for the national interest of the country in the long run. It is further argued that India's place in the world can be determined by its place in the immediate neighbourhood. On the other hand, overcoming the challenges posed by China as an economically, technologically, militarily superior country certainly is an uphill task before the present dispensation.

- It is to be admitted that relations with the neighbours cannot be operated in the ambit of a zero-sum game. In this connection, it can be said only changing the names of different initiatives would not serve India's objective to emerge as a great power; what is required is a well thought-out policy-strategy, treating all neighbours on an equal footing, proper utilisation of diplomatic and intellectual talent that can help in wiping out misapprehensions and misperceptions against India which in turn would largely increase trust among neighbours and make the South Asian region peaceful and India a vibrant country.

INDIA-CHINA RELATIONS POST WUHAN SUMMIT

India China: Why is Modi meeting Xi now?

Shashank Joshi, BBC News, 26 April 2018

- Last year, India and China were locked in their most serious border crisis in the last three decades. China's state-controlled media was issuing near-daily threats of war, as both sides built up forces on the edge of the tiny Kingdom of Bhutan.

- But the meeting does not come out of the blue. After the border dispute was defused in August, Mr Modi and Mr Xi broke the ice at the Brics summit in

September, alongside the leaders of Russia, Brazil and South Africa.

- A flurry of high-level visits to China followed, including by India's foreign secretary, national security adviser, foreign minister and defence minister.
- In March, Mr Modi followed up with fulsome congratulations to Mr Xi on his re-appointment as president, saying it showed Mr Xi enjoyed the "support of the whole Chinese nation".
- In recent days, China reciprocated. It will resume sharing hydrological data on the rivers that run into India and has offered to re-start low-level military exercises; both activities were suspended during last year's crisis.
- So why is this thaw occurring now? There are several reasons. Firstly, India believes that last year's crisis marked a dangerous phase in the relationship and that tensions need to be kept in check—especially with national elections in 2019. More broadly, China's economy is five times bigger than India's and its defence spending is three times as large. While India has a local military advantage at many points on the border, it still needs time to build up its strength.
- Secondly, India hopes to secure Beijing's cooperation on several issues where China's role is crucial, such as putting pressure on Pakistan-based terrorist groups and securing India's admission to the Nuclear Suppliers Group (NSG), a body that controls nuclear trade.
- Thirdly, India is responding to an uncertain period in world politics. India's concern is that Beijing will improve ties both with Washington, because of the North Korean crisis, and with Moscow, because of the rupture in West-Russia relations, all at Delhi's expense. Better, in this view, that India hedges its bets now.
- China is eager to dampen India's hostility to the scheme (BRI). It is also concerned about last year's meeting of India, the US, Japan and Australia—informally known as the Quad—after a decade-long hiatus, and their joint efforts to develop alternatives to the BRI. By engaging Mr Modi, Mr Xi hopes to slow India's steady drift towards America and its allies.
- On the ground, the dispute at the heart of last summer's standoff is dormant rather than resolved. China has built up its forces a stone's throw from the flashpoint, while India has upped its own presence and patrols the border more aggressively.
- The Indian Navy, whose most important task is now watching the Chinese naval vessels that roam the Indian Ocean in growing numbers, has recently

signed agreements giving it access to the facilities of the US, France and Oman.

Narendra Modi–Xi Jinping meet: Wuhan talks reflect China's acceptance of India as a major Asian power

Tara Kartha, First Post, 29 April 2018

- Certainly, Wuhan is a type of engagement that is new to India-China relations, and reflects Beijing's public acceptance of India as a major power—at least in the Asian region. The informal summit style, the breaking of protocol in terms of welcome to the Indian leader, and a reversal of the acrimonious tone in Chinese media, all seems to indicate that Beijing has calculated that the Indian prime minister would welcome such a public acclamation just prior to elections.

- It is also equally a quiet acceptance that Prime Minister Modi is there for the long term, at least for the next five years. Oddly, the same perception may have driven Indian diplomacy in recent months.

- The Wuhan meeting's actual outcomes will only be apparent in the months ahead. In public talks and tweets, Prime Minister Modi in his customary style, opted to raise ground level issues through the "STRENGTH " strategy, which stands for Spirituality, Tradition, Trade and Technology; Relationship; Entertainment; Nature Conservation; Games; Tourism and Health and Healing.

- It is as well to remember, however, that the amount of travel between the two countries has increased exponentially, with the number of Indian tourists alone to China expected to reach 50 million, given a year-on-year 4.6 percent increase.

- We may have far less in dollar terms, but we have fewer countries to spend it on. Chinese 'aid'—defined loosely—was spent in some 138 countries. We need to concentrate on only about half a dozen.

- Meanwhile, all indications are that New Delhi at least has a vision for the long haul. The prime minister's own enunciation of a "new Panchsheel" built around "shared vision, better communications, strong relationship, shared thought process and shared resolve" may seem rather flowery for a relationship that is to be based on pure national interest. But it is certainly far better than the language of a "friendship that is higher than the mountains and deeper than the sea" that has become standardised in Beijing's dialogues with Pakistan.

Why Modi and Xi Jinping are new grandmasters of the geopolitical chess game
Minhaz Merchant, DailyO, 1 May 2018

- The Modi–Xi bilateral in Wuhan marked only the opening move in an elaborate chess game between the duo.
- Afghanistan is the chess board.
- Enter Afghanistan. Xi knows that the United States is already encouraging India to play a larger economic role in Afghanistan. The decision by Xi and Modi to work jointly on economic projects in Afghanistan satisfies three Chinese concerns and two Indian ones.
- First, India-China infrastructure projects will indirectly draw India into the BRI which, as Xi announced late last year, will extend to Afghanistan.
- Second, for that to happen, peace must return to Afghanistan with the Pakistan-sponsored Taliban joining an Afghan coalition government at some stage. The China-Pakistan Economic Corridor (CPEC), part of the BRI, already faces security threats from Baloch insurgents. Restoring peace in the region is therefore key to BRI's success. India's economic role in Afghanistan, now backed by China, can help.
- Third, a deeper economic partnership in the region between India and China will, Xi hopes, help wean India away from the US orbit of influence. Xi is keenly aware that by 2030 the world's three largest economies will be the United States, China and India. In this geopolitical triangle, China and the US will form the two largest angles and India the smallest. But though the smallest, India will be the swing power. Whoever it aligns with—China or the US—will have the edge.
- Xi sees US-China rivalry in Cold War terms. As this century unfolds, India will increasingly play, in this new Great Power rivalry, the role Britain played during the Cold War between the US-led West and the Soviet Union.
- Xi knows that India and the US are developing a strong strategic military partnership. That is why he played the "pan-Asian" card with Modi. In Wuhan, Xi spoke emphatically of China and India as Asian powers building a "globalised and multipolar world" together.
- As a shrewd strategist, Modi sees two benefits from Xi's gameplan. The first is neutralising Pakistan. While Xi has his own geostrategic reasons for drawing India into a pan-Asian orbit, Modi knows that joint India-China economic projects in Afghanistan will cool Pakistan's fevered opposition to India's growing role in a country Islamabad has long coveted as part of its strategic depth theory.

- The second benefit for India in Xi's new overtures is that a joint India-China co-operation lowers the temperature on the eastern front. With India's military still under-equipped to fight a two-front war, a modus vivendi with Beijing will help the Indian Army focus on counter-terrorism operations in Jammu & Kashmir and infiltration of terrorists across the Line of Control (LoC).

- As Jane Perlez wrote in *The New York Times*: "China finds itself removed from the center of the rapidly unfolding diplomacy, and is unusually wary about Mr. Kim's objectives in reaching out to his nation's two bitterest enemies (South Korea and the United States).

- Increasingly isolated and in Trump's crosshairs, Xi's pragmatism has compelled him to launch his charm offensive and seek co-operation with India rather than confrontation. The possibility of Doklam 2 has significantly receded.

Xi Jinping and Narendra Modi have jump-started a new era in China-India ties

Sourabh Gupta, South China Morning Post, 7 May 2018

- Modi, like his predecessors Manmohan Singh and Atal Bihari Vajpayee, has been quick to pivot from hawk to dove and unreservedly engage Beijing in good faith whenever an opportunity in bilateral relations presents itself.

- The Xi-Modi meeting was notable on two counts: for what was agreed upon and (with requisite political will) can be expected to be implemented; and for what the meeting denotes within the broader context of three decades of Sino-Indian ties since normalisation in the late-1980s.

- In terms of symbolism, and its connotations going forward, the Wuhan meeting will be primarily remembered as a moment when a Chinese and Indian leaders jump-started a fresh, virtuous cycle in Sino-Indian relations. In this regard, the Xi–Modi summit falls squarely in the category of two previous meetings.

- In November 2000, prime minister Atal Bihari Vajpayee's principal secretary, Brajesh Mishra, paid a secret visit to Beijing to resolve bitterness following New Delhi's caustic accusation that China's hostility and policies were key drivers of its May 1998 nuclear tests. In June 2003, Vajpayee paid a landmark visit to Beijing, setting in motion a process that in 2005 led to a set of political parameters to resolve the long-standing boundary question.

- First, each cycle over the past two decades has witnessed an initial focus on repair and on-the-ground stabilisation of the boundary, followed by an intensive and successful effort to narrow the underlying dispute at the negotiating table. The current cycle is likely to be no different—although it will have to await Modi's re-election as well as the roll-out of a more astute special representative (who doubles as New Delhi's China point person and boundary negotiator).

- Second, New Delhi's relations with Washington as well as the issue of the subcontinent's nuclearisation have never been far from the surface.

- History will show the informal summit in Wuhan as a relatively small but nevertheless noteworthy event. For that, Xi and Modi deserve credit. If they can translate the foundation that they have laid into a durable arrangement on their contested boundary, history will even record their contributions generously.

The Modi–Xi Wuhan Summit fixed the growing power imbalance between India and China—somewhat

Shyam Saran, Scroll.in, 16 May 2018

- The informal summit reflects the unusual and somewhat similar leadership qualities of the two men:
- One, both leaders have a high degree of self-assurance and belief in the value of leader-to-leader engagement transcending the tools of traditional diplomacy.
- Two, statements emerging from the two sides after the summit suggest that the leaders were responding to the growing uncertainty in both the regional geopolitical landscape in Asia and the world.
- Despite the disruptions caused by US President Donald Trump's policies, the Chinese had, until recently, been confident about managing US relations, avoiding trade-related disputes and offering cooperation in constraining North Korea from pursuing its nuclear program. This confidence has been badly shaken with China blindsided by developments on the Korean Peninsula where a North-South détente is taking shape without a Chinese role
- Renewed emphasis on the "strategic and global dimension" of India-China relations goes beyond the dynamics of bilateral relations. This is also reflected in the additional measures announced to strengthen peace and tranquillity on their border.
- Three, India has also been impacted by the shifting currents in the regional and global landscape, and better relations with China provide the nation with much needed breathing space, particularly in its own periphery. Not that China will give up steady penetration of India's South Asian neighborhood or

the Indian Ocean. However, China may advance at a slower pace than before. Improved India-China relations also constrain the temptation of India's smaller neighbors to wave the China card in squeezing concessions.

- The prospect of India and China working together on a joint project in Afghanistan blunts India's declared opposition to China's Belt and Road Initiative even as Pakistani concerns about Indian influence in Kabul go ignored.

- The Wuhan Summit has restored the balance to some extent, but this can only be sustained if India narrows the gap through more rapid buildup of its economic and military capabilities.

The ghost of Wuhan will haunt India for years

Pravin Sawhney, The Wire, 6 July 2018

- China appears to have checkmated India's foreign policy choices by a strategic masterstroke: the Wuhan understanding which has created a new model of engagement called 'China India Plus'.

- The Wuhan understanding, which is the consequence of Doklam, is not a modus vivendi as the two sides have done in the past, but a transformational moment in bilateral relations.

- Once Chinese build-up in various domains of war started within months of the tactical crisis, its tangible assets like new roads, aircraft hangers, military construction and missile firings in Tibet informed India that it had bitten more than it could chew. China, it was clear, had the capability to fight a non-contact war (through its space, cyber, electromagnetic domains, its range of accurate cruise missiles and armed unmanned vehicles), which India could not match. Once the reality hit, Modi, who did not want a bigger Doklam before the 2019 general elections, sought and met President Xi Jinping for the informal Wuhan summit. Undeniably, China's military coercion—which is always supported by credible military power—had won the day for China without it even firing a shot.

- Meanwhile, while welcoming Modi in Wuhan, Xi offered the 'China India Plus' proposal. Appearing benign and futuristic, it states that India and China (Two Plus) should coordinate their development and connectivity projects to help the neighbouring countries in order to ensure Asia's rise. While Two Plus One for Afghanistan was agreed at Wuhan, Xi, taking the Wuhan understanding further, recently offered the Two Plus One to visiting Nepal's Prime Minister K.P. Sharma Oli, who was pleased with it. Xi could now offer this new model to the Maldives, Seychelles, Sri Lanka, Bangladesh, Myanmar and so on.

- The Wuhan understanding has created a catch-22 situation for India: It can neither afford another Doklam nor partner with China on connectivity projects for two reasons. One, the worldviews and, hence, foreign policy objectives of India and China are at sharp variance. China, to quote Mao Zedong, 'everything under heaven is in utter chaos; the situation is excellent' views the world as passing through the geopolitical flux of multi-polarity after the Cold War bipolarity, to eventually become bipolar, with China and the US as the two poles.

- The second reason flows from the first. China's hard power is strides ahead of India and a catch-up is not possible.

- India's woes would not end here. It would become increasingly difficult for Modi to streamline its strategic intent with the US and the Quad, especially for the Indo-Pacific region. Moreover, India would not be able to neglect its ties with Russia, which is not only India's biggest defence supplier, but also its sole partner for defence-technology transfer.

INDIA-RUSSIA RELATIONS

A tame outcome at Sochi

Kanwal Sibal, India Today, 25 May 2018

- Surprisingly, the press release India issued on the Sochi summit was unusually bland and less informative than the statement issued after Wuhan. A much more positive message on sensitive issues should have emanated from Sochi to reassure public opinion on the state of India-Russia ties. There is no reference to CAATSA or US sanctions policies other than the two leaders reiterating the significance of long-standing partnership in the military, security and nuclear energy fields and welcoming the expanding cooperation in the energy sector. Iran or JCPOA are not mentioned even indirectly. The wording on terrorism and Afghanistan is thin. The reference to a multipolar world order is banal. The decision to intensify coordination, including on the Indo-Pacific region, catches attention because Russia avoids the term 'Indo-Pacific' due to its US-led anti-Chinese connotations.

- The only rational explanation for this low-key press release is that India is being careful in the public projection of the informal summit with Putin so that its task of engaging the US positively on issues that adversely affect Indian interests is not made more difficult.

Modi's personal touch to India-Russia relations

Nalin Kumar Mohapatra, The Pioneer, 2 June 2018

- The one-day visit of Prime Minister Narendra Modi to Sochi on May 21 heralded a new beginning as far as the question of India-Russia relations is concerned. It can be termed as a new initiative because the visit of Modi to Russia took place when the relation was slightly strained. This can be partly attributed to Russian policymakers' ambivalent policy on giving sophisticated weapons to Pakistan (known for sponsoring cross-border terrorism) and keeping mum on Chinese aggressive policy towards India. The third issue is Moscow's engagement with Taliban which certainly created jittery among the policymakers in New Delhi. The fourth concern is low level of bilateral economic relations between these two countries which certainly provide opportunity to introspect why after so many years the mutual economic relations are not on a higher pedestal.

- Modi's intention to add a new substance to the gloomy bilateral relations between India and Russia can be evident from the fact that before leaving to Sochi, Modi on his personal twitter account (as quoted on the PMO website) stated "the talks with President Putin will further strengthen the Special and Privileged Strategic Partnership between India and Russia". One interesting inference can be concluded from the twitter message that Modi intended to give the informal relationship to a new "strategic level" between these two civilisational powers.

- The most intriguing aspect of Russian engagement with Taliban came to light when just after signing the Sochi Informal Summit declaration with India, Russia sent a feeler to Taliban leadership for negotiation as reported in newspapers.

- The second issue which cropped up during Modi's interaction with Putin is to maintain strategic equilibrium both at the regional as well as at the global levels.

- India-Russia cooperation can act as a hedge against expansionist policy of other external power which may have a spillover-effect on the security of both the countries directly or indirectly.

- Another critical area that got full attention in the Informal Declaration at Sochi was cooperation in the field of energy cooperation. Since the signing of the Sakhalin deal, India has signed deals in the Siberian, Far East and Arctic regions of Russia.

- What is worrisome in India-Russia relations is that the economic cooperation has not reached its potentiality. One may add a footnote here that while India's economic cooperation with the EU, the US and China is growing, that with Russia is quite stagnant. In this regard, the operationalisation of the International North South Transport Corridor Project (INSTC) will facilitate greater economic cooperation between the two countries.

- The informal meeting between Modi and Putin can be remembered for one thing that both the leaders gave personal touch to strengthen the bilateral relationship between the two countries.

Future of the India-Russia relationship post Sochi summit
Shruti Godbole, Brookings, 2 July 2018

- Sochi summit—the two leaders upgraded this traditionally close relationship to a "special privileged strategic partnership."
- While there has been some improvement in economic relations between India and Russia in the last two years, the relationship today essentially hinges only on military technological cooperation, where Russia supplies about 60% of India's imported military equipment by value. This dependence on military technical cooperation to sustain the bilateral relationship might be problematic in the long run based on India's economic growth projections and doubts about Russia's ability to satisfy Indian demands.
- On the other hand, it is not just Russia that is worried about the India-US relationship. India too has concerns about Russia's growing relationships with China and Pakistan, and its contentious relationship with Washington.
- After the Ukraine crisis in 2014, the Russia-China relationship has become stronger, with important implications for India and other rising powers. Both Russia and China are being challenged by the United States, politically, economically, and strategically. While China has been able to sustain competition with the United States, a weak Russian economy is increasingly making Russia dependent on China for economic cooperation. This dependency can further extend to political and strategic domains over time.
- Russia's position on areas of tension in the world, whether it is Ukraine, Georgia, West Asia, Afghanistan or North Korea, appears to openly challenge US predominance. This tension catches India between its growing strategic partnership with the United States and its dependence on Russia for defence technological needs.
- Despite these strains, a strong India-Russia relationship is important because it gives extra manoeuvring space for both countries vis-a-vis other actors.

- From the Indian perspective, there is scope for improvement in trade between Russia and India if the international North-South corridor through Iran, and the Vladivostok-Chennai sea route can be operationalised. India can benefit from hi-tech cooperation with Russia in the fields of artificial intelligence, robotics, biotechnology, outer space and nanotechnology. It can also cooperate with Russia on upgrading its basic research and education facilities. There is scope for growth in the energy sector, beyond mutual investments. Mutual benefits in trade of natural resources such as timber, and agriculture can also be harnessed.

- Putin has made a conscious attempt to energise his relationship with Japanese Prime Minister Shinzo Abe. Russia has also been trying to develop ties with Vietnam and other Southeast Asian countries through the East Asia Summit and ASEAN. Given India's long-term association with these countries, India can help Russia in navigating these relationships.

INDIA-EU RELATIONS & NORDIC SUMMIT

Europe, India and Modi: It's time to start over

Shada Islam, The Wire, 17 June 2015

- First, after a year of little or no high-level contact, Delhi and Brussels appear ready to resume negotiations on the much delayed Bilateral Trade and Investment Agreement (BTIA), a comprehensive deal covering all areas in goods, services and public procurement in both markets.

- Second, India's new economic programme opens up fresh avenues for increased EU-India synergies which go beyond the two sides' traditional interaction. This could include cooperation in areas where both sides have a strong economic interest such as infrastructure investments, sustainable urbanisation, innovation and synergies between "Digital India" and the EU's agenda for a Digital Single Market.

- The EU has made clear that it is targeting the emerging well-off Indian middle class for enhanced market access in automobiles, wines and spirits, and cheese. Brussels is also calling for reform in Indian laws on intellectual property rights, trade and environment, and trade and labour and wants liberal access in insurance, banking, and retail trade. India, for its part, is insisting on more labour mobility, professional work visas and recognition as a data secure country to attract more European investments in its high tech sector.

- Also, while India may not want such counsel, the EU is well-placed to share its experience in building a single market, economic reform and modernisation, cutting back over-regulation—the new Commission priority—and improving the business environment.

- In order to get India and the EU talking to each other on these and other equally interesting topics, Modi's "can do" spirit needs to filter down to different, less adventurous, echelons of the Indian bureaucracy.
- Above all, both sides must take a fresh look at each other.

Modi in Europe: Relaunching the EU-India Strategic Partnership
C. Raja Mohan, Carnegie Europe, 29 March 2016

- As a leader with sharp political acumen, Modi also understands the current traumatic moment in Europe after the March 22 terror attacks in Brussels and the November 13, 2015, attacks in Paris. As Brussels copes with an unprecedented threat enveloping it, Modi will hope that Europe can better appreciate the terrorist challenge that India has continued to endure since the late 1980s.
- India's past neglect of Europe was in part due to a lack of attention and capacity. New Delhi neither understood the significance of the European project nor mastered the technique of navigating Brussels for its national benefit. India found it easier to focus on bilateral partnerships with key European actors like the UK, Germany, and France with which it had historic relations.
- If Europe had no powerful champion in New Delhi, Brussels too found it rather hard to deal with the ponderous Indian bureaucratic system.
- But his plans to visit Brussels in April 2015 were vetoed by Italy, which was locked in a diplomatic row with New Delhi over the arrest and trial of two Italian marines for the killing of two fishermen off India's coast in 2012. Italy claimed Indian courts had no jurisdiction in the matter.
- Modi in typical fashion ordered his diplomats to find a way out. India has now joined an arbitration procedure and has agreed to abide by the verdict of the international tribunal that will rule on the matter. By moving the issue out of the bilateral ambit, Modi has cleared one of the current hurdles in India's political engagement with Europe.
- If problem solving has been one of the trademarks of Modi's foreign policy, the other distinguishing feature has been the determination to put Indian diplomacy firmly in the service of India's developmental goals.
- India and EU were due to resume the trade talks in 2015. But New Delhi pulled out at the last minute when Brussels banned the sale of 700-odd

pharmaceuticals from India. Now, Modi is also eager to have some of the current European restrictions on the movement of Indian professionals lifted. And he wants Brussels to give India's IT sector data security status, which is critical for expanding the sector's business in Europe.

- Brussels too needs Indian professionals to boost Europe's economic competitiveness. The EU is also seeking better market access in India for a number of its goods, including wines and automotive parts. There is much room here for some give-and-take.

- Beyond the commercial arena, Modi will want to generate a deeper political understanding of how to cope with the rapid breakdown of the old order on the Eurasian landmass and the adjacent waters of the Pacific and Indian Oceans.

- The rise of China, the assertiveness of Russia, and the temptations of retrenchment in the United States make it a lot harder for New Delhi and Brussels to cope with the rapid change in the Middle East and the Far East.

Where Do European Union-India Relations Stand?

Ankit Panda, The Diplomat, 31 March 2016

- Speaking in Brussels, Modi highlighted India's uniquely high growth rate, which continues to be the highest among large emerging economies, outpacing China, Russia, Brazil, and South Africa—once its bedfellows in the BRICS grouping. Modi told EU leaders that India was the "lone light of hope" in the world economy.

- On energy, the joint statement refers to the outcomes of the December 2015 21st Conference of Parties (COP21) outcomes, including the India-led International Solar Alliance.

- While the latest EU-India summit doesn't foreshadow a sea change in the relationship, there are some important differences from the outcomes of the 2012 summit. For instance, the EU appears more interested in India's regional role as a major power. Where the 2012 joint statement omitted any mention of Afghanistan, for example, the 2016 statement states a "commitment for a sustainable, democratic, prosperous and peaceful Afghanistan," suggesting that the EU recognises India as a significant regional player. Moreover, Wednesday's joint statement mentions the South Asian Association for Regional Cooperation (SAARC), unlike the 2012 statement.

- Moreover, in what represents a victory for the Modi government, the EU-India summit emphasises India's position on recent political developments in

Nepal (with regard to the country's new constitution) and the Maldives (with regard to Abdulla Yameen's increasingly anti-democratic tendencies). Among other global topics, the joint statement references the Joint Comprehensive Plan of Action with Iran, North Korea's recent nuclear testing, and peace in the Middle East.

EU-India summit: slow progress, except for security deal
Stefania Benaglia, EU Observer, 9 October 2017

- The 14th EU-India Summit held in Delhi last Friday (October 6th) was not a summit of big announcements. But it succeeded in maintaining the political momentum created by the last summit in March 2016, which came after four years of frozen relations. The summit confirmed that on several issues the strategic orientations of the partners are mostly aligned. It is now time to align the policy agendas.

- The EU and India should now focus on transforming political declarations into actual policy. The two parties already hold several policy dialogues but these have been confined to bureaucratic exchanges, in which the counterparts discuss without much real commitment or therefore progress.

- To move out from its impasse, there is the need for concrete steps, such as facilitating officer exchanges between Europol and Indian Security Agencies— agreed upon this week—to enhance security cooperation.

- In a volatile world orphaned of US leadership, India is looking at the EU as an island of stability and even urging it to upgrade its role as global security provider. In this context, and in line with ongoing discussion on the future of European Defence, the consolidation of the European Defence and Technological Industrial Base (EDTIB) including by supporting its export, would strengthen the EU stand as global security provider.

- India still fails to see the added value of dealing with the EU rather than bilaterally with member states. In addition, Indian officials sometimes hold the conviction that EU competences can be overturn by dealing directly with member states on issues, such as trade, on which the EU has exclusive competence.

European Union and India are natural allies
Arun K. Singh, Hindustan Times, 10 October 2017

- The 14th India-EU summit, held in Delhi on October 6, drew attention to an important dimension of India's foreign policy and international economic engagement which normally receives scant public or analytical attention.

- EU, with its present membership of 28 countries, constitutes India's largest trading partner, accounting for more than 100 billion euros, in a balanced trade relationship. With investments in India of US$83 billion over 2000-2017, it is 24% of total FDI flows into the country. 6,000 European companies are present in India. The Indian origin community, at 2.1 million, is not insignificant, even though less than the 3.5 million in the US. France, a leading member of the EU, is an important strategic partner, with high technology cooperation in defence, space, and civil nuclear. 50,000 Indian students are in EU in higher education, with 5,000 having been provided ERASMUS scholarships.

- The European Investment bank has committed Euros 1.5 billion for the year, with loans supporting the Bengaluru metro project and a solar project.

- Engagement with the EU also enables India to balance some of the unhelpful trends emerging from the US, and to reinforce those that meet its interests. Many of these were reflected in the joint statement issued following the summit.

- On Iran, both supported staying with the Joint Comprehensive Plan of Action, since Iran has maintained its commitment, contrary to the now anticipated decertification by the US administration.

- In an op-ed on October 6, Juncker said "European Union and India are natural partners", the "bond is built on our shared beliefs", and that "the strength of the law outweighs the law of the strong" (the opposite of what China is doing in South China Sea), and there was a need to work "with like minded partners".

- There were specific references to terrorist incidents in India, which India had linked to Pakistan, and Pakistan based terrorist groups and individuals.

- In another oblique negative reference to Pakistan "both sides stressed the responsibility of those who support DPRK's nuclear and missile programmes".

Modi reboots India's connect with Nordic nations after decades

Vivek Katju, Asia Times, 18 April 2018

- Recognising that Swedish technology can be useful in some crucial areas, Modi responded purposefully to Lofven's desire to develop bilateral relations. Consequently, then-president Pranab Mukherjee visited Sweden in 2015.

- With the ice broken, Lofven visited Mumbai in 2016 to take part in the

"Make in India" week. He held in-depth discussions with Modi and the two decided to intensify economic and technological contacts, including in the defense and security fields.

- Sweden has an advanced defense industry, and with India now determined to develop its own, it makes good sense to foster partnerships with it. Renewable energy, urban waste management and innovation were also identified as focus areas for collaboration.

- Modi's Stockholm visit takes the 2016 process forward. Most noteworthy is the decision to sign a confidentiality agreement for the safeguarding of Swedish defense technology. This underlines the determination to act purposefully in defense manufacturing industries.

- The India-Nordic summit sent clear signals to both Donald Trump's America and Xi Jinping's aggressive China. At a time when President Trump is challenging open and inclusive global trading systems, the summit emphasised "the importance of rules-based multilateral trading systems as well as open and inclusive trade for prosperity and growth." Europe is worried about the imposition of selective duties on some product lines and Trump's protectionist approach. India shares these concerns and has articulated them previously.

- Nordic countries have substantial interests in the Chinese economy, but this did not constrain them from joining India in calling for the upholding of "the rules-based international system". This is an unmistakable reference to China, which is disregarding international conventions and rules as it expands its international influence.

- Modi had told a Danish minister whom he met at the margins of a "Vibrant Gujarat" event in January 2017 that Holck should be extradited to India. The Indian Central Bureau of Investigation put in a fresh extradition request last year and the Danes again asked for assurances.

Why Narendra Modi reaching out to Nordic nations is both historic and important

Harsh V. Pant, DailyO, 20 April 2018

- This was not only the first visit of an Indian Prime Minister to Sweden in 30 years but also an attempt to reach out to the wider Nordic region with the first India-Nordic summit which saw India interacting with the Prime Ministers of Denmark, Finland, Iceland, Norway and Sweden on a single platform.

- New Delhi's focus, for far too long, has been on traditional Western powers, with the US on one side and major European powers like the UK, France and Germany on the other. The result was a complete neglect of advanced

Nordic nations with whom India shares some significant political and economic complementarities and which rank highest in various human developments indices. The Bofors scandal too cast its own shadow on relations with Sweden in particular, with reluctance on the part of India to move beyond past troubles. On the other hand, the Nordic states too were absorbed in trying to manage their European identities in multiple ways and India was not really on their radar.

- But with the changing global context in which states like China and Russia are busy remoulding the rules of global governance to their advantage and with India standing out as an economic powerhouse with strong democratic credentials, the discourse in the Nordic states too has undergone a dramatic shift. A strong partnership with India is seen as not only desirable but also imperative of changing global realities.

- In Sweden, Modi galvanised top Swedish firms to invest in India, underlining the importance of strong bilateral business relations for the people of the two countries. Sweden has been a strong supporter of India's "Make in India" campaign with the Swedish Prime Minister leading a big delegation to the Mumbai summit in 2016.

- India and Sweden are working on reviving their traditionally strong defence ties in light of the latter's interest in proposing the Saab Group's Gripen-E single-engine jet fighter for the Indian Air Force and with a Request for Information having been issued earlier this month to Stockholm. India and Sweden have decided to set up a common task force on cyber security and are working towards finalising a bilateral agreement on exchange and mutual protection of classified information for cooperation in the defence area as well as encouraging private sector stakeholders to develop supply chains for small- and medium-sized enterprises with major defence and aerospace original equipment manufacturers.

- The highlight of Modi's visit to Sweden was the signing of the Joint Innovation Partnership pact and adoption of the Joint Action Plan.

- The Swedish government will be providing more than US$59 million (Rs 387 crore) for innovation cooperation with India in the field of smart cities and sustainability, two key priorities of New Delhi. With the Joint Action Plan, meanwhile, the two nations will try to enhance cooperation in key areas of renewable energy, women's skills development and empowerment, space and science, and health and life sciences.

- In this context, India received key support from the Nordic countries for its membership of the Nuclear Suppliers' Group (NSG) and a seat at the UN Security Council as a permanent member. The NSG support from the Nordic states is particularly significant because there was a time when these states had adopted a strong moralistic approach on India's nuclear programme. Today, there is a recognition and acceptance of India's credentials as a responsible nuclear actor despite not being a formal member of the Nuclear Non-Proliferation Treaty (NPT).

INDIA-SOUTHEAST ASIA RELATIONS

The India-ASEAN Partnership at 25

Ashok Sajjanhar, IDSA Comment, 4 January 2018

- The Look East Policy registered impressive gains for 20 years after its inception. Having become a sectoral partner of ASEAN in 1992, India became a dialogue partner and member of the ASEAN Regional Forum (ARF) in 1996. India and ASEAN entered into a summit partnership in 2002, the 10th anniversary of LEP, and launched negotiations for a Free Trade Agreement (FTA) in goods in 2003. These discussions culminated in a bilateral deal being concluded in 2009 and becoming effective in 2010. Bilateral trade and investment showed impressive gains in the first decade of this century. While bilateral trade increased from USD 2 billion in 1992 to 12 billion in 2002, registering a growth of 12 per cent annually, it zoomed to 72 billion in 2012 with a cumulative annual growth rate of around 22 per cent over the preceding 10 years. India's two-way trade with ASEAN now stands at approximately USD 76 billion. India and ASEAN missed out on achieving the two-way trade target of USD 100 billion set during the Commemorative Summit held on the 20th Anniversary of the bilateral partnership in 2012 in New Delhi. The India-ASEAN Free Trade pact in services and investments, which was concluded in 2014 and came into effect a year later, has the potential to reduce India's trade deficit with the region as also impart a strong impulse to bilateral exchanges. India is also a part of the ASEAN-led Regional Comprehensive Economic Partnership (RCEP), which, when concluded and implemented, will cover almost 40 per cent of the world's population, 33 per cent of global GDP and 40 per cent of world trade.
- Currently, there exist 30 different dialogue mechanisms between India and the ASEAN states focusing on a range of sectors. These comprise an annual Summit and seven Ministerial meetings focused on a variety of areas that

include foreign affairs, economy, environment, tourism, etc. The ASEAN-India Centre (AIC), established in 2013, has enhanced the strategic partnership by concentrating on policy research and recommendations as well as organising meetings between think-tanks and similar institutions in India and ASEAN countries.

- Connectivity between India and ASEAN, particularly Myanmar and Thailand, has emerged as a significant element in cementing bonds between the two regions.

- Two major connectivity projects, viz., the Trilateral Highway between north-east India and Myanmar and onwards to Thailand (and Laos and Vietnam) as well as the Kaladan multi-modal transit and transport project, have been under implementation for several years. The NDA government has taken it up seriously. It is highly likely that both will soon become operational.

- Relations with ASEAN have become multi-faceted to encompass security, connectivity, strategic, political, space technology, counter-terrorism and anti-insurgency operations, anti-radicalisation, trade and investment, maritime security and defence collaboration, in addition to economic ties.

- Prime Minister Modi has travelled to Singapore twice, once to attend the State funeral of Singapore's first Prime Minister Lee Kuan Yew in March 2015, and again to mark the 50th anniversary of the establishment of bilateral relations and establish a strategic partnership in November 2015; to Myanmar twice, once to participate in the East Asia Summit (EAS) and the India-ASEAN Summit in November 2014, and again on the way back from China in September 2017; to Malaysia in November 2015 for a bilateral visit as well as to attend the EAS and the India ASEAN Summit; to Laos in September 2016 for the EAS and India ASEAN Summit; to Vietnam on a bilateral visit en route to China in September 2016; and, to the Philippines to participate in EAS and India-ASEAN Summit in November 2017. He also made a short stopover in Thailand on his way to Japan in November 2016 to pay respect to the venerable, departed king Bhumibol Adulyadej. Visits from India have been reciprocated by high level visits from ASEAN States to India. Relations, which were earlier seen as lackadaisical, are again assuming renewed vigour.

- India and ASEAN account for about 30 per cent of the global population (i.e., 1.85 billion people) and a combined GDP of approximately USD 5.1 trillion. Together, they would form the third largest economy in the world.

Asia's newest love story: Modi and ASEAN are lost in each other's eyes

Sriram Iyer, Quartz India, 26 January 2018

- In fact, he has to thank the people of ASEAN for being ranked the third most-popular world leader by a Gallup International Association (GIA) survey in collaboration with CVoter International, released in January 2018.
- In all, Modi's global ratings were up by a net four points, thanks to a 26-point boost from the ASEAN.
- Hanoi's affection for Modi may have stemmed from its need to counter the neighbourhood bully, China. Modi struck the right chord when, in November 2017, he told an ASEAN summit in Manila that India advocated the settlement of disputes (in the South China Sea) via peaceful means and as per international law. This is not something China likes to hear; it wants to settle the issue bilaterally.
- The term Indo-Pacific has now gained currency, suggesting that the region spanning the Indian and the Pacific oceans is now being viewed organically as one in security terms.
- The two countries deepened their defence ties in December 2016. Widodo drew parallels between India and Indonesia as victims of terrorism and the need to work together to combat extremists.
- The Philippines, on the other hand, wants inexpensive medicines from India. President Rodrigo Duterte has invited Indian drug makers to set up facilities in his country. However, it's not just about cheap medicines. In November 2017, the two countries signed four agreements in defence, logistics, agriculture, and micro, small, and medium enterprises. The Philippine National Police uses Mahindra cars.
- The ASEAN has a trade deficit of US$77 billion with China and a trade surplus of over US$45 billion with the US, according to ASEAN data from November 2016 (pdf). The TPP was meant to be a counter to China's economic hegemony in the southeast Asia, but the US put paid to the plans.
- Meanwhile, India-ASEAN bilateral trade reached US$71 billion in 2016-17, constituting around 10% of India's total global trade, according to IHS Markit. The firm sees the potential to at least double this number to around US$140 billion by 2025.

India's pivot to Southeast Asia

Simi Mehta, Asia & The Pacific Policy Society, 2 March 2018

- In his Republic Day editorial that appeared in 27 newspapers and in 10 languages, Prime Minister Narendra Modi focused on the shared values and common destiny between India and Asean, which have moved on from being dialogue partners to strategic partners.

- The idea that India should enlarge its engagement in the region was also evident this year in the quadrilateral grouping of India, US, Australia and Japan. India's Ministry of External Affairs has maintained that the Quad partnership is to ensure freedom of navigation in the region's oceans, indicating growing concerns over China's continued build-up in the South China Sea.

- Second, there are economic imperatives behind New Delhi's engagement with Southeast Asia. Taking advantage of mutual geopolitical insecurities, India has consistently pressed for greater economic integration with Asean nations and has sought to present itself as an attractive investment destination to them.

- During the Republic Day celebrations in New Delhi, Modi offered to set up digital villages in Cambodia, Laos, Myanmar and Vietnam by utilising India's US$1 billion line of credit to Asean for "connectivity, culture, and commerce". In July 2017, India's then-foreign secretary Subrahmanyam Jaishankar described connectivity as the "new Great Game".

- With the signing of the Asean-India Agreement in Services and Investments, Asean and India are likely to benefit from an extended market, where air connectivity aims to play a pivotal role.

- On the other hand, the Asean exhortation for India to "stand with Asean" to conclude the Regional Comprehensive Economic Partnership (RCEP) by 2018 did not achieve concrete commitments.

- India's protectionist instincts have impacted its regional profile and highlighted its weaknesses, leading to frustration among other member nations by slowing down or impeding the negotiations. This could jeopardise India's regional status in the eyes of the Southeast Asian nations.

- Furthermore, some of New Delhi's consolations for Asean members, like its 2015 offer for access to India's indigenous satellite navigation system, the GPS-aided Geo Augmented Navigation (GAGAN), received no uptake from the nations of Southeast Asia. They instead chose the alternate offer from China.

- The third imperative of India-Asean relations is socio-cultural. India has recognised the importance of its commonalities with Southeast Asia in civilisation, culture, religion and tradition and has sought to exploit these to build close linkages with the Asean countries. Southeast Asia remains an attractive destination for Indian tourists given its historical sites and affordability.

- Unfortunately for New Delhi, the repeated use of the term Indo-Pacific by the Indian side during the Commemorative Summit was met with no candid citation from the Asean side. Only the press note of the Indonesian foreign ministry noted that President Jokowi had proposed to invite key countries in the region to discuss the Indo-Pacific concept. "I suggest that this concept should be developed based on openness, inclusiveness, based on the spirit of cooperation," said President Jokowi.

INDIA-WEST ASIA RELATIONS

India's Israel-UAE balancing act As PM Modi to tour Middle East
Rajeev Sharma, The Quint, 16 January 2018

- India is all set to give a new thrust to its 'Look West' foreign policy and also counterbalance its ties with Israel by engaging the Arab world, as Prime Minister Narendra Modi is all set to embark on a three-nation Middle East tour from the second week of February to Oman, the United Arab Emirates (UAE) and Palestine.
- This visit is symbolic, as it will show not just the domestic audience but the world that the Modi government is engaging with one and all, without fear or favour and without any predilections or prejudice.
- This trip is an attempt by the Modi government to strike a balance between India's ties with the Islamic world on the one hand, and with Israel on the other.
- Modi's main agenda in the UAE will be to remind Abu Dhabi about their promised investment of US$75 billion in India; not a cent has come from the UAE since this promise was made by their authorities two-and-a-half years ago, when PM Modi last visited the UAE.
- This investment, coming from a predominantly Muslim nation, would allow the BJP (which is seen as an ultra-right wing party) to prove to the electorate its credibility in the international community.
- If this investment comes through, it would also allow the Modi government to score brownie points over arch rival Pakistan, which has traditionally had very close relations with UAE.
- The reason for this is that the UAE wants counter-guarantees from the Indian government, something Modi can't do. India has given counter-guarantees only once in the past—in the Enron case, which had caused India to burn its fingers.
- For a large number of Indians, Oman is second home. The number of Indian expatriates in Oman is 8,00,749 (as of April 2017) and the number of Indian

workers including professionals in Oman is about 6,90,163 (as of October 2017). No wonder then that four Indian Prime Ministers have previously visited the Sultanate—Rajiv Gandhi (1985), PV Narasimha Rao (1993), Atal Bihari Vajpayee (1998) and Manmohan Singh (2008).

- The highest level of visit to Palestine from India has been by the then President Pranab Mukherjee in October 2015, although the then Palestinian President Yasser Arafat had visited India several times, and current Palestinian President Mahmoud Abbas visited India in the years between 2005 and 2012, and most recently in May 2017.

As PM Modi embarks on historic West Asia tour, the optics are significant
Kabir Taneja, News18, 9 February 2018

- During this visit, Modi is set to become the first Indian Prime Minister to visit Palestine after becoming the first PM to visit Israel in July last year. What works in India's favour here is the tight-rope balancing act it pulls off in the region, successfully dealing with the various power centres, religious and sectarian crevasses and economic interests without breaking any relationships.
- The fact that Ramallah is aware and acceptable of India's growing relations with Israel, and Tel Aviv knows of India's long-standing stance on Palestine and support for a two state solution, and both Israel and Palestine accept India's relations with each other emboldens its 'non-aligned' position in the region, perhaps the only diplomatic space in the world where the very idea and implementation of non-alignment still bears fruit in the current climate.
- The turn observed by global economics over the past decade has not only put developing economies in Asia at the centre of the global growth story but also re-shaped how countries in West Asia approached India.
- With Asian economies becoming majority oil buyers, West Asian economies increasingly depended on these sales to power their domestic economics as other Western markets moved swiftly to renewables or, in the case of the US, became energy self-sufficient thanks to its shale boom. This shift gave India an upper hand in negotiating larger political and trade deals, with long-standing sore points of cooperation such as counter-terrorism and labour rights becoming more favourable to Indian demands and requirements, which had been undercut by the Gulf capitals for a long time.
- Both Oman and the UAE also present further opportunities for India to increase its trade base. Modi will become the fifth Indian Prime Minister to

visit Oman since the first visit by Rajiv Gandhi in 1985.

Modi's balancing act in the Middle East

Mustapha Karkouti, Gulf News, 13 February 2018

- India is now the largest market for Israeli military products, buying around US$1 billion (Dh3.67 billion) annually of weaponry in recent years. Though it does not represent more than 2 per cent of India's entire world trade, but it equals 45 per cent of Israel's total military sales.
- In a way it is, mainly for two reasons. First, it is the first visit ever by an Indian prime minister to the Occupied Territories. Second, it seems the visit was intentionally done through a direct helicopter flight from the Jordanian capital, Amman, rather than a hyphenated drop over after visiting Israel last July, as many world leaders usually do. Prior to visiting Ramallah, India's prime minister met Jordan's King Abdullah during which he discussed the peace prospects following the announcement of the US president, Donald Trump, to recognise [occupied] Jerusalem as the capital of Israel.
- But the world's international relationship in 2017 has considerably changed from what it was in the past. As the former Soviet Union collapsed, the non-alignment bloc, of which India was the leading player, gradually withered away. The new millennium has witnessed the birth of the so-called Brics countries, a lose association of five major emerging national economies: Brazil, Russia, India, China and South Africa. However, the question remains whether Modi's India will be able to energetically facilitate conditions to revive the Middle East peace process where many regional and international players have miserably failed.

Modi in the Middle East: A Diplomatic Masterstroke for India or Playing with Fire?

Kamal Alam, Al Sharq, 21 February 2018

- Under Modi, India stands as one of the foremost supporters of not just Palestine but also Israel's arch enemy the Syrian Arab Republic and the Islamic Republic of Iran which is amongst India's key economic partners. And whilst the headlines in Pakistan are of a conspiratorial India-Israel embrace against Muslims—Narendra Modi has also been bestowed the highest civilian honour by Saudi Arabia—an award never conferred to any Pakistani Prime Minister. This balancing act of being Israel's strategic defence partner has not stopped India from strengthening its ties not just with the Arab states in the Levant but also the Gulf states of Saudi Arabia and the United Arab Emirates.

- So how has Narenda Modi overturned a traditional cautious approach to the Middle East with a proactive all-encompassing embrace of the region?

- Post-independence India under the watchful eye of Jawaharlal Nehru had firmly established its credentials as anti-colonial and imperial state which was against British and French aggression in the Suez. Along with the nationalist Egyptian President Gamal Abdel Nasser, Nehru led the anti-Western alliance which also meant firm support for Palestine and an opposition to Israeli territorial plans. This also brought India closer to the newly independent Algeria, pro-Soviet Syria and the Palestinian guerrilla movements based in the Levant. In the decades to come India stood firm in core relationships with the nationalist Arab governments whilst maintaining minimum relations with the pro-American states of Saudi Arabia, Jordan and the newly established GCC states. Until 1992, there were no formal ties with the State of Israel until the then Prime Minister Narasimha Rao reached out set up an embassy in Tel Aviv. Since then in just over two decades India has become the largest importer of Israel's weapons in the world, a top destination for Israeli tourists especially the conscripts leaving military service and one of Israel's key economic partners.

- Indeed the Israeli Prime Minister during his current visit has hailed Modi as a 'revolutionary leader' and the public and private ties between the two states are hitting new heights. Preceding Netanyahu's trip to India, Modi became the first ever Indian Prime Minister to visit Israel

- Whilst there is a clear convergence of Indian and Israeli defence interests in the fields of avionics, drones and the Silicon bubble—Israel also understands and respects India's historic commitment to Palestine—indeed a space could be opening up for Indian mediation and diplomacy between the two as the Americans have clearly lost their role according to the Palestinian President.

- A clear sign of India's influence and alliance with the current Palestinian leadership can be seen in the recent sacking of the Palestinian envoy to Pakistan who appeared in a rally in Islamabad with India's most wanted man Hafiz Saeed.

- Israel for all their enmity of the Iranian leadership has not been able to challenge India's closeness with Iran. At the same time, Modi has capitalised on the Emirati and Kuwait disgruntlement with Pakistan on their refusal to send its troops to Yemen. Modi became the first foreign leader to address a public gathering of expatriates in the UAE. The UAE Crown

Prince was the chief guest on India's national day and the Emirati forces paraded side by side India's in a big blow to Pakistan's claim as the guardian of the Gulf. The UAE even backed Indian military action against Pakistan based militants after the Uri attack. Under Modi India has also signed a historic strategic defence partnership with Saudi Arabia and Qatar has started investment in the Indian economy under Modi's watch.

- Most remarkably Indian support to the Syrian President Bashar al Assad and his government has taken a very public and strategic stance; the foreign, finance and intelligence ministers have all made trips to Syria regularly.

- However with the great balancing that Modi has undertaken between the Gulf countries and Iran, Iran and Israel it has also brought great risks. Ayatollah Khamenei for the first in over two decades criticized Indian on its Kashmir stance by stating that the people of Kashmir are oppressed, a stance that backed the Pakistani version of the international issue. Iran seems to be worried about the increasing closeness of Israel and India and whilst so far there have been no major ruptures in the very important Iran-Indian economic ties, it is clear that Tehran is not too pleased.

INDIA-AFRICA RELATIONS

India's Modi sets sights on Africa

Gabriel Domínguez, DW, 23 October 2015

- But just how strong are Indian-African ties? Economist Biswas explains that although previous Indian governments may have been relatively low key in terms of stepping up trade ties, India's private sector has been much more dynamic. "The significant presence of an Indian diaspora in many parts of the continent—countries such as South Africa, Kenya, Tanzania and Mauritius—has led to strong entrepreneurial ties in sectors such as retail services, mining and commodities trading," said the analyst.

- And although only Nigeria and South Africa make it among India's top 25 trade partners, analysts say New Delhi is keen on diversifying into new regions, especially French- and Portuguese-speaking countries such as Senegal and Mozambique.

- A number of Indian multinationals already have significant interests and investments in the region, with strategic sectors including agribusiness, pharmaceuticals, information and communications technology (ICT), and energy.

- In fact, African countries, in particular Nigeria and Angola, now account for more than a quarter of India's oil and gas imports—a diversification strategy aimed at reducing New Delhi's traditional dependence on the Gulf states, as Constantino Xavier, a researcher at the Washington-based Johns Hopkins University, told DW.
- And as Xavier points out, ties are also strengthening on the security front. "East African coastal states from Somalia to South Africa, including also the Seychelles, Madagascar and Mauritius, are all key partners in India's efforts to establish leadership in the Indian Ocean Region, from combating piracy to securing sea lines of communication and disaster mitigation."
- India is also the largest contributor to UN-mandated peacekeeping and other operations in Africa, with more than 30,000 personnel involved in 17 of 22 total missions in the region since 1960.
- India provides a useful model for democratic development. Indeed, the world's largest democracy is increasingly responding to requests from African governments to share its democratic experience, offering training on electronic voting systems, parliamentary procedures, federal governance, and an independent judicial system to strengthen the rule of law.

PM in Africa amid a trade slump

Suhasini Haidar, The Hindu, 23 July 2018

- However, given declining trade and investment, Mr. Modi will face the challenges of Chinese competition and unfulfilled expectations during the visit, according to the latest data.
- Despite the ramping up of high-level visits, various studies and statistics show that Indian interest in the Africa growth story has not kept pace, and even declined through most of the period. The greatest slump appears to have been in investment figures.
- According to the "World Investment Report for 2018", issued by the United Nations Conference on Trade and Development (UNCTAD), Indian FDI in Africa in 2016-17 at US$14 billion was even lower than it was in 2011-12 at US$16 billion. In fact, with the exception of the 2015 figures, which jumped due to a single investment of US$2.6 billion by ONGC Videsh Ltd. for a stake in the Rovuma gas field of Mozambique in 2014, Indian investment in Africa has steadily decreased year-on-year since 2014.
- While one of the issues has been the investment climate in African countries

itself, which has seen FDI flows drop 21% in 2016-17 according to UNCTAD, India is the only one of the big investors in Africa to have reduced its investment.

- China, for example, increased from 2011-12, when its investment levels were identical to India's at US$16 billion, to a massive US$40 billion in 2016-17.
- A similar slump both in actual and comparative terms has been seen in India-Africa trade figures from 2013 to 2017, when export and import figures fell from US$67.84 billion to US$51.96 billion. The China-Africa bilateral trade, in comparison, has hovered around the US$170 billion mark.
- One of India's biggest problems has been its concentration on East African trade and investment opportunities, as well as a dependence on petroleum and LNG, say experts. India's exports to African countries have also been dominated by petroleum products, and a diversification is needed to broaden economic engagement.

How Modi's Africa tour is a welcome but late move to counter China
Prabhash K. Dutta, India Today, 24 July 2018

- PM Modi's visit to Rwanda was the first such visit by an Indian prime minister.
- China is the largest economic partner of Rwanda. Over 70 per cent of country's roads have been or are being built by Chinese companies. Chinese investment in Rwanda is in the tune of US$400 billion in over 60 projects over last decade or so.
- China established diplomatic relations with Rwanda in 1971. On the other hand, Rwanda opened its High Commission in India in 1999 and sent its first High Commissioner in 2001. India is yet to open its High Commission in Rwanda.
- China is the biggest supplier of arms and weapons to African countries.
- India does not export much arms to African countries but it provides training to many countries that buy weapons from China. So, India trains African soldiers carrying Chinese weapons. Sensing an opportunity, China has launched a massive training campaign in Africa. It has opened centres in Tanzania, Rwanda, Uganda, Kenya and Burundi.
- China has 43 active diplomatic missions in Africa against India's 29. The Modi government recently decided to open 18 new missions across Africa.
- After his election in 2013, President Xi Jinping chose Africa for his maiden foreign trip, which he followed up with two more tours during his first tenure.

He is back on Africa tour in his second term. India is playing a catch up game in Africa.

Is Narendra Modi's India-Africa partnership policy working?
Rajiv Bhatia, Quartz India, 10 September 2018

- Every major player—China, Japan, the United States, Russia, the Association of South East Asian Nations, besides the former colonial nations—is enhancing cooperation with it.
- India's president, vice president, and prime minister have made more than 25 visits to African capitals during the past four years.
- Peacekeeping has been a vital element of the India-Africa partnership since 1960. Over 6,000 Indians currently serve in peacekeeping operations in African countries. About 70% of 163 Indians, who lost their lives while on duty, did so in Africa.
- New Delhi's decision to open 18 new diplomatic missions in Africa in the next few years, which will take the total number to 47, reflects its new Afro-centric approach.
- Project partnership, fuelled by the government's Lines of Credit (LOCs) and managed by Exim Bank, needs to show improvement. A total of 166 projects are officially listed for the period 2002-17, involving concessional credit of US$9.31 billion. The difficulty is that of this amount, contracts of the value of only US$4.83 billion (51%) have been signed, and an amount of only US$3.95 billion (42%) has been disbursed. The limited absorption capacity of recipients, procedural delays, and lack of interest among established Indian corporates are the main constraints.
- India committed to providing 50,000 scholarships during 2016-20 and setting up a variety of skill development institutions at bilateral and regional levels.
- Among projects under the International Solar Alliance, a sizeable share of India's concessional credit has been earmarked to African nations.
- Finally, people-to-people links continue to develop—but in a sub-optimal way. Inadequate growth in tourism, lack of direct flights by Indian carriers, underutilisation of public diplomacy as a tool, particularly by the African side, and below-par engagement with civil society, strategic, and academic communities, constrain the growth of dynamism and substance in exchanges between Indian and African Third Spaces (beyond the government and business sectors).

INDIA'S ENTRY INTO MTCR, WASSENAAR ARRANGEMENT AND AUSTRALIA GROUP

MISSILE TECHNOLOGY CONTROL REGIME (MTCR)

India joins Missile Technology Control Regime. Top 5 things to know
Kallol Bhattacherjee, The Hindu, June 27 2016

- The Ministry of External Affairs said India's MTCR membership would help in "furtherance of international non-proliferation objectives," even as a statement from the MTCR chair at The Hague said India would enjoy "full participation in organisational activities, including the October 2016 plenary of the regime in South Korea."
- Membership of these groups would help India trade more effectively in critical high tech areas.
- MTCR: Top five things to know:
  - MTCR membership will enable India to buy high-end missile technology and also enhance its joint ventures with Russia.
  - MTCR aims at restricting the proliferation of missiles, complete rocket systems, unmanned air vehicles and related technology for those systems capable of carrying a 500 kilogramme payload for at least 300 kilometres, as well as systems intended for the delivery of weapons of mass destruction (WMD).
  - India's efforts to get into the MTCR also got a boost after it agreed to join the Hague Code of Conduct, dealing with the ballistic missile non-proliferation arrangement, earlier this month.
  - India's membership had been blocked in 2015 by Italy, which seemed to link it to the standoff over the detention of the Italian marines. With the return of the second marine, Salvatore Girone, to Rome on May 29, the sources said, "Italy is no longer blocking the consensus."
  - China, which stonewalled India's entry into the 48-nation Nuclear Suppliers Group (NSG) at the just-concluded Seoul plenary, is not a member of 34-nation MTCR.

India joins MTCR: 7 things the country stands to gain
Ashna Mishra, The Economic Times, 12 July 2016

- India has officially joined the Missile Technology Control Regime (MTCR) as a full member, three days after its failed NSG bid due to stiff opposition from China and other countries like South Africa, Norway, Brazil, Austria, New Zealand, Ireland and Turkey. (June, 2016)

- As India becomes the 35th member of the MTCR, here are seven things that you should know:
  1) Benefit to ISRO (access to cryogenic technology) 2) Sale of BrahMos 3) Procurement of Israel's Arrow II missile 4) Buying surveillance drones 5) Boost to Make in India 6) Step closer to NSG 7) One-upping China.

WASSENAAR ARRANGEMENT
Why is Wassenaar Arrangement important to India?

V. Sudarshan, The Hindu, 16 December 2017

- December 8, 2017: The Wassenaar Arrangement is a grouping of 42 countries, of which India is the latest entrant (on December 8) that seek to bring about security and stability, by fostering transparent practices in the process of sale and transfer of arms and materials and technologies that can be used to make nuclear weapons with a view to prevent any undesirable build-up of such capabilities. By doing so the grouping hopes to stymie destabilising developments. A further aim is also to prevent these proscribed items and technologies from falling into the hands of terrorists as well.
- Significantly, one of the purposes of the arrangement is to "enhance co-operation to prevent the acquisition of armaments and sensitive dual-use items for military end-uses, if the situation in a region or the behaviour of a state is, or becomes, a cause for serious concern to the Participating States."
- India will be able to more easily access dual use technologies and materials and military equipment that are proscribed for non-participating members. India will also be able to sell its nuclear reactors and other materials and equipment indigenously produced without attracting adverse reactions. It will also be in a better position to collaborate with other countries in developing such capabilities.

Significance of Wassenaar Arrangement for India

Dipanjan Roy Chaudhury, The Economic Times, 12 July 2018

- The decision was taken at the two-day (Wednesday & Thursday) plenary meeting of the grouping in Vienna.
- Besides USA, Russia and France played key roles in ensuring India's membership to Wassenaar Arrangement. French Ambassador to India Alexandre Ziegler congratulated India on "joining" the Wassenaar Arrangement. "One more recognition, after MTCR, of the growing role India plays in today's world," he said. India joined MTCR, another key export control regime, as a full member in 2016.

- "India would like to thank each of the forty-one WA Participating States for their support for India's membership. We would also like to thank Ambassador Jean Louis Falconi of France, 2017 Plenary Chair of the WA for his role in facilitating India's accession to the Arrangement. India also notes the valuable contribution of Japan and France as co-rapporteurs, and Ambassador Philip Griffiths, Head of WA Secretariat, for their guidance during the preparatory process. India's entry into the Arrangement would be mutually beneficial and further contribute to international security and non-proliferation objectives," MEA said in a statement after WA decision.

Wassenaar Arrangement Admits India as Its 42nd Member
Ankit Panda, The Diplomat, 8 December 2017

- Formally known as the Wassenaar Arrangement on Export Controls for Conventional Arms and Dual-Use Goods and Technologies, the organisation is designed to regulate the export of sensitive technologies that could possibly lead to "destabilising accumulations," according to its guidelines.
- Since its founding in 1996, the Arrangement has become an important component of the global nonproliferation regime, with member states exchanging information on their transfers of conventional weapons and dual-use goods to states outside of the arrangement.
- To be admitted to the Arrangement, states must meet certain criteria, including acquiescence to a range of global nonproliferation treaties, including the Nuclear Nonproliferation Treaty (NPT).
- India's admission to the Arrangement is not predicated on this requirement; New Delhi has never signed the NPT and has sought to burnish its nonproliferation credentials through its behavior and policies since its nuclear breakout in 1998.
- Though admission requires consensus, the United States' backing for Indian admission into the Arrangement—reaffirmed prominently by the Obama administration—helped New Delhi's case.
- India's admission to the Wassenaar Arrangement was in part facilitated by China's nonparticipation in the Arrangement. (Beijing does informally maintain export control standards largely in line with those required by the Arrangement.)
- India's membership in the Wassenaar Arrangement partly hinged on a lack of consensus, with Italy having objected to New Delhi's participation until the two countries repaired their bilateral relationship this year following a multiple-year spat over the fate of two Italian marines who killed two Indian fishermen

in 2012.

- Earlier this year, India had updated its export control lists to bring them in line with international standards, including those required by the Wassenaar Arrangement.

AUSTRALIA GROUP

What Does India's New Australia Group Admission Mean for its Old NSG Bid?
Rajeshwari Pilllai Rajagopalan, The Diplomat, 1 February 2018

- The support to India's membership within each of these regimes reflects India's clean track record with regard to non-proliferation. India asserts that its accession to these global technology clubs is "mutually beneficial and further contribute to international security and non-proliferation objectives." This represents a significant change in Indian attitudes: India had for decades criticized these arrangements.
- But it should be noted that there has been a significant change in the attitude of the non-proliferation order towards India too, from seeing India as a country of proliferation concern to a partner. Members of these regimes accept now that bringing India within the tent is in their own interests both because of India's growing profile in the technology exports and the overall changing political equations between India and the major powers.
- The Australia Group was set up in 1985 specifically "to ensure that exports do not contribute to the development of chemical and biological weapons." The initial focus of the group was on chemical agents, but by the 1990s, the mandate was expanded to include biological agents as well. The export control lists of the Australia Group are considered fairly comprehensive and go beyond even the scope of the Chemical Weapons Convention (CWC) and BTWC.
- Though both sides have tried to revive their relations, irritants do keep popping up. China, on its side, has been critical of India's increasingly closer ties with the United States and its allies such as Japan and Australia. All of which means that for the time being at least, India may have little hope of seeing its NSG membership actually achieve success.

EDITORIALS ON MODI'S FOREIGN POLICY—2017-18

India and the world: Foreign policy in the age of Modi
Manoj Joshi, Observer Research Foundation, 8 March 2017

- Prime Minister Narendra Modi's foreign policy has been characterised by great energy, a desire to break the mold of the past and a penchant for risk-taking. Given the vigour he has imparted, foreign relations should have yielded more significant results. They haven't. This is not only the fault of poor conception and implementation of some initiatives, but to the fact that in foreign policy there are external variables outside your control.

- Even before the Modi government assumed office in May of 2014, certain trends in foreign policy had hardened. 1) The Special Representative process of resolving India's border issue with China had reached a dead-end. 2) The same had happened with the composite dialogue with Pakistan. Actually, minus a Pakistani effort to punish the perpetrators of the 2008 Mumbai terror strike of November 2008, the very basis of a bilateral dialogue to resolve issues had been undermined.

- To secure its periphery, New Delhi must deal with its biggest foreign policy challenge—moderating, if not breaking, the China-Pakistan alliance. Short of this, it remains limited to managing its relationships with the two in a sub-optimal manner. As of today, however, the Modi government appears to be faltering even in this task.

- The new Indian assertiveness was also visible in Sri Lanka where New Delhi helped cobble an alliance that saw the defeat of Mahinda Rajpakse in the presidential elections. The man who defeated the LTTE became anathema to New Delhi because of the burgeoning links between Sri Lanka and China. More than this, though, New Delhi was alarmed by the docking of Chinese submarines in Colombo harbour in 2014 and 2015.

- But the visits to the island republics of Mauritius and Seychelles have been useful in developing India's maritime domain awareness scheme, as well as its naval posture in the Indian Ocean.

- Modi's obsession with "terrorism" from Pakistan is puzzling considering that since 2011 we have not suffered a mass civilian casualty attack. It appears to be designed to appeal to the domestic electorate.

- The one area where India has had unalloyed success is in its relations with the United States. This is not because we have an identity of interests, but a congruence of needs that the other can fulfill.

- Relations with Japan are a subset of ties with the US, and again, serve mutual needs—India wants Japanese investment and technology, while Tokyo seeks India's participation in the East Asian coalition.

- What about the main agenda: seeking an economic transformation of India? According to the government, Modi's foreign visits have resulted in a sharp rise of FDI into India. In 2015, for example, India attracted US$44 billion a

29 per cent jump over the figure for the previous year. The figure could be higher for 2016, but it needs to be recalled that the 2012 figure was US$46.55 billion, and so to attribute the growth to Modi's foreign policy alone would be an error.

- China continues to swarm over us in South Asia. The latest sign of this has been the US$24 billion aid, loans and investment commitments made by Xi Jinping during his visit to Bangladesh in 2016. As it is, all three of the wings of the Bangladesh military are equipped with Chinese equipment.

- A major problem in India's foreign policy is its illusion that it is somehow competing with China. We are certainly a budding rival of China, the only one with sufficient physical size and population to offset its power. But we are a long way from actualising the potential.

Prime Minister Narendra Modi's Hug Diplomacy Fails

Antony Clement, Modern Diplomacy, 17 February 2018

- Two years ago, without doing any homework or planning, Modi travelled to Pakistan from Afghanistan to greet his counterpart, the then Prime Minister Nawaz Sharif, to wish him well on his birthday. He hugged Sharif and spent only two hours with him to try to sort out the 70-year outstanding divergence between India and Pakistan.

- Modi strategically hugs fellow world leaders. He has no strategic perception. He believes only in the power of his personal charisma in dealing with foreign policy matters. This strategy has failed considerably with China and with our other immediate neighbors, but he neither intends to accept these mistakes, nor is he interested in learning from them.

- Under his administration, we lost numerous soldiers in fighting with Pakistan terrorists, experienced a 100-day shutdown in Kashmir, blindly allowed a Pakistan team to inspect our Pathankot Air Force Station, and generally continued down a visionless path in foreign policy. These indicate that Modi's defensive and offensive strokes against Pakistan have failed completely, including the most politicised 'surgical strike' that did not contain the terrorists from Pakistan. Today, the Modi government is searching for policy directions in handling Pakistan, but sat in a corner like a lame duck.

- In the beginning, when he took office, Modi perhaps believed that 'everything is possible' in international affairs simply by virtue of occupying the prime minister seat. Further, he thought that all his visits abroad would bring a breakthrough. His hugs with counterparts, various costume changes, and the serving of tea, indicate that our prime minister is using soft power approaches. These approaches were used by our first Prime Minister Nehru whilst India did not have a strong military or economy. However, India is not today what it was in the 1950/60s. Presently, hugging and changing costumes will not necessarily keep India influential in international relations, especially at a time when the world is undergoing multi-polar disorder. However, he is in continuous denial that his paths are wrong, especially in dealing with our neighbors.

- India's 'aid diplomacy' to Afghanistan in various fields has been increasing day after day, including infrastructure development and the training of Afghan security forces. Yet, India's influence in Afghanistan is in disarray. Former Afghanistan President Hamid Karzai said, "India should have its own policy on Afghanistan". However, Modi's policy makers in New Delhi are expecting the US President Donald Trump and Secretary of State Rex Tillerson to maintain India's active and significant role in Afghanistan.
- Modi's mute approach to the Rohingya crisis speculates India's major power ambition. This is a serious setback to India's diplomacy: it is now pushing Myanmar to get support from China, along with our neighbor Bangladesh, in resolving the crisis with Rohingya refugees.
- China has now realised that her weaved network against India can be strengthened easily in the Indian Ocean, because New Delhi only displays silent concern.
- Modi cannot understand the setback he is facing with China, Pakistan, and our other neighbors. In comparison, Vajpayee's or Dr. Manmohan Singh's combined simple charisma as leaders or economists with appropriate home-work in the past; has caused tremendous results in foreign policy, including expected results in Indo-US nuclear negotiations. This is completely missing in Modi's administration.

All Modi has to show for on the world stage are minor victories and major mistakes

Girish Shahane, Quartz India, 26 April 2018

- India's foreign policy objectives have remained consistent for the last 25 years through a number of changes of regime, differing more in emphasis than in fundamentals.
- Modi can be more openly pro-Israel than any Congress prime minister, not having to contend with a large Muslim membership with strong anti-Zionist

feelings. Behind the scenes, though, Israel's weapons exports to India have risen consistently as has trade and technology transfer between the two nations. We have experienced nothing like the whiplash shift marking the entry of Donald Trump into the White House.

- Logic suggests that in a situation where policies are nearly identical, implementation will make the difference. It suggests, as a corollary, that Modi, a charismatic, industrious, ambitious man determined to stamp his name on history, would be a better vehicle for furthering India's bipartisan foreign policy goals than his predecessor, who possessed far less real power. Yet, Modi has no signature achievement to compare with Singh's bold push for the US-India civil nuclear deal at the cost of the Congress's alliance with the Communist parties, whose reflexive anti-Americanism balked at the agreement.

- The trajectory of India's worsening relationship with Pakistan hints at the downside of having a larger-than-life figure like Modi at the helm. Everything becomes about him in a way that isn't in the nation's best interest. The dangers of megalomania have been brought into sharp focus by Trump's rise, and Modi suffers the same disease, though its symptoms aren't as manifest in his case.

- The absence of long-term planning indicates that the bullet train is a vanity venture along the lines Modi recommended during his days as Gujarat's chief minister, stating that we should build a high-speed rail link as a way of showing the world our strength, irrespective of whether it would be popular with commuters. How a Japanese-designed rail link could be marketed as a sign of India's strength is another matter.

- While it hasn't pulled any stunt as crazy as the note swap in the international arena, and continues to exude authority and credibility, the administration's foreign policy performance has lacked vision, and produced few tangible gains even in terms of augmented exports in new markets. It has been frequently confused and pursued an ad hoc, personality-driven style that has contributed to a worsening of relations with most of our neighbours.

- Modi is like a stylish batsman of whom much is expected but who consistently fails to deliver big scores. Four years on, he's put far too few runs on the board while Xi's been on a century spree. It might be time to accept the man's technique is fatally flawed, and drop him from the national team.

The Nehruvian Style of Modi's Foreign Policy

Brahma Chellaney, The Open Magazine, 18 May 2018

- Modi's stint in office has clearly changed Indian politics and diplomacy.
- The political stability Modi has brought, coupled with his pro-market economic policies, tax reforms, defence modernisation and foreign-policy dynamism, has only helped to further raise India's global profile.However, India's troubled neighbourhood, along with its spillover effects, has posed a serious challenge for Modi.
- The combustible neighbourhood has underscored the imperative for India to evolve more dynamic and innovative approaches to diplomacy and national defence.
- India's ability to secure its maritime backyard, including its main trade arteries in the Indian Ocean region, will be an important test of its maritime strategy and foreign policy, especially at a time when an increasingly powerful and revisionist China is encroaching on India's maritime space.
- But like his predecessors, from Jawaharlal Nehru to Manmohan Singh, Modi took office unschooled in national security. The on-the-job learning of successive leaders, coupled with their reliance on bureaucrats that have generalised knowledge and little time for forward thinking, has blighted national security since independence. Prime minister after prime minister has bypassed institutionalised processes of policymaking and pursued a meandering, personality-driven approach to diplomacy.
- Modi is no exception. In fact, his recent Reset 2.0 with China shows that he does not believe in the 'once bitten, twice shy' adage. His Reset 1.0, which was launched soon after he came to office, backfired conspicuously.
- As anyone who has interacted with Modi in person will attest, he is a soft-spoken, attentive and magnetic personality—a contrast to the voluble, rabble-rousing Modi on the campaign trail. Those who meet him are charmed by his disarming ways. That may have helped foster Modi's abiding faith in the power of his personal diplomacy.
- To be sure, Modi has used his personal touch with some effect, addressing several world leaders by their first name and building an easy relationship with them. In keeping with his personalised stamp on diplomacy, Modi has also relied on bilateral summits to try and open new avenues for cooperation and collaboration. Yet, in terms of tangible gains for India, his personal diplomacy has little to show, other than with Japanese Prime Minister Shinzo Abe.

- Truth be told, Modi's personal diplomacy mirrors that of the man he intensely dislikes, Nehru. Politically and ideologically, Modi has little in common with Nehru.
- India faces major foreign-policy challenges, which by and large predate Modi's ascension to power. India is home to more than one-sixth of the world's population, yet it punches far below its weight.
- While Modi has found it difficult to contain cross-border terrorist attacks from Pakistan or stem Chinese military incursions across the Himalayan frontier, he has managed to lift the bilateral relationship with the United States to a deeper level of engagement.
- Modi's separate informal summits with Xi in Wuhan and with Russian President Vladimir Putin in Sochi underscore India's strategic imperative to develop a semblance of balance in relations with different powers, including reversing the declining trajectory of the once-special relationship with Moscow.
- Modi, more fundamentally, sees himself as a practical and spirited leader who likes to play on the grand chessboard of global geopolitics.
- Modi's various steps and actions have helped highlight the trademarks of his foreign policy— from pragmatism and minimalism to zeal and showmanship. They have also exemplified his penchant for springing diplomatic surprises.
- The truth is that, in terms of concrete results, Modi's record thus far isn't all that impressive. His supporters, however, would say that dividends from a new direction in foreign policy flow slowly and that he has been in office for just four years.
- If foreign policy is shaped by the whims and fancies of personalities who hold the reins of power, there will be a propensity to act in haste and repent at leisure, as has happened in India repeatedly since independence.
- Unfortunately, Modi's 'Make in India' initiative has yet to take off, with manufacturing's share of India's GDP actually contracting.
- Although he came to office with a popular mandate to usher in major changes, his record in power has been restorative rather than transformative.
- As for foreign policy, India, despite absorbing greater realism, remains intrinsically cautious and reactive, rather than forward-looking and proactive

Successful security plan, foreign policy hallmark of Modi govt

Shishir Gupta, Hindustan Times, 27 May 2018

- However, the Modi government's main success lies in its diplomatic and security engagement of West Asia and the Association of South-East Asian Nations (Asean) and that too at a time when the dark shadow of the so-called Islamic State had loomed large since 2014. Before the advent of Modi, governments used to look towards Sunni West Asia through the prism of Pakistan and hence were reticent in making overtures towards countries in the region.
- The result is quite evident in a single mention of Jammu and Kashmir in the Organisation of Islamic Cooperation's Dhaka declaration this year; Bangladesh was at the forefront of support for India's claim to observer status in the OIC. With Prime Minister Modi's personal diplomacy working on global leaders, including the rulers of Saudi Arabia and the UAE, the days of Indian fugitives and terrorists taking refuge in these two kingdoms or for that matter anywhere in West Asia are practically over.
- While the US, Japan and France are India's core partners, Prime Minister Modi has managed to forge a personal bond with Russian President Vladimir Putin and Chinese President Xi Jinping through candid conversations.
- The sub-nationalism of the two regional parties in the Valley have confused the population between self-rule, autonomy and Indian nationalism. The answer to this only lies in Pakistan reining in extremist groups and disassociating itself from a self-made Kashmir cause.
- Apart from Pakistan, the Modi government has expanded cooperation with nations in its immediate and extended neighbourhood. Close relations have been established with Myanmar, Bangladesh and Afghanistan; ties with Sri Lanka and Nepal have been brought back on track and are on the mend with China and the Maldives.
- A strong electoral mandate is directly and not inversely proportional to effective national deterrence and foreign policy.

India's foreign relations are in tatters and the Modi government has only itself to blame

Shekhar Gupta, The Print, 30 June 2018

- India's decline from global consciousness has been as rude as its rise was steady and smooth.
- Recent pro-active blunders have made India's external relations a man-made disaster.

- Two external negatives were not the Modi government's fault: The rise of Trump and a new Chinese assertion. Trump's actions, particularly the change in Iran policy directly led to rising oil prices, destabilising India's domestic economy and politics. The Chinese push for CPEC, unmindful of Indian concerns, and its moves in Sri Lanka, Nepal, the Maldives and Bangladesh showed that China is no longer willing to leave the subcontinent as a zone of India's pre-eminence.

- The Modi government's greatest blunder is to exploit sensitive external relations in its domestic politics. The first essential attribute of successful leaders in history is strategic patience. They move firmly, but never get so committed publicly as to deny themselves room for manoeuvre, front, back, sideways.

- In all major state election campaigns he made his foreign policy "conquests" the centre-piece, and it worked. But there are perils in declaring victory too soon. It narrows your strategic space. Instead of keeping quiet as the past governments did, it made one set of local, tactical and limited "surgical" raids into a feat rivalling the securing of Siachen in the spring of 1984.

- Similar misjudgements were made on trade. Radical controls on prices of medical devices especially stents were made a part of election discourse. It closed your options when Trump, even more transactional, reacted.

- It is risky to keep punching above your weight, as India has been lately.

- Self-congratulation is a most tempting trap you set for yourself. For four years India has been celebrating becoming a "natural strategic ally" of the US, but has let its military decline.

- Four years have effectively seen four defence ministers, the current one being an ineffectual photo-op caricature. Our military pensions budget will exceed the salary budget in two years and both are already way above the capital budget.

- Declining military might is compounded by economic slowdown. You can fool your people by changing how you calculate your GDP. It becomes dangerous when you start believing it.

- It's time to stop breathless celebration. It will be wiser to take a deep breath, make a reality check, and introspect.

Modi's tilt to Washington in foreign policy damages ties with Beijing

Zhang Jiadong, Global Times, 20 August 2018

- It appears that India wants to seek close ties simultaneously with different countries. However, India's "partnership" actually makes it a soon-to-be ally of the US and the West, and also the US' "major defense partner" and "major non-NATO ally." It sours the strategic cooperation between China and India. In 2017, Indian troops illicitly entered Doklam, an undisputed Chinese territory. It is Modi's attempted break of the alleged China's containment policy toward India, and also a strategic risk.

- Modi has restructured the foreign policy decision-making team. He did not pick any member of the team from the time Indian National Congress was in power. Although it is in keeping with party politics, Modi also kept a distance from the team of former prime minister Atal Bihari Vajpayee, a member of the ruling Bharatiya Janata Party (BJP), who passed away last week. As a result, Modi's foreign policy team has been left with neophytes in foreign affairs. The efforts of previous leaders in promoting China-India relations were not carried forward.

- President Xi visited India in September 2014. Although his visit drew a lot of attention, its strategic meaning didn't receive due attention. India focused on resolving specific bilateral issues, but it neglected former Chinese and Indian leaders' consensus: the two countries should seek cooperation in the whole world.

- Thus, China and India have changed their focus from establishing a new world order to grappling with complicated bilateral relations, especially territorial disputes.

- After Modi assumed office, India's foreign policy leaned to the US. India is promoting relations with the US, winning economic interests and coping with "China threat." It uses the strategic dispute between China and the US to maximise its interests. That has become a new strategy for India's major power relations.

- China basically failed to pull India back to a traditional, neutral policy, and had to choose the old policy of supporting Pakistan. All this led to the 2017 Doklam standoff.

- Modi will continue to play a special role in China-India relations. He is like Jawaharlal Nehru, Indian's first prime minister, who showed a change in his own policies. Nehru failed to use the two countries' friendship and then made a break with China. Likewise, Modi showed a friendly gesture at first, but because of later indiscretions things went close to a military conflict. However, Modi is more pragmatic. After relations nose-dived, he tried to fix it to serve his political interests.

Postscript

Modiplomacy was cast in a Shakespearean mould because the fluctuations in foreign policy were like the shifting fortunes of the Bard's heroes on account of changed circumstances and arrival of new dramatis personae. The unpredictability of US President Donald Trump had radically changed the global context of Prime Minister Narendra Modi's foreign policy.

The situation appears to have suddenly changed as this book goes to the press. Modi has gone down in history as the only foreign leader to have greeted his diaspora in the United States in the company of the US President. The mutual admiration expressed by Modi and Trump and the commitments they made to work together at the 'Howdy Modi' event in Houston have raised hopes of a new dawn in India-US relations.

Significant progress was achieved in several areas of concern such as trade, terrorism, Kashmir and migration. Trade negotiations were reported to be nearing closure. Trump strongly supported the elimination of 'radical Islamic terrorism', including from Pakistan, and declared that he will mediate between India and Pakistan only if both countries agree. He also said the US is proud of the migrants from India and is ready to 'fight for them'.

Modi and Trump declared themselves as the 'best of friends' and stressed that India-US relations had never been better. The chemistry between them seemed to augur well for the strategic partnership, even as observers are on a wing and a prayer for greater stability and predictability in bilateral relations.

Having had the experience of turbulent India-US relations in the last three years, Modi has no intention to put all his eggs in the American basket. His visit to Vladivostok, Russia and his discussions with President Vladimir Putin in early September were as significant as his visit to the United States. It had three components, all of them equally important: a bilateral visit, the annual summit and the Eastern Economic Forum as the Chief Guest. A Joint Statement, 'Reaching new heights of cooperation through trust and partnership' consisting of 82 paragraphs, issued after the visit was a virtual compendium of activities, which would take India-Russia relations to a higher level.

Good relations with China are also very much in Modi's agenda and he is following up on his efforts to reset relations with China, which began in Wuhan last year. A return visit by President Xi is likely to improve relations, though China has not shown any signs of changing its positions on the issues of contention, particularly the border and its strong support to Pakistan.

Modiplomacy rolls on in innovative ways, dealing with global issues through a string of bilateral relationships and interventions at the multilateral fora. Modi 2.0 is poised to achieve the results of the many initiatives that he had taken during his first term.

Index